The Iron Man

James William Hague

Giles H Brearley F.C.M.A.

Typeset and printed on behalf of the authors by Sherwood Print and Finishing Ltd.

First published 2011

ISBN 978-1-904706-88-5

James William Hague- The Iron man.

(British Heavyweight Champion 1909-1911)

Contents;

Foreword

Iron Hague

I feel privileged and proud to be asked to write this foreword to a book on "Iron" Hague of Mexborough. He was the first Yorkshire man to win the English (later, in 1909, renamed the British) Heavyweight Title. The mere name "Iron" Hague conjures up a fighting image; "Iron" = something immensely strong, seemingly unbreakable; "Hague" = Earl Douglas Hague, the famous British Army commander.

It may seem strange that someone from the South East corner of Kent has been asked to write an introduction for a Yorkshire man but Aylesham, being a mining village built nearby Snowdown Colliery in 1926, always consisted of miners from all over the British Isles with a large number coming from Yorkshire, especially from the areas around Mexborough. The "old timers" from that area were full of stories of the famous "Iron" Hague and, as a boxing fanatic who learnt to read from the "Boxing News" before I started school, I had therefore read about him.

He always interested me, especially the stories of his dynamic punching power which enabled him to win the English title from the then champion, "Gunner" Moir, a man who had lasted ten rounds in the world title challenge.

Yet, "Iron" Hague ko'd him in the very first round. Then he met the legendary Sam Langford, the "Boston Tar Baby" and although defeated in four rounds, "Iron" Hague had scored a genuine knock down over Langford with his famed right hand ("Dirty Dick"), a feat claimed by very few and the thought of what might have been if "Iron" hadn't injured his right hand in landing this knock down punch. But even more, what could he have achieved if only had listened to wiser heads and not been lulled into believing that his powerful punch would carry him through without the need of strenuous training.

I was and still am amazed at the various photos of him in which he always appears to have a real "beer belly". Never mind the stories of a hard training grind and over the years. At Colindale Newspaper Museum, starting in 1960 as I researched various sporting papers together with Yorkshire papers covering his career, I could only wonder why no-one had written a book on this amazing man who had seemingly thrown away a God-given gift along with all his hard-earned money.

Now, Giles Brearley has turned out what I can only describe as not only a long overdue book but one that has been diligently researched and is highly readable and deserves to be on the bookshelf of all boxing fans.

Harold Alderman (MBE),

Aylesham

Kent Boxing Historian

Awarded BBB of C Exceptional Award for Services to Boxing on 29 November 2009

London Ex-Boxers ASS,

Alf Paolozzi Award 2007

Introduction

By the time I was born, Iron Hague had been deceased for some four years.

As I grew up in the South Yorkshire Town of Mexborough, his name and stories used to periodically surface, stories that seemed, on the face of it, to be greatly exaggerated but stories that others swore were factual right down to the finer points. Over the years, I picked up other stories here and there, all adding to my knowledge on the Mexborough Wizard.

In my youth, I developed a great interest in boxing. I have fond memories of all my family glued around a radio set at 3am in the morning listening to the latest Cassius Clay fight being broadcast live from the U.S.A. Title fight after title fight were listened to or watched with a great fascination, particularly the heavyweights. I met many former fighters over the years. I was delighted on a business trip to Australia, to find myself sat next to Henry Cooper for breakfast for each of my three days in Brisbane. To my disappointment, he refused to talk about boxing, only about golf and the then state of the country.

One day, I bumped into local author, Barrie Chambers, who told me he was researching Iron Hague. He had accessed all the local news articles over the years. These he compiled into date order and enhanced them with additional boxing data.

Barrie correctly pointed out that if Hague been from anywhere else in the UK, other than the Dearne Valley, his exploits would have been printed to excess and a monument erected in his honour.

Remarkably, as a town we had nothing to commemorate him. The Dearne Valley has had plenty of famous sons and daughters but for whatever reason, was always a little reluctant to shout about them. Barrie did a great job completing his project producing a very informative book called "A Champions Diary." Sadly, Barrie died shortly after its publication.

I had always promised myself that one day, I would write a definitive book on our Mexborough boxing hero. Over the years, while carrying out other research, I recorded and stored any information I unexpectedly came across about Iron Hague in readiness.

One or two forages down into London, visiting various archives, proved to be very valuable unearthing even more material. Whilst the local press gave valuable information, the National's and local London papers would often give extra detail and a more unbiased view on events.

I also found that many of the people Iron boxed wrote their own memoirs in later years and many referred to their encounter with our Iron, which was very useful.

One great source of facts and data that materialised was that unbeknown, Iron in 1928, had given a series of detailed interviews to a journalist about his early life and boxing career.

These notes did help confirm finer details of many events and provided much more additional information.

One problem that had helped fuel legends and myths over the years was that Iron was always very reluctant to talk in great detail of his past experiences. Even to his close family he did not reminisce

In particular, like many soldiers, he was very reluctant to relate about his First World War experiences. The harshness experienced and the great losses of comrades prayed very hard on his mind. To research his military career, I enlisted the help of the Grenadier Guards archivist, Lt Colonel Seymour. He was very helpful and managed to uncover the details of Iron's wartime deployment and detailed service.

I did receive a lot of encouragement to write and deliver this publication and was pleasantly surprised at the number of willing helpers I encountered along the way.

I was very ably assisted by Swinton Heritage researcher, Ron James, who spent hours trailing through various news archives. Ron should be a "national institution" in his own right, his willingness and enthusiasm are an asset for any historical society. Ron also uncovered en-route, details of his own forebear, who proved to be a relative of Iron Hague and who achieved some national boxing success himself. I was also very ably assisted by Harold Alderman, the noted boxing historian. His knowledge on boxing's history was invaluable. It did not matter who the boxer was, Harold would know all about him in some detail. He knew not only of events over the years but also about the whole politics surrounding it all at the time.

BBC Radio Sheffield in 2009 did a special broadcast based on Iron's life. It was timed to be a 100 years on from his glorious win. I was asked to do the introductory interview for the programme with Roney Robinson, which I duly did.

The programme was very well received and it spurred me on to start and assemble all my notes and put pen to paper.

So without further ado, please read on and I hope you enjoy Iron Hague's story.

Giles H Brearley FCMA
November 2010

Chapter 1
Family Origin

Inside the Tavern the open windows caused the air to swirl round, dragging along the thick tobacco smoke that was being exhaled from numerous; pipes, roll your owns and cigarettes. The miners of Denton colliery were once again not in a happy mood. The management were appearing to be very dogmatic in their response to the appearance of thicker dirt bands in the seam. The wages were set to suffer yet again.

Denton was situated some 5 miles east of Manchester city centre, near Stockport. The Colliery, originally called Ellis Colliery, originated from the 18th century exploiting the numerous shallow coal seams that prevailed and was the town's largest employer. Coal mined from here fuelled Manchester's industry and kept the cities home fires burning.

One attendee, who just listened to the banter and was unusually quiet, was James Hague. "What's up with you?" asked his long time fellow hewer, "You've usually got plenty to say on these matters."

Denton Colliery near Manchester where the Hague family had worked for generations.

Turning to him, James Hague muttered "We are off Tom, I've had enough! I've got my lads to think of now and this is not for them. We've been miners here for the last three generations but what's the future now hold for them or for their kids?"

James had recently lost his wife, Phoebe, and was now single handedly bringing up his two sons, 15 year old James and 13 year old John. They still lived at their little rented cottage at 10 Bond Street in Denton.

James, the eldest son, was already working down the pit alongside his father and soon John would be joining them. Since Phoebe had died, there were now times when young John was left to his own devices as James and John worked out their shifts down the mine. Reports had been drifting back how young John, known as 'Bazzo', was getting into more and more fights round the town and making a name for himself for the wrong reason. He even chased a bear round a visiting circus rink pretending to wrestle the animal, showing to the astonished onlookers his great bravado with no fear.

Everyone had to work in the Hague household and before her premature death, Phoebe had fetched in a wage working as a weaver. Without that extra money, it was becoming very tight. To help make ends meet, James had took in a young lodger called John Hall, which had helped. The reduced future wages from the pit however were now to be the final straw.

"I've decided we are going to join the Yorkies" James murmured to his old pal. His friend was taken aback. "I say everyone, have you heard Jamesie boy here, he is going to join them 'Yorkies', so another one flies the nest". James was bombarded with questions from his fellow drinkers, "Are you sure you are doing the right thing?", "But you are leaving all your friends!", "what's so good about it over there?", " The best thing to come out of Yorkshire is the Manchester Train", "Look does tha know what tha doing?","The Hagues have always been a part of Denton, you can't go", "Thas kept that bloody well secret".

There had been a steady exodus in recent years of miners moving from Denton to the new deep mines opened up in the Dearne Valley in South Yorkshire. Here, newly built accommodation awaited the successful applicant. The seams were thicker, the wages were higher and it would take son John away from the trouble he was getting in. James saw the move as securing a better future for the lads and importantly, the opportunity for "he" the widower to start again.

The sinking of two shafts had taken place in 1863, creating the Denaby Main Colliery. The owners were Messrs Pope and Pearson. The Barnsley Bed was reached in September 1867 at a depth of more than 422 yards. In 1893, the company also opened out Cadeby Main Colliery. As early as 1867, there began the building of houses to accommodate the workers and their families. The layout of the village was very reflective of the style created by the 'Industrial Revolution'. The streets of terraced houses ran parallel, all with bottom views towards the colliery. Shops, schools, churches, public houses and parks were also included in the new infrastructure. A few weeks earlier, James had taken the train over the Pennines to Sheffield and then caught a connecting train onto Mexborough. Whilst there, he went to see a Deputy at Denaby Colliery and secured employment as a hewer. The South Yorkshire area had seen a lot of migrants moving from Scotland, Ireland, Newcastle and Lancashire to fill the huge number of new jobs generated from the sinking of several new mines. As a newcomer, James felt he wouldn't really feel any exclusion as there was a whole new generation of outsiders all now thrust into a new comradeship.

Surface view of Denaby Main Colliery where James secured work.

He was also put onto a house in Mexborough that was up for rent. He met the landlord and shook on the deal. Now he also had somewhere to move into, a back to back terraced house on Woodruff Row, just off the town centre, near the Brickyard. The pieces were now all in place. The essential belongings they had were sent on by train so the spring of 1882 saw the arrival of some new Mexborough residents, "The Hagues".

James not only secured employment for himself but also for both of his sons. They all worked at Denaby Colliery and for a while, there were three wages coming into their new house. The physical graft now expelled by youngest son John tempered some of his waywardness and all settled down.

One young lady who caught young John's eye was Ann Bennett. A year younger than John, she was the daughter of William Bennett and his wife Joannah. The Bennett's also lived at Woodruff Row and so were neighbours. The Bennett's were a family well known for their great sporting prowess. William, born in 1853, was nicknamed Micky. He was the eldest of three brothers, his siblings being Walter (Cocky) and Harry (Tip). He played for Mexborough Town but went on to become centre forward for Sheffield Wednesday. He was with them in 1889 when the club had became a founder member of the Football Alliance. He was the first of the town's residents to achieve professional status.

By 1884, Johns love for Ann had blossomed and they were married. John was aged 16 and his bride was 15. They initially lived with James but later secured a house at number 8 Charles Street. These terraced houses were built in the 1870's in what had

William Bennett poses in a Sheffield United playing strip – 1890s.

been the grounds of industrialist Samuel Barkers residence 'Mexborough House'. John was something of a sportsman himself. He played for the "west end" football team who hailed from the Roman Terrace end of town. He was also a useful runner, competing in local cross country races. Another of his talents was that he was a good "clog dancer". He had learned this as a youngster on the Lancashire streets. The predominant style of Lancashire clog dancing was termed 'heel and toe.' Many of the steps emulated the sound of the shuttle and other parts of the cotton spinning and weaving machinery. It was a very common form of entertainment. The miners and mill workers shoes were made with wooden soles which sounded every time they walked and facilitated the dance rhythms.

The marriage was happy and a series of children were born to them. The eldest was James William born on the 6th November 1885 followed by Phoebe born in 1888, John born in 1891, Lily born in 1894, George born in 1899 and latterly Agnes, born in 1902.

Daily life in the Hague household went on much as for many of the town's residents. John worked as a miner and provided a regular weekly wage, he thought he ruled the roost. The regular income put the food on the table, Ann kept the home together and showered them all with her love.

John's father, James moved in with his other son, at a property known as "Railway Gates" near Adwick on Dearne following his son's marriage to Wath girl, Ellen. There was a strong interaction of all family members, particularly with the Bennet's whose sporting achievements were accelerated with the continuing achievements of Cocky. The town boasted football and cricket teams with a keen following. Both the Hague's and the Bennett's became involved front line with the teams, being equally comfortable kicking a ball or wielding a cricket bat.

At the age of five, James William was taken by his young mother, Ann, from their home up Lower Dolcliffe Road then onto Garden Street, to the Infants school. The school had been newly built of stone in 1878 and in 1890, was still comparatively new.

The children's education was versed around the three "r's; reading, writing and arithmetic. The discipline was, by today's standards, probably quite brutal. One female teacher dragged a girl by the hair and hit her in the face causing a concussion and the doctor had to be sent for. Excessive measures were frowned upon and the teacher was cautioned. Another teacher who thrashed a child with a bicycle tyre, was encouraged to resign.

On a cold spring morning in 1891, the children were in the playground engaged in various play activities. Six year old James William was showing off some marbles his father had bought him when the school bully approached. He towered above his proposed younger victim. He lay claim to the shiny round pieces of glass clutched in James' hands. James offered to fight him and the bully eagerly accepted believing he had a softie in front of him. The marbles were thrown down as James launched himself, small fists blazing, attacking the aggressor. The other children made a ring around them shouting them on. The two aggressors went at each other like a pair of young bulldogs. By the time the teachers realised what was happening, young James had outfought the dazed bully and defended his corner admirably. Victory was in the air. Unfortunately, he was sent to see the headmaster who gave him six of the best with the cane. This feat was then duplicated by John when he returned from his shift

Garden Street Infant School (now demolished) which Iron Hague attended, where he picked up his lifelong nickname of "Iron.".

at the pit and learnt his young son had been fighting.

This became a regular occurrence as fighting became a regular feature of young James William's life. He would not cower down to anyone. He was well built compared to his other class mates, blessed with his father's spirit and full of the Bennett's powerful sporting prowess. It little mattered to John whether his son had won or lost a street fight, down came the strap in retribution. On discovery of his son fighting, a good hiding was always delivered in the old fashioned way; James William thought his father had been endowed by God in this way to deliver this punishment. The beatings became so regular, James accepted them as invariably part of the end purse of the fight. John was trying to instil discipline into his son but as he fought more than most, it did seem harsh.

Many rumours circulated in later years as to how James William received the nickname "Iron" Hague. Banded about for years was that a teacher hitting his bare backside with a cane and getting nowhere announced you must be made of Iron. It was stated he was impervious to pain, hence the name.

The real reason however Iron revealed was that in a playground incident, an assailant realising his hopelessness, threw a half brick at James' head splitting it wide open. Being the toughie he was he, wrapped a handkerchief around the cut and held it in place with his cap. Upon entering school, the Master asked him to remove his cap. Boys did not ever wear a cap inside school. Young James responded by saying, "Please sir, my head is bleeding very fast and so I am afraid to take my cap off". The teacher thought at first that this was intended as a joke but he soon realised the seriousness of the wound when the cap was removed. "Good God," said the teacher "and you never complained, you must be made of Iron." James had the wound cleaned, clipped and dressed. He then emerged at the other end with the life name of "Iron Hague".

Establishing yourself as "Cock of the Class" invariably brought on challenges over the years as different maturity rates affected the boys and they fancied their chances. "Cock of the School" brought even more challenges as the boys of Dolcliffe Road, Doncaster Road and the National Church of England School flexed their muscles, all hoping to be the "Supreme School Champion".

Fights down at the Leach (waste land at the side of the canal) were a regular occurrence. Iron often fought for coppers, with the winner taking all. If his mother got wind of it she used to appear with a rolled up washing line to belt him with. At the sight of her, off he would run. When his father found out he had been fighting, he knew what to expect. This however, did not deter him.

He also proved himself in swimming, using the river Don and the canal to regularly out swim his fellows, particularly when the summer months were blessed with warm sunshine. He used to love taking part in strength trials against the other kids, taking

Early postcard showing children posing aside the River Don .This was a popular summer pastime as their were no swimming pools in Mexborough and most children learnt how to swim in this river. Iron excelled at this.

his powers of endurance and resistance to the ultimate.

Rarely did a month go by at school without some major incident or fight taking place. To quell the situation and instil a feeling of discipline, the teachers at Garden Street School made young "Iron" the school monitor. He handed out the ink and the pens and he made sure his fellow pupils didn't abuse it. Some of the kids used to shout out as they received a "cufter" from Iron for a bit of a try on. The teacher used to tell them to shut up it, was just a love tap.

Despite this role, young Iron absconded from school on many occasions. The headteacher would often turn up at the Hague house to enquire where he was. His mother would go out looking for him and chastise him over his persistent truancy. This did impact on his schooling, leaving him well short in the 3 "r's" skills. This impacted onto the rest of his life.

Chapter 2
The Colliers Life For Me

As the year of 1898 progressed into summer, there began a strong debate in the Hague household as to where should James William work. His thirteenth birthday was on the 6th November 1898 whereupon he would then leave school and be expected to into enter the world of work and that of a premature manhood.

Life down the pit did not appeal to young Iron and fierce arguments took place. Mother Ann always took her sons side (mothers and sons!). These discussions continued right into autumn when John decided enough was enough. One final fierce argument took place which settled the matter. "If he doesn't want to go down the pit then listen to him!" Ann cried. James shouted up "I want to be a boxer." "Boxer?" replied John "I'll give you all the boxing you'll get my lad. Down the Pit you go, same as your father, your grandfather and great grandfather before him". That was the end of the matter, John's word was final. Down the pit young "Iron" would go.

John Hague's approaching the deputy to get young Iron a job was a formality. Iron was duly set on at Denaby Colliery as a pony driver.

Pit Pony and driver underground at Denaby Main Colliery.
This was Iron's first job on leaving school.

The pit employed some 1568 men underground and 501 men were surface workers. Iron was responsible for leading a pony up to the districts, attaching the filled coal tubs and transporting them back to the pit bottom for winding up to the surface. He would also take out empty tubs and supplies to the coal hewers and road headers. Iron answered to the head horseman who supervised their welfare.

He ensured they were fed and watered and had sufficient clean straw. The food for the ponies was kept in a raised granary above the ambulance station to discourage the rats and mice. The exact amount of food was taken down each day for the pony to feed on as surpluses would encourage vermin, even underground.

Each pony had its own stall near the pit bottom. The pony drivers often took extra treats like carrots and grass to bond with their animal. The ponies were notorious characters and would refuse to move if one extra tub was attached to their load. They knew exactly the number of tubs they would pull. There was no kidding them on by slipping an extra one on.

One acquaintance Iron met at Denaby was Tommy Stokes. He was a boxer of some local repute being dubbed the "The Yorkshire Pitman Champion". He was aged 19, some 6 years older than Iron and born at Denaby. He had been on the boxing circuit the last couple of years and done very well in such a short time. As they queued with the line of miners to take up their place on the chair that would take them underground, they used to spar up to each other. To Tommy Stokes, it was good fun but to the young Iron it was a serious opportunity to measure himself up. It was the start of a long relationship between the two. Iron would talk Tommy through the fights he had had and Tommy would burst into a flurry in the form of advice for the growing lad.

Tom Stokes in fighting pose.

As a market town, Mexborough saw a lot of miners at the weekends enjoying their drinking sprees. Pits were operating at Manvers, Kilnhurst, Denaby, Wath and Warren Vale, all within a few miles of the town. Street fights regularly prevailed and young Iron used to bear witness to these as the juvenile onlooker. Every now and again, the word would go round that a proper fight was in the offing. These always interested

Iron and he endeavoured to enjoy the spectacle. These fights were often to prove something, settle a dispute and were always bare knuckle and brutal.

It was the first day of spring 1899. There was a keen hoar frost and new Constable Hurst of Mexborough had been up since an informant had banged loudly on his door at 5.00am. Despite the sport of bare knuckle fighting being illicit, it still occurred. The use of 'Bare Knuckle' was made illegal right from the start of the Prize Ring back in 1700. This fight ban continued right until the 'Bare Knuckle' practice officially ended in 1867 following the introduction of the Marquis of Queensbury rules for boxing with gloves. Despite this, some continued its practice as being the only true way of deciding who was the best.

Linked to these fights was the illegal betting that always took place. It appealed to many. The order from the top of the police command was to stamp them out.

These fights were the bane of Constable Hurst's life. There was an assortment of venues in the locality that had been used in the past but the exact location was always kept as a tight secret until just beforehand. Sometimes, "dummy crowds" would be sent to two or three places causing the police's resources to be spread very thinly.

He now stood on the hill at the top of Clay Lane (Clayfield Road) and as a consequence of the frost, was able to pick up a trail. The men appeared to be heading towards Barnburgh. He followed the footprints of 15 or 16 people down to the River Dearne. These footprints were then joined by a further group who had approached from the direction of the Denaby Pit. All footprints then headed in the direction of the Barnburgh Crags. The crags were created as a result of a natural fault line thrusting a limestone escarpment above the sandstone bedrock. The presence of mature trees and enclosed small grassland paddocks made it ideal for the purpose of a fight venue.

Constable Hurst was in plain clothes and walked alone. With his cap pulled well down he simply nodded his head as he passed straggler groups. As a new constable, he wasn't yet well known and it was easy for him to blend into the growing assembly of spectators. Youngsters were sent out to various lofty points on the crags acting as lookouts, their job was to warn of the approach of any police.

At 7am sharp, the men at the front were encouraged to join hands to form a ring. A line, known as a scratch, was drawn down the middle of the ring by the dragging of a foot sunk deep into the soil. Four men who he recognised who were recent arrestees were; Grainger, Longley, Mannion and Humphries. They entered the ring. Mannion and Humphries were acting as seconds to the fighters and the other two acted as ring assistants.

In anticipation of great ensuing entertainment, the mood of the crowd began to become more excitable. A huge cheer went up as two well known prize fighters entered the ring – William Blount and Thomas Ryder. There was a score to be settled and today was the day. The Seconds began to help the fighters to strip to the waist.

The fighters then placed the toes of their right foot onto the scratch line. The contest then began.

The fight was being run on the London Rules which meant no hitting below the belt, gouging or kicking. Constable Hurst, hemmed in near the front, witnessed three twenty minute gruelling rounds. He would be a valuable witness to these events. The Sergeant would be well pleased with him.

Unfortunately, the young lads acting as look outs were not as vigilant as intended as their heads were turned watching the fight; they never noticed the string of police rushing up St Helens Lane having apparently been alerted by a Harlington resident. All of a sudden, a cry went out with the realisation of several uniformed constables in their presence. The fight stopped and chaos reigned, the air was filled with the sound of police whistles and shouts to "remain where you are". The bookies tables were speedily folded up with their owners dragging their case and boards into the adjoining woodlands.

The attendees fled in all directions. Constable Hurst identified himself to the raiding officers and pointed out the ring leaders who were successfully arrested.

One of the youngsters who fled that day was fourteen year old Iron Hague.

The banter and sparring of Iron with Tom Stokes continued for nigh on two years. Over this time, Iron the juvenile, was growing. He was getting broader, deeper chested and taller as he grew into manhood. When aged 15, Iron decided that he had listened to Tommy enough and now wanted to step into the ring proper.

One spring morning of 1900 Iron proclaimed, "Tommy, I want to have a serious fight with you. I am tired of these friendly scraps between us." Tommy agreed to the request and arrangements were made for a 29 round fight on the following Sunday morning with a purse of a pound a side.

The news about the fight went round the community like grease lightening. The contest was to take place on the field adjoining the colliery, sandwiched between it and the river Don. That morning, a large crowd assembled all wanting to witness this spectacle. A large portion had walked over from Mexborough, keen to see their fellow citizen Tommy Stokes, up against this young pretender. It was, in reality, a growing boy fighting an experienced mature fighter, which added to the awe of it all.

As the fight commenced the crowd went quiet and then burst into a roar. The two boxers stood toe to toe for the first three rounds giving each other "what for". There was little footwork and dancing around and the ring could have been the size of a doormat. One thing Iron realised this time was that every punch thrown by his opponent was very hard. He had not experienced anything like this before. In past street fights, the odd punch had a meaning to it but Stokes' punches all counted. A noisy steam train hurtled through the nearby crossing and nobody even turned to look at it, the crowd were engrossed.

By the start of the fourth round, young Iron was actually feeling unwell and suffering from double vision. He saw seven Stokes' looking at him. He quickly pulled himself together the best he could. He pulled an almighty punch from somewhere that swung round and hit Stokes right on the forehead. The impact knocked Stokes senseless and he was out for the count. All of a sudden it was all over.

A group of the onlookers, realising Stokes would not get up, suddenly surged forward surrounding Iron. They were cheering and shouting and he was showered with adulation. He had been cheered many times by a few onlookers but this was something new.

Other than the victory, there also had been other things that had happened that day in the field. Life's shackles were sprung open. The boy in Iron Hague had been well and truly chased away. In his mind, Iron knew it was now time for him to move on.

The Monday morning saw Iron walking to Denaby Pit with his friend, Albert Taylor, for the day shift. As they crossed over the River Don after leaving Mexborough Iron paused, "I've done Albert, you won't get me down the pit ever again." Albert stared on in amazement as Iron threw his Dudley flask high into the air and then watched it splash into the middle of the river. They both stared as it bumped about in the swirling waters. The pit buzzer suddenly screeched out and Albert rushed to the Pit gates, while Iron rushed home.

Chapter 3
A Fair Opportunity Presents Itself

John Hague did not take it well that his son had walked from the pit. He learned of this bravado from a deputy in the Staff of Life public house, situated on the town's High Street, probably not the best way for him to find out. Yet more arguments took place at home as John felt his son was wayward and needed putting straight. Mother Ann defended him to the hilt and would hear none of it. John however was a step ahead, "Don't think you are going to be hanging around all day with these fanciful ideas. I've spoken to Sid Barnes and he is going to set you on at Barron's Glassworks, they want some labourers so go down and see him tomorrow." Not the exact news Iron had expected but typical of John, his Father. John was a hard task master.

The living costs of the Hague household at this time were:-

	Shillings	*Pence*
Rent	*3*	*3*
Bread and flour	*3*	*0*
Meat	*4*	*5*
Fish	*0*	*11*
Bacon	*0*	*11*
Eggs	*1*	*0*
Milk	*1*	*3*
Cheese	*0*	*6*
Butter	*2*	*0*
Potatoes	*0*	*10*
Veg and Fruits	*1*	*1*
Rice tapioca, oatmeal	*0*	*6*
Tea and coffee	*0*	*5*
Sugar	*0*	*11*
Jams, marmalades etc	*0*	*10*
Sundry	*2*	*0*
Total	**23s**	**10 pence**

The average wage then for a labourer was 28 shillings per week (for an average 53 hours working week). The 5 shillings or so spare a week would provide for clothing, health and any leisure. So obviously, money was tight and Iron's contribution into the pot was badly needed. They lived like many others at the time, only four weeks away from the workhouse. When times of extra expenditure where identified John would work extra hours at the pit.

One place where Iron used to slip away to in order to find a sympathetic ear was to his mother's brother's house, Walter Bennett's (nicknamed Cocky). He was continuing on the families sporting prowess and playing professional football. He had helped Mexborough Town FC win the Midland League in 1897/98. In the 1895/96 season he had scored 82 goals, 19 of them in two matches alone. He was snapped up by Sheffield United from Mexborough for a £40 transfer fee. He had enjoyed great success at Bramall Lane and was popular with the crowds. He helped them win the championship.

He was just about to be selected for the England team. As much as Iron felt his father didn't understand him, he felt Cocky did. Cocky still helped promote football in the town and Iron was often his young helper.

William "Cocky" Bennett donning his England cap.

One thing that greatly fascinated 15 year old Iron was the boxing booths at the travelling fairgrounds. The boxing booth worked by hoping that some local lads would fancy their chances, put the gloves on and have a go at one of the resident boxers. If no one could be found, they would put on a boxing exhibition boxing each other. This was done softly, softly so as not to hurt each other. The larger crowds though were to be always found whenever a local lad was having a go whereupon the mood of the boxers would change as they wanted to inflict harm as quick as possible to save wear and tear on themselves.

Iron, from age 14, always used to approach the booth for a contest but got rejected, being told to come back when he was a man. As he filled out and developed more of a physique, he was taken more seriously. On his first venture into the booth's ring, he blooded the nose of his opponent. The showman became very wary of young Iron and realised he was one to keep an eye on.

When the Feast came to Mexborough that summer, it had hardly finished setting up camp when young Iron appeared looking who the boxers where. The show was being run by a man dubbed as "The Professor". He had a few seasoned lads in his stable. His heavyweight was introduced as Bill Somebody, the 11 stone champion of Somewhere. When the gloves were held up invitingly, Iron shouted "Chuck 'em over here." The Professor beckoned to Iron, "I know you and if you come in, you'll have to play light, d'ye hear?"

Troop of boxers awaiting their public at this travelling boxing show. Iron Hague loved to volunteer to fight them and to take them to the wire.

"All right" replied Iron, "I won't hurt him, chuck us the gloves." Their bout was the third up with two lighter weights boxing first. The task was to last three rounds as the challenger. If so doing, you received a cash reward. With Iron's fight, all went well for two rounds. Iron sparred good-humouredly and light. Bill Somebody thought he would take advantage of the situation and delivered a full right to the body. Iron responded with a right and a quick left punch that sent Bill to the deck. When he got back up, Iron ploughed back into him unmercifully with punches both to the head and body. The Professor shouted "Time, time!" but Iron was so fired up in a frenzy, he ignored it. Bill Somebody fearing the worst jumped out of the ring into the audience. Iron leaped after him and chased him to the end of the tent where he knocked him out with a huge left to the chin. The professor came running over screaming. Iron simply said, "You should have told him to play light, not just me." The show was over.

Iron was not a particularly accomplished scholar and would often hide the fact with acts of bravado or silences. He needed time to study what was written. At Barron's Glassworks the next day, foreman Sid Barnes produced the paperwork for employment. He commented as to the time that Iron was taking studying the papers, "Are you going through everything lad?" Sid enquired. He wasn't, he hadn't got past the fifth line. He just then signed the page and handed it back. He was to start the next day at 6am on the day shift. His job would be to take the blown glass bottles and stack them into crates and then take them to the despatches yard, where he would help load up the carts and barges. Barron's was the largest employer in Mexborough with the factory premises straggling down from Hope Street right down to the canal side. The business was established back in 1850 by Thomas Barron and his father Joseph. At their peak, they were producing 144000 bottles per week. Just as Iron was leaving, Sid shouted to him, "I understand of thi father that thar a rum lad with the fists, well don't think there's any of that here tha nos."

His reign at Barron's as it happened, did not last too long.

In 1901 when aged 16, he overheard someone reading the South Yorkshire Times that there was to be a fair at Wombwell and it would have amongst its attractions a boxing booth.

A view of Barrons Glassworks which stands at the side of the South Yorkshire Navigation Canal at Mexborough , where Iron later worked.

Inside Barrons Glassworks where bottles were blown, Iron's job here was to crate up the blown bottles.

With no more ado, he set off on foot to walk the seven miles to the fair. Iron claimed that even if there had been a train service, he could not have used it as his father always ensured he had no money. It took him less than two hours. Once there, it did not take Iron long to find the boxing booth. It was an impressive large marquee with a raised platform entrance. Iron found it fascinating. This was just what he was looking for. A large sign proclaimed the forthcoming action:-

BOXING TONIGHT

KILLEM DIEHARD

"The Man Eater from Philadelphia."

BATTLING BUSKER

Who fears no man.

COWBOY HUMPHRIES

The Champion of the Western World

After an hour or so, the door on the marquee was flung open and a man beating a drum emerged. Iron remembers that he looked like a circus freak. He weighed about 25 stone with a large head, a large nose and a large body but with the tiniest of legs and all balanced on child's feet. This gentleman was known as "Tiddler" and was the proprietor, manager, announcer, drum beater, money taker and mopper up of beer.

Having now got the attention of a crowd, he started his banter:-

"Gentlemen, I have the greatest pleasure to introduce to you Killem Diehard, the "man eater" from Philadelphia. Diehard fears no man, he is the victor of a thousand fights. He is a terrible negro."

Staring at the coloured boxer, Iron thought how ugly he was. His ears were virtually gone and his nose was as flat as a steam iron. Iron thought that if he had been the victor of a thousand fights, he must have lost ten thousand.

Tiddler then went on to introduce his other two fighters, Battling Busker and Cowboy Humphries. If you believed Tiddler's patter, they were nearly all as good as world champions.

Tiddler's final line was "If there are any gentlemen in the audience who would care to put on the gloves and have four rounds with any of these boxers then please step forward."

Iron shoved his way through the crowd to the front. "I would like to," he declared. Tiddler's fat face wobbled from side to side, "And who do you want to fight with?"

he enquired. "The black man," Iron replied. Iron made his way into the tent and was pulled aside by Cowboy Humphries to wait in the wings until the marquee filled up. The public stormed in, putting their three pennies admission into Tiddler's bucket, which he gratefully received.

Humphries then told Iron to enter the ring and threw a pair of gloves at him. However, for Diehard, Battling Busker helped him put on his gloves. Seeing Iron struggling, a member of the audience helped Iron fasten on his gloves. Iron waited in the ring corner expecting Tiddler would make some kind of announcement; he did not, he simply called "Times out" to start round one.

Diehard rushed straight at Iron like a mad bull, punching wildly. He managed to catch Iron on the nose the chin and deliver several blows to the head. After a minute of this one sided affair, Iron managed to push Diehard away and started to fight him proper.

Suddenly Tiddler called "Time - end of round one." Iron stood ready for round two, now a lot better prepared. As in the first round, Diehard rushed again at Iron but this time, he was met with a mighty left hand punch straight in his face. This was followed by a strong right hander clean on the jaw. Diehard snorted out and fell through the ropes and through the marquee cover to disappear from sight. The crowd cheered out loudly. This black aggressor had been beat by a local boy – Iron was the Champion. Tiddler was clearly not pleased at the events and reluctantly paid over the purse.

Iron, the victorious, then walked around the rest of the fairground taking in the attractions. Suddenly, he sensed he was being followed. He looked behind and saw non other than Diehard, Cowboy Humphries, Battling busker and Tiddler talking amongst themselves and pointing over to him. Sensing an attack, Iron adopted a fighting pose and faced the posse as they stopped a few yards short of him. Tiddler stepped forward and thrust out his hand to gesture a handshake. Iron was very nervous about this but shook his hand vigorously. Then in turn, the boxers all did the same.

Tiddler told Iron that they would all like him to join them and become part of the fairground show, was he up for it? Iron was taken aback, he had never expected that. The lure of the fight was too much for him and he agreed he would join them. They all shook hands again. Tiddler explained a financial arrangement for the would be boxer and confirmed they were leaving Sunday to go on tour through Staffordshire and Lancashire. They all went back to the boxing booth and talked to each other, becoming friends. All he had to do now was tell his mother and father.

Iron started to talk to his father about his experiences at the Wombwell fair but clearly he wasn't interested. How could he try to explain when all his father ever wanted him to do was to listen to him? There was probably a conflict of personalities. John's view was that all this fighting was a distraction to proper employment, in his eyes being a pugilist was not a job or respectable. It all just developed into a row. Iron abandoned the talk and left it.

On the Sunday morning at 7am, Iron slipped out of the house. He took one final look back, paused just for a moment, then he off went on his way. He knew his mother, brothers and sisters would be devastated but it was something he had to do. He mistakenly thought his father didn't care less. John was oblivious to his departing son, sleeping off the Saturday night ale from the Bulls Head. Iron scampered through the empty streets, there was no turning back. He was on his way – he had run away from home.

Chapter 4
You Set Them Up And I Will Belt Them

The two hours journey was a hard walk for Iron as he carried a case with his belongings in this time and it was heavy. Iron was greeted as a long lost son when he arrived at the Wombwell fair booth. Tiddler put his arm around him and proclaimed, "Our Iron's here now lads." Iron helped his new found fellows pack up the marquee and pack the equipment into the horse traps. Then they set off on their way. For Iron, the spirit of adventure had never been higher.

After four days on the road, the horse drawn procession pulled into a field near Stafford. That was to be their set up. Iron set about helping with great zest. Who would turn up to test him he wondered? He had no fears or trepidation, it was more of a "he couldn't wait" feeling. Tiddler decided to make Iron the star turn of the show. As they waited in the marquee, Tiddler went out with his drum beating to draw in the crowds.

He introduced "The Iron Man" to the crowd and offered a £1 to anyone who could last four rounds with him. Iron looked up and down the crowd expectantly. There was only a single taker up and not what he expected. A large woman with a red drinker's nose demanded a go. They all started laughing, which incited her even more. When Tiddler tried to reason with her as to the absurdity of the situation, she pushed Tiddler aside and launched herself at Iron, slapping him across the

The Boxing Booth Show, reloaded up and on the road.

face. She screamed at him, "There, how do you like it?" Her language was full of expletives and her insistence of a boxing challenge grew. All of a sudden, Tiddler shouted out" Is there any woman in this audience who would like to have a go with this fighting Venus?"

A woman's voice then shouted out, "I will." That did it. With full furore, she leapt into the crowd shouting, "Where is the cat? I will scratch her eyes out." She grabbed the hair of the first woman she could see. The woman then defended herself and a tug of war with their long hair took place. The heads were going too and fro accompanied with shrieks, screams and groans. Eventually, a policeman came on the scene and the fight was halted. Tiddler declared it a draw to the riotous crowd.

As the tour progressed through Staffordshire, Iron took on men of all sizes. Not one had lasted four rounds and collected the celebrated pound prize. Most of the opponents were felled in the first round, often from the first blow. Others hung on until the second round but very few reached the third round. No one succeeded in reaching that elusive fourth round.

For Iron, it was good experience as he came across so many different fighting styles. One thing Iron respected with these have a go pugilists was that they had guts. It was not unusual for one of the opponents defeated to appear again the following night to have another go.

This occurred in Hanley, one stiffly built ginger haired fighter who had been put down in the second round the night previous turned up again. He had a bonzer of a black eye but still wanted to fight. This time Iron put him out in the first round. He then turned up the third night with two black eyes wanting to have a go yet again.

Feeling a little sorry for him, Iron only tapped him a little in the first two rounds to give him some encouragement. At the start of the third round, the challenger lunged at Iron and landed a right punch right between the eyes. Iron responded with some attacking flurries finally landing a killer punch on the chin end. It took 25 minutes to bring the challenger around. He didn't turn up again.

They had remained in Staffordshire for six months before travelling into Lancashire. The shows flowed and the fighting continued. Between four and twelve men were fought by Iron on every day's opening.

At one show in Lancashire after two years on the road, Iron had a real test. Following Tiddler's introduction, a young fellow made his way to the ring. Tiddler told him to take his coat off but instead he stripped down the waist. He had come prepared. The young man called Smith had one of the finest physiques Iron had ever seen. He was about 6 feet 2 inches tall and had arm muscles like duck eggs. He carried no fat anywhere. He was some three inches taller than Iron with a longer reach, which could be very dangerous.

As Iron looked over, he noticed Tiddler sneak a drink from his beer jug. Passed shows had learnt him that he only did this if he feared the worst. Tiddler clearly thought that this modern day Samson would make mince meat out of Iron and he would be paying the £1 purse out.

As round one got underway, Smith stepped forward in a businesslike manner and started sparring away. In one instance, as Smith dropped his guard for just a second, Iron was straight in there with a right blow. With great speed, Smith corrected the move and blocked the punch. This knocked Iron off his feet onto the canvas. Iron was up within a second but it gave Smith great confidence. He lunged forward and landed two decent punches onto Irons temple. Iron retaliated with a fast punch under the chin. He seemed unperturbed with this. Then round one ended.

Tiddler took a long drink out of his beer jug before announcing round two. In this round, Iron adopted a strategy of hard selective punches to knock Smith out. This failed as he was too guarded and the more he got the more he seemed to thrive on it.

As the third round commenced, Tiddler's behaviour went erratic. Iron had never seen him behave quite like this before. He marched up and down the marquee throwing his arms about shouting, "Knock him out." Killem Diehard tried to calm him down but it was in vain. At the end of the third round, Tiddler was still dancing and throwing himself about. He approached Iron before the fourth and threw his arms around him. "Knock him out" he spluttered in his ear repeatedly. He had had too much beer and Iron had had enough. With no further ado Iron turned and hit him with a right hander so flooring Tiddler. Luckily for him, he fell on a pile of shavings.

In Tiddlers absence, Killem Diehard called for the fourth round to commence. Smith waded in with a right punch to Iron's temple. This was answered with three swift punches to the face. Smith felt these and appeared to weaken. These were followed by planting a punch to the ear followed by a left hook. Down at last went Smith. Iron had done it but that was a hard fight.

Killem Diehard stooped over Smith with a view of helping him up but a woman in the audience thought he meant mischief and whacked him over the head with a bottle she had secreted in her coat. Diehard's head was bleeding and in response, he turned round and struck out at the woman. Within a few seconds, the whole place was in uproar. Everyone was fighting each other. A group armed with chairs were hell bent on stomping Iron and the boxers. The situation was serious. It became obvious the crowd had come to see their local boy Smith whack the boxers but it wasn't to be. Iron crawled out under the marquee into the fairground still stripped to the waist. He went to his caravan for safety. He could here police whistles blowing all around.

The situation was absurd. Iron packed his belongings into his case and headed off for the railway station. It was time to return home to Mexborough. He had been away two years and that was long enough. Within thirty minutes, he was sat in the third class carriage on the steam train and was heading back.

Chapter 5
Home Is Where You Hang Your Head And "Up the Town"!

Iron had not been home or corresponded with his parents for some two years. He was suddenly racked with feelings of guilt. He knew his absence would have caused agony even though they knew he was alright. As he made his way up Station Road from the railway station, all sorts of thoughts raced around his head. What if they had moved? What if they had left the district?

Iron paused outside the door and tapped loudly with the knocker. Presently, he heard a bolt being drawn back and then the door opened. There stood Ann. She cried out, "Oh its William! Dad come quickly, its William!" She then threw her arms about his neck and started crying. A lump entered Iron's throat and tears ran down his hardened cheeks. Iron was motionless, speech failed him. This man, who in the last two years had fought hundreds of men and beat them all was, for the first time in his life, knocked out by his mother's tears. John entered the room and they stared at each other. John then lunged forwards and hugged him. The prodigal son returns. Iron related his adventures of the last two years to the eager listeners. At the end, Ann made Iron promise that he would give up this 'wild beast' sort of life, as she called it and return to civilisation. Iron was so taken aback, he promised his mother he would not fight again. She savoured this moment as she could see a twinkle in his eye as he said these words. She knew it wouldn't be long before he was back to his old ways.

Cocky Bennett helped Iron by getting him the job of groundsman at the Athletic Football ground at Hampden Road. Here, he had to keep all the pitches flat and mowed, the white lines white and ensure pitches were set up with nets, etc, as needed. It was now November 1903 and Iron was still only 18 years of age yet had seen so much. Unfortunately, as with any fighter of proclaim, trouble was waiting for him just round the corner.

Cup fever was in the town. The Mexborough Montague Hospital Cup had been keenly fought over for a number of years. This pre-Christmas third round tie on the 12th December 1903 was between Mexborough Town FC and Highthorn FC of Kilnhurst.

Kilnhurst was situated at the other side of the Don Valley to Mexborough and was about three miles away. Highthorn itself was no more than a few cottages and farms that abutted the village. Kilnhurst was quite unique in that for its size, it contained a lot of serious heavy industry. The village boasted a colliery, an ironworks, a brickyard, a glassworks as well as being surrounded by farms.

The village had its own Co-op who's origins were back in the 1860's. It dominated the main thoroughfare on Victoria Street and acted like a department store for the area. The Kilnhurst residents were viewed as being parochial and if you upset one, you upset them all.

Highthorn had won the cup in spectacular style beating Wath the previous year and were looking for a repeat performance. Some 600 spectators had assembled to watch the game. Spirits were high and drinking in the town's public houses beforehand had been widespread. The day, although fine, was bitterly cold. The ground was still soft and slippy and made goalkeeping very hard. Play was intense from both sides and by half time, Mexborough led 1-0 but the pressure was very much on. In the second half, Mexborough missed a penalty, but as the closing minutes came a long shot from Town forward, Hall, landed the firm decider. The visiting fans went into uproar as they believed the ball had gone out of touch on the sideline just beforehand. The referee, Mr Grayson of Sheffield Woodhouse, had to stop play for a full ten minutes. One of the Highthorn players strongly remonstrated with the referee. The situation got even more heated being drawn on by the visiting crowd. Suddenly, in temper, the player struck out and punched the referee with a fist to his head. The low police presence at the game made matters very tense but nontheless, two constables marched onto the pitch and arrested the Highthorn player.

The supporters were by now jostling up to each other. One of the visiting supporters was William John Hewitson. He was known as "The Champion of Kilnhurst". He was 6 feet tall with a thickset build and towered above everyone. He was a bit of a bully in nature and unbeaten in his previous battles, he firmly believed he was invincible.

The football crowd was now engaged in a vicious fight and heads were knuckled on both sides. The police managed to bring things under control but it was obvious that the Kilnhurst men were quite embittered. Hewitson, as his parting shot, told the assembled Mexborough crowd, "Fetch Mexborough's best and I will show you what victory really means."

So now a pugilistic challenge was to be settled, Kilnhurst's best would take on and beat anyone from Mexborough. Iron as it happened was not at the game. He was out of town. He probably saw enough of the place in the week as groundsman without putting free overtime in. One thing that later annoyed him was the discovery that one of the visitors in the turmoil had took the match ball away with them.

Some of the Kilnhurst men who were regular drinkers in Mexborough were still around town at 9pm and goading the local lads, "So who is going to be your man then? My, you've gone a bit quiet." The problem was that the lads knew Iron was their man but they couldn't find him. He wasn't at home. He wasn't with friends. He had disappeared off of the radar. They needed to check with him first.

One of the lads asked John Hague, who was in the Bulls Head, where Iron was and he cut up a bit suspicious as to why he wanted to know.

In Iron's absence, Ernest Rawson, who had done quite a bit of bare knuckle in his younger days jumped in with both feet, "Tell your man 10 shillings a side, bare knuckle under Prize Ring rules. We will see you at 8am in the morning at Old Denaby Woods." He hoped that he had done right as great reputations were at stake here.

The Kilnhurst lads managed to just get back to the Commercial Hotel in the heart of their village where King Hewitson kept court. He was more than up for it. Just as the word then sped round Kilnhurst it was equally doing the rounds in Mexborough, and also in Denaby at the pit where Iron used to work.

The last train from Doncaster limped into Mexborough station at 12.18am. Iron alighted and speedily made his way to Woodruff Row for some well earned sleep.

At 6am on the Sunday morning, the door knocker at the Hague household at Woodruff Row was repeatedly banged. "Who the bloody hell is that?" boomed out John's voice from the front bedroom. Iron rushed downstairs and was surprised to see Ernest Rawson and his pal standing there. They quickly explained the situation and Iron jumped straight in. He was well up for it. He went back upstairs and after explaining to John, it was nothing, speedily got dressed and left the house. "I bet it isn't" muttered John as he watched him disappearing downstairs once more.

The appointed Mexborough meeting place for all involved with this battle royal was on the canal bank near Ferryboat Lane. Iron was taken aback. When he arrived there

The ferryman couldn't believe his luck with all the early morning passengers wishing to travel over to Old Denaby from Mexborough.

out of the darkness to see some 400 people assembled, they gave him a thunderous ovation. Onwards from there meant they needed to cross over the River Don via the hand propelled ferry boat. The ferryman couldn't believe his luck when he was knocked up to transport hundreds of people over the river when he may only do 100 in a full day.

As the party crossed over the railway line to enter the lane that ran up to the village, a sole cyclist could be seen heading towards them like the clappers. He had been sent ahead by Rawson to check things out. He told as to how the police had got to know of the fight and a load of them had secreted themselves in the wood. "They were," he said "as thick as flies, hidden in every nook and cranny." It was obviously a joint police operation as Mexborough alone couldn't have raised this manpower.

Just like the prize fighters of days gone by, the party was determined that the police should not ruin the day and an alternative venue was quickly decided on. The game plan was for Iron and his followers to march across the fields following the River Don towards Hooton Roberts and stage the fight there. The onlookers were to split up into small groups and to travel down several of the alternatives routes that presented themselves. The cyclist was despatched to tell the Kilnhurst lads what was happening. The fight did not now take place for some three hours to give everyone time to arrive there. It was thought wise to do this rather than run any risks.

Hewitson was a miner, as was his father, and resided at 46 Hooton Road, Kilnhurst. He was around 14 stones in weight with a height advantage. He was twenty three years of age and a good four years older than his challenger, Mexborough's man of Iron. The changing of the fight venue meant the Hewitson family home was situate only a half mile away. The field for the contest was at the side of Hooton Cliff and somewhat out of the way. As 11.45am approached, almost 500 people were assembled in the field in preparation to witness the fight of the decade. As Iron approached the centre of the field, Hewitson said nothing and just stared at him. It was obviously his technique, one that is still used by the fighters of today. If pulses were running high, it didn't show anywhere.

Iron stripped down to the waist and started to stretch his arms and move his neck from side to side. He looked fit, as did the champion of Kilnhurst. They always say a fighter needs a few key qualities. He needs power and fitness but importantly, he needs to possess that killer instinct. When he fights, he has to mean it and enter the contest without fear or trepidation. Both men seemed to tick all these boxes.

They were just about to start the fight when a voice could be heard yelling out, "Stop, stop! I will not have you fighting in my field." Approaching them was the farmer, armed with a hedging bill. He was dressed with gaiters and matching jacket. He had a red face and huge side whiskers.

He was overweight and clearly had exerted some effort to run up from Elm Tree

Farm which was at the edge of Kilnhurst. He muttered he would fetch the police. Rawson met the farmer as he reached the crowd and got him around the neck and told him to keep quiet. Rawson then let up his grip and tried to reason with the man, but the farmer was having none of it. The mood of the crowd was one of increasing intimidation towards the farmer. Rawson ordered him to stand there, pointing at a spot on the ground.

Rawson then went into discussions with Hewitsons seconds. "He is your man what are we going to do?" chimed up Rawson. "We've dodged the Mexborough Police and we don't want this tiller of soil spoiling all our efforts." One of the seconds said he knew the farmer. He was a very religious man and obviously did not show up earlier as he would have been at the service up at St Thomas Church, adding that the vicar up there does go on a bit.

One of the crowd suddenly produced a rope and cries rang out to tie the farmer up and throw him in the hedge bottom until the fight was over. The suggestion was from a bookmaker who clearly did not want his gaming book for this day to be thwarted. The Kilnhurst lads did not really fancy doing this. They would have to live with all this long after the fight was finished. Fearing for his safety, the farmer started shouting out for help from the police, who were nowhere to be seen. Rawson then had a brilliant idea. "Right" he said, "give me a hand, we are going to carry the fat little bastard over here." They took him to where the fighters stood and plonked him down on a makeshift chair. He protested but it was in vain as the crowd encircled making it nigh on impossible for him to get out. Suddenly, one or two policemen started appearing but they did nothing and just stood about here and there. They weren't in strength and could have been waiting for reinforcements. An off the cuff conversation with one of them confirmed they were in reality as keen to see this fight as anyone but they needed to hurry.

The battle was now to commence in earnest. In lieu of the trickle of police, it was decided to save time to dispense with rounds and go straight for it to the finish. It was the 13th December and unlucky for somebody. As soon as they stood facing each, other Hewitson lunged forward and planted a lovely punch on Iron's nose. They were off. For a couple of minutes, the boxers were toe to toe both showing great aggression. In the fourth minute, Hewitson landed an uppercut which knocked Iron off his feet and down he went.

The crowd started shouting for him to get up which he did with great speed. The punch was noted and felt.

The fighting then settled down and was not as fierce, probably being influenced by Iron to allow him to recompose. After five more minutes, Iron caught Hewitson with a mighty left hook that sent him reeling backwards. He was down on the ground but rallied to his supporters screams to get up and wade in. He duly responded to Irons surprise and though dazed, boxed on. He was more defensive but a stray punch managed to knock Iron down again. After about thirty minutes fighting, Hewitson seemed to find some unspent energy and suddenly upped the ante. Iron had kept picking away with jabs, starting to mark his man. Hewitson by now, did not look a pretty sight but remarkably, he boxed on.

Hewitson's face now showed the punishment it had absorbed; one eye was virtually shut and the other badly bruised. Even though there were visible marks and swelling to ribs and body, Hewitson still would not give in, the boxing went on. Observers noted how Iron also started showing the battle scars from this fight. No one could go through this ordeal without paying the price, it certainly was a fight to the bitter end. On the thirty fifth minute, Hewitson's corner suddenly threw in the sponge signifying the end of the fight. Hewitson was finally beaten but what a job it had been.

Remarkably, Iron's backers who put up the money for the fight, donated him some 2 shillings for his efforts. They had done very well thank you, for just standing around. A bucket was passed round for the loser who ended up with 10 shillings 6 pence. It demonstrated that it really was a mugs game when the loser gets more than the victor.

In later years, Iron often used to quote that "It is on record that the last great fight with bare knuckle took place at Farnborough between Tom Sayers and John Heenan about 1854. But you can take it that the last bare knuckle fight under Prize Ring rules was between Hewitson and me at Hooton Roberts and it was in 1903."

After the fight ended, the crowd quickly dispersed fearing the arrival of police on mass at any time. Iron and his men headed back to Mexborough with the satisfaction that the best man Kilnhurst had was proved to be no match for Mexborough's own champion.

It was about 2pm before Iron trundled over the threshold of the family home at Woodruff Row. His mother swooned at the sight of her son, seeing that he was in a pitiful condition. She made him look into a mirror, pointing out lumps of torn flesh and swellings.

She kept repeating, "What will your father say, what will your father say?" Iron gazed at his reflection, blocked out his mother's wails and gave a wry smile despite feeling sick and dizzy.

After sponging him down, she wanted him to take some food but he found that he could not fully open his mouth and had no hunger feelings. If he was the victor what did the challenger look like? Ann took the beef steak she was to prepare for him and cut it into strips and slapped it on the facial swellings securing it there with bandages.

She was a big believer in raw meat healing cuts and bruises. Iron later recalled and commented that the dinner he thought he had earned was instead hung around his face.

Mexborough Police Station can be seen towards the middle of the picture as an assortment of buildings. Iron Hague was taken here and charged after the Kilnhurst bare fist fight.

He could not find comfort in laying down because of the soreness of his ribs. The only comfort he found was by sitting up in an upright position. When John arrived home, he was not best pleased. He had heard what had happened from the many town citizens who kept stopping him to congratulate him on Iron's success. When he burst through the door, he wanted to wade into Iron as he had always done over the years. The sight of Iron though with his injuries made him hesitate. Instead, he threatened to plant his foot firmly on his backside, the only uninjured part left. John went on and on about the morals of it all. He felt long gone from his own youth and had lost any sympathy for a young man's sowing of wild oats. Iron responded by saying that he had now some 10 shillings to show for his efforts so all was not in vain. What were a few bruises?

As the day shift policemen checked in on the Monday morning at the Low Road Mexbororough police station, a message awaited several of them.

"You have to be back here for 9am, the Superintendant is coming." That meant serious business. At 9am prompt, the meeting commenced. The Superintendant took it personal that despite excellent intelligence, they were unable to stop a prize fight right in their backyard. They were a laughing stock. The fact that some police were even amongst the spectators he found even more unbelievable. Sergeant Morris tried to defend the officers by saying they were so highly outnumbered by the mob present, their life could have been at risk without sufficient police numbers. Even the press were aware of the fight and attended. The Superintendant found it all very embarrassing. It was made very plain that this matter had to be brought to an end in the police's favour. Two sergeants and four men were allocated to fetch the fighters in, one team to Kilnhurst and one team to Woodruff Row.

One of the young officers present went into the backyard to use the outside toilet. He was a neighbour of Ernest Rawson's and was actually a spectator at the fight. By chance, Rawson was passing by, they glimpsed each other.

Upon seeing Rawson, he beckoned him over and whispered, "We are on our way up to Iron's house, we are under orders and have to fetch him in."

Rawson just nodded, turned and ran up onto the High Street and onto Woodruff Row. He knocked and burst into Iron's house in the same second, taking the occupants by surprise. He spluttered out to Iron, "Quick, make yourself scarce, the police are on your track." Iron, somewhat taken aback asked, "Who's given the game away, I thought we had eluded them?" "So did I," was Rawson's response "it must have been that dirty old farmer bloke, it will be useless trying to deny you have been in a fight, that is unless" Rawson paused "you tell them you have been run over by the steam roller."

The reason for this humorous comment was because of the frenzied activity on High Street as preparations were made to lay new tram lines. The use of a steam roller was a novelty to the townsfolk.

Suddenly, there was thunderous repeated banging on the front door. Rawson, like a rat up a drainpipe, shot out of the backdoor. Iron felt indifferent to anything that would happen and calmly opened the front door and asked if he could help them? The burly policeman and his sergeant were not amused. Iron was arrested to appear at Doncaster West Riding Court the next morning. He was charged with breaking the peace by indulging in a fight at Hooton Roberts. A similar raid had occurred in Kilnhurst so the Tuesday morning saw Iron and Hewitson once more stood side by side.

The chairman of the magistrates was perhaps a fight fan as he appeared sympathetic to what had gone off. Iron decided to speak for himself. He explained to the bench as to how this fight was a personal vendetta just between the two of them that ended up getting blown out of all proportion. The sergeant contested this because of the detailed organisation that had gone into the event. The magistrate wasn't swayed by the sergeant's angle on things and to the disappointment of the police, only bound each of the fighters over for six months to keep the peace. Iron winked at his arresting officer as he left the court.

Chapter 6
A "Stand In" Opportunity Eventually Prevails

Iron had to keep his head down now to avoid perhaps being jailed for any breech of his court order.

He was keen to further his boxing skills and career. He spread the word that he would fight anyone for money. The town at this time did not boast a boxing promoter or a suitable venue to stage contests.

He was persuaded to commence formal training under the watchful eye of former fighter and town resident, Shep O'Brien. He showed great promise and Shep told everyone about Young Iron whenever he could. Shep recognised that Iron possessed a great punching power, the like of which most boxers would die for. One of the party tricks Iron would do for any onlookers was to start punching panel doors hung from beams on chains. He would belt the strong outer frame then finish with a frenzy smashing all the panels and then finally splitting the frame straight into two.

Iron had no manager looking after him and was trying to secure fights himself by asking around the venues, without luck. The use of managers was becoming evermore popular, originating in the USA. It was now taking over in England and many aspired to fill the roles.

After a moribund period, an offer arose out of the blue for a fight to be squeezed in at short notice which Iron jumped at. It was at the Labour Hall, Manchester on the 4th August 1904 against a Mr A White of Burton on Trent. The fight proved to be a testing one for Iron. There was no knock out or outstanding boxing, just a steady amble through. Nerves may also have had something to do with it. The fight lasted for eight rounds and Iron won on points. So although the fight was dull, it was his first professional fight and he won. It was also a payday and funds were urgently needed.

The only other opportunity emerging for Iron that year was for an exhibition fight on the 22nd November. This was to be a three rounder against the Elland Boxer, Jack Lamb. The fight took place at the circus arena, pitched at Warrington. Boxing exhibitions always provided the boxers with a bit of income and in those times, had become a popular feature of entertainment. Exhibitions of boxing even started to feature on the stage, in variety, with many top fighters of the day all taking part in them. The pay for this was often very good and if you were a heavyweight, you got the most. A top fighter got £200 a week for appearing in a regular show.

It served its purpose as £25 was paid for Iron's services. That was equivalent to 10 weeks working for his dad.

This was hardly the best start for a serious fighter intent on beating all comers. He badly needed someone to be handling his corner and looking after him.

There was to be a boxing contest at Doncaster Drill Hall, which was situated on Frenchgate, on the 2nd January 1905 and Iron was looking forward to witnessing the spectacle. Pat Mannion, who lived in Denaby, was the Yorkshire Pitman's champion. He was matched against Dan Lewis, a coloured boxer middleweight of great repute, who lived in Sheffield.

Two days before the event, Mannion fell victim to a dreaded flu bug and was confined to his sick bed. The Doncaster promoter, Mr Smith, now had a problem as this was his star billing. After general discussions with people in the know, he was told to contact the up and coming Mexborough lad, Iron Hague, he could save the day. Now this was an opportunity; to be able to box right in one's own backyard.

Mr Smith had to ask directions to Woodruff Row after leaving the train but was soon put right. He was given a warm greeting and Ann made her guest a cup of tea whilst he waited for her husband and son to return. They didn't have to wait long. John arrived first and Iron arrived just after him. After a quick discussion, which received John's approval, Iron agreed he would step into Mannion's shoes, the fight could go ahead. There was however a problem. The way the fight game worked, Iron needed a backer to put up a purse. John said he had an idea. He was very friendly with the landlord of the Bulls Head who was a great sports fan, he may help. With no further, ado he threw on his coat and shot up the High Street returning shortly afterwards. "Mr Biggs will put up the purse for Iron," John announced, "the fight can go ahead."

The contest was to be over twenty rounds of two minutes duration and be for "a pony" (£25) a side using four ounce gloves. Iron, aged 19, was weighed in at 11 stones 7 pounds. This was about one and a half stones heavier than Lewis and he was some four inches taller but despite this, the bookies money was still on Lewis as he was by far the more experienced fighter, with a reputation of being a hard hitter. The odds started out the night as evens but had drifted to 5 to 4 by the start of the contest. Lewis was aged 24. Iron had come across Lewis several times before in the past on the boxing booth circuit. He had boxed with him in several exhibition bouts when a member of the public had not been forthcoming. Lewis had boxed extensively for the Gal Hague booth in the travelling fairs. Despite the common surname, Gal Hague was a relative of Lewis and not Iron.

On the night of the fight, the regular crowd at the Drill Hall was swelled by an influx of Mexborough citizens wanting to see Iron perform, now with gloves on and in a regular fight. There wasn't a seat left in the house. Iron was certainly building up his fan base.

On the night, Iron's seconds were his trusted trainer, Shep O'Brien, Dudley Long and J Dalton of Rotherham. The referee was well known local fighter Percy Lavcock, the timekeeper was none other than Pat Mannion, the fighter who Iron had stood in for. One wonders whether Mannion was in fact in trepidation of Lewis or only partially recovered from his flu.

The fight opened with Lewis lunging forward and landing a full left into Iron's face. This riled Iron and he responded with both fists flying but Lewis simply stepped out of reach. Iron's tactics were to go for Lewis's body with weakening slams. Lewis's tactics centred on delivering head punches that would daze his opponent. Indeed in the first round, Lewis had two very near misses which if connected, would have put paid to Iron. Iron did however score sufficient points to make the round even. For the next round, the skilful Lewis kept his young opponent at bay the best he could with a demonstration of speed stepping. Iron's body blows though kept finding their way through Lewis's defence and started to take their toll. During the one minute break, Lewis seemed to recover well for the third round. In the third round and within a minute, Iron managed to pin his man into the corner and pummelled him. With a mighty right hander, he then punched Lewis through the ropes and out of the ring. His seconds tried helping him back in but he was not having any of it. The fight was over, he was counted out.

Iron stood victorious. He was pleased with it all having had little time to train, he had fought from the rough.

Frank J Law, proprietor of the Montague Arms and Iron Hagues much loved manager.

Iron afterwards commented as how he had never fought someone who moved around as much as Lewis. He was like a dancing cock nipping in with a light blow and then nipping out again.

Back in the changing rooms, Iron was slumped down on the bench when there was a knock at the door. Dudley Long, Iron's second, with cigarette blazing answered the door. He was confronted by a gentleman immaculately dressed wearing a black fedora hat. "I would like to see Mr Hague," the gentleman informed him. Long immediately recognised him as Mr Law, the landlord of the Montagu Arms Hotel, Mexborough. Addressing him as "Sir", Long graciously let him in and Iron propped himself back up from the bench to meet him.

Having Frank Law come to see you was akin to a Mexborough Royal visit. Iron also knew who he was but pretended he did not, just like his friend. Law congratulated him on his win. He told Iron how he had been at the ringside and how he was a good judge of fighters.

He wondered if Iron wanted to take up boxing professionally as he was looking for a new fighter to promote. Iron took all of ten seconds to think about it. "I would love to be a professional," he retorted in response. The two of them shook hands vigorously both feeling they had pulled off a coup. It was agreed a meeting would be set up with Iron's father, John, to get his approval. That could have been a problematical meeting for a stranger but with Frank Law in front of him, it would be a lot easier as his business acumen, and high local respect went before him. Interestingly, Iron was aged 19 and headstrong, but still sought the approval of his father. The age of 21 was always classed as the presenting of the "key of the door" to your children.

Francis John Law was born in 1858 at West Melton. His family had been there for several generations previous. As a youngster, he worked in the bowels of the newly sunk Wath Colliery. This, he quickly, established was not for him and he went into the licensed trade. He was renowned as being a good all round sportsman and also boxed himself. He was involved in one memorable fight at the Newhill Fair. His opponent was Jack Glenn who had been injured underground at Stubbin Colliery previously. He was apparently thereafter left such that he was now impervious to pain and drove on when other men would have stopped. They fought under the English Rules for ninety minutes and even after all that time, there was still no advantage identified to either fighter. When both fighters were finally spent and drained, the fight was declared a draw.

Frank also won a few local running races, establishing an "all rounder" reputation for himself. His family were entrepreneurs and Frank also had the flair. As a young man, he borrowed some working capital and bought the stock and the lease of the Queens Hotel at Winterwell, West Melton. This he kept for ten years, during which time he married Miss Jane Cook, who was a local girl, their children, son John and daughter Kate were born there.

Frank then went on to take over the Cross Keys Hotel situated on Doncaster Road, Wath on Dearne. He retained this for some eight years. Whilst there, he became involved with his father, John and his uncle, George Law, operating a small colliery at Firth Lane, West Melton. They also owned the small brickworks at Packman Road. They sponsored the Newhill Cricket Team and Frank was one of its best players.

With his built up wealth, it meant he had sufficient capital to bid and acquire the prestigious Montagu Arms, Montagu Square, Mexborough upon its coming on the market. This was the biggest hotel in the area with many letting bedrooms.

An early shot of Montague Square, Mexborough, with the Montague Arms on the right hand side. The town's bank is straight ahead. It was here that Frank Law opened Iron a personal bank account

In addition to the bar areas, it also had dining and meeting rooms and to the rear, a large stables were spread around an open quadrangle. It was a large employer in the town employing, many bar staff, cooks, maids and domestics , a cellar man, handyman, stabling and horse keeper and carriage staff.

The hotel was built by the Montagu family of High Melton so proudly bearing their family name. These were often glory badges for the gentry, having the pub/hotel on your estate named in honour of you. This put your stamp onto the area. It was a sight to greet your visitors and emphasised your power grip.

Recently the Prince of Wales Theatre had been built right alongside and this had brought the business on even more. Many of the stars of the day stayed at the Montagu lifting its fashionability. Many landlords throughout the area aspired to own and run the Montague Arms hotel but few had the necessary capital to do so.

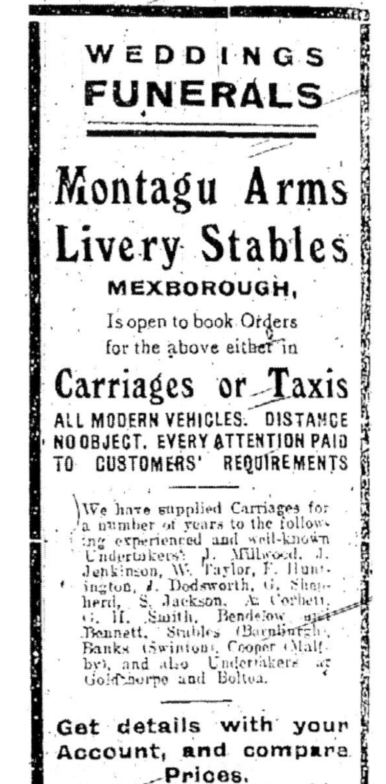

Advert from the Montague Arms – 1909

The following Saturday morning at 11am prompt, Frank Law was knocking on the Hague's front door on Woodruff Row. An arrangement had been made to meet with Iron's parents for exploratory talks and hopefully to seek formal approval for Frank's plans. The door was answered by Iron himself who beckoned Frank to come in. Inside the small front parlour, Ann Hague had ensured that everything was put neatly away and gave the ambiance that it was always kept like that.

Frank was greeted by John wearing his Sunday best shirt and a black tie. Although John did not acknowledge the fact he knew Frank Law, he most certainly did. After the introductions, Frank got down to explaining his interest in boxing and how he felt Iron had great talents in the ring. He outlined his plans for training and going forwards, he wanted to sign Iron up into a formal management agreement.

At first, John seemed very reluctant but warmed to the situation as the meeting went on. Finally, John stood up and said, "The lad has been fighting since he was six years old and he's made nowt out of it yet. If you can put him in the way of making a living by fighting, well jolly good luck to the both of you." He outstretched his hand to Frank and the deal was done.

A proper gymnasium was set up in what was known as "the Low Drop". This was where the hotel dipped down two floors from the High Street level to rendezvous with the land below. The gym had a sparring area, skipping area and was equipped with punch bags and an assortment of training aids.

It was a proper training HQ. Frank invited John to come round and have a look at the gym facilities, which he did.

Since John consented, he started to take a greater interest in his son's boxing and the training routines. He started spending more and more time there. At last, father and son stood side by side in a great admiration for each other. Over the years, Iron had always shown the greatest respect and fear of his father. They had argued countless hours, now all that was behind them. For John, it gave him a new pride. Word about Iron going professional went around Mexborough faster than a west wind. Everywhere John went he was asked by enquiring citizens as to "What is the latest?"

As part of Frank's deal came a joint backer. To go up the ladder, you had to be able to put up high stakes which were way beyond the reach of many.

This role was filled by Thomas Weston. He was aged 58 at the time. He was the landlord of the Reresby Arms at Denaby and a very successful businessman. He was born in 1847 in Halesowen, Worcestershire. His wife Elizabeth was from Sedgefield, Staffordshire. He had left home at the age of 15 and moved three miles away to Rowley Regis (part of east Birmingham) where he became an apprentice cordwainer to Henry Raybould. Following on from this, he went to work in the coal mines. He was married in 1869 and his son Eli was born in the following year, 1870. Thomas drifted into inn keeping taking over the Junction Inn at Methley near Leeds. He

Mr & Mrs Thomas Weston, Iron Hagues backers.

did this whilst still working at a local mine. He later moved to Mexborough in South Yorkshire and took over the Union Inn at the corner of Quarry Street and Doncaster Road in Mexborough. He traded this successfully and then took over the Bulls Head on the town's High Street, which was more central. He had amassed sufficient capital to make a big move. He took over the Reresby Arms on Doncaster Road at Denaby, which also served as a hotel.

If there was one thing about him, it was he knew how to make a business crack. He quickly upped the profile of the place and the hotel rooms were always full. As a former working man, he understood his customers. He always put a bit back across the bar for them in the way of occasional free pints or a bit of food. Every new face appearing was always greeted with a welcome from the landlord himself. He flourished in the pioneering days of the time. Denaby was a relatively newly built mining town and buzzed with activity. Although he was very successful, earning a lot of money, he was also very benevolent. He gave away a great deal of money in the form of Pensioner Treats, helping the poor of the parish and anyone else he thought deserved it. He was viewed as a kind hearted sentimental

A picture of Doncaster Road, Denaby Main, with the Weston's Public House ,the Reresby Arms (the Pig) to the left hand side (now demolished).

soul, but there was another side to him. He was keen on every kind of sport and was a very shrewd judge of raw sporting talent.

He ran the Denaby United Football Club for many years when Denaby played as one of the finest in the Midland League. They were best the district had ever seen. One great tragedy in his life was the premature death of his son Eli whom he doted on. Eli was buried at Mexborough Cemetery where a portrait of him was attached to the huge domineering gravestone marking the burial spot. For several years on the anniversary of the funeral, Thomas hired a full funeral outfit to revisit the grave and rededicate it to him.

Thomas was a keen boxing fan and was a member of the National Sporting Club in London. When his friend, Frank Law, approached him to be co-backer he already knew of Iron. He had seen him fight and thought him very worthy of an investment. Now this part of the deal was done, there would be sufficient clout to go all the way if Iron could hack it.

The way the system worked was that a purse was pledged by the backer for their man to win. This would be matched by the other side. After the fight took place and a winner was proclaimed, the losing boxer's backer would pay his money over to the other backer. It was a bit like a private bet. This would then be paid over to the boxer with a percentage being deducted and paid to the manager (often a third). In addition, the backer paid the fight preparation training costs, ie sparring partners, accommodation, etc. The backer made his money from controlling the side stakes that went on the outcome. Unofficially, it was his cost to secure the betting rights. In addition, the boxer would receive a lump sum in prize money put up by the venue.

The Montagu Arms was a large building and the gymnasium room was of a good size. As Iron got into his training routines, it was easy to get distracted as people wandered down from the public bars to stand with a beer watching the business in hand. Iron did get used to this but always maintained he could not train as serious as when behind a closed door with his sparring partners.

The old saying is "what goes around comes around" and that was the case for Iron's first fight in Frank Law's stable. The opponent was none other than his old adversary Tom Stokes. Stokes had always felt bitter about his performance against the younger Iron those few years ago and saw this fight as an opportunity of rectifying the records.

Iron, undeterred, quite fancied the prospect. The fight was to be in the February of 1905, a regular bill at the Doncaster Drill Hall. Surprisingly, it turned out to be a bit of a one sided non event. Iron was now some four years older than when they last met and his physique was now much stockier and he had had all the boxing booth experience. He was now a much different animal.

The fight, listed near the bottom of the bill, lasted for eight rounds before Iron knocked his opponent out, notching up his first professional 'Knock Out' win. The fight met with a good crowd response, he was a local youngster and they liked him. Stokes soon rallied round, not believing his fate. He went and shook hands with Iron to show good sportsmanship.

As the summer trundled on, a visiting fairground to the town brought with it "Watsons Boxing Booth". This was run by Jim Watson of Leeds. Iron, unsurprisingly, acquainted himself with the owner reliving with him his previous experiences of the booths. Watson offered Iron a regular job which tempted him greatly. As he later quoted, "The experience one gains whilst with a boxing booth is invaluable. True, some of your opponents are very crude and know little about the noble art but even they are apt to spring a surprise on one often when least expected. Therefore, it means that one has always to be alert and in the pink of physical fitness, otherwise disaster may follow on."

The difference this time was that Iron did not stay away as before but travelled only intermittently to various accessible venues. This meant he was available for anything his manager could organise for him. Iron saw it as a way of intensifying the training by keeping up the demands of him. This arrangement lasted for several months.

In March of 1905, Frank Law confirmed to Iron the next fight would be tough and was very important to their going forward to the bigger time. It was to be at the Doncaster Drill Hall against Dick Parkes of Goldthorpe. Dick was an experienced heavyweight of 13 stones who carried the title Pitman's Heavyweight champion of Yorkshire. He had fought Mannion of Denaby and took the title a few months earlier. The fight was being billed as "For The Heavyweight Champion of Yorkshire" and it was a title Frank Law desperately wanted his man to have.

Dick Parks – opponent and trainer.
Former Pitmans heavyweight champion.

It was decided that a harder training programme would be undertaken. Unfortunately, the interruptions to Iron's training routine continued with a large number of well wishers wanting to watch him train. They would edge down from the public bar, firstly putting their head round the corner and then standing full in the doorway. They would then be joined by one or two others and start encroaching inside. They often would fetch him a beer down for him for later as a gesture; the sight of five beers awaiting Iron was not uncommon. As sessions were coming to an end, even fish and chips turned up. One underlying problem with Iron was that he radiated a lot of self confidence. He never felt that he had to train excessively as he was that good.

Frank Law, deciding not to jeopardise this fight, contacted his friend, a fellow boxing fan who was the landlord of the White Swan at Wickersley near Rotherham. Iron and two trainers were sent there to set up camp and train in peace. Rooms were made available and the outbuildings facilitated a dedicated gym.

The training consisted of plenty of running. This saw early morning pounding round the villages of Maltby and Braithwell in a circular route. This was followed up by an hour's skipping. Increasing overall power was encouraged with working of the medicine ball. The sessions then always ended up with intense sparring, a punishing routine for anyone.

8th April 1905 was the night of the contest. It was being billed as "The Best Heavyweight Contest of the North". The admission money had been increased accordingly to 2 shillings and 6 pence (half a crown) as a minimum for the night, which was a big thing and certainly verging on profiteering.

A little annoyingly, Iron was billed as being Ian Hague. This happened many times throughout the years as people misconstrued Iron for Ian. It got to a point where Iron stopped correcting them. Ian was used as a result of a misunderstanding by journalist George M Wells of the Sheffield Telegraph. He was the sports writer as well as the local correspondent for the Sporting Life. He corrupted the Mexborough man's moniker by misunderstanding dialects. He thought that "Iron" was a Dearne Valley slang pronunciation of the Scottish Christian name "Ian". He reported on this revelation in an early article he wrote on Iron and other journalists followed suit. Iron himself came to accept it as a slang way of writing Iron and so it stayed.

The fight was scheduled for twenty, two minute rounds. Dick Parkes was aged 27, 5 feet 9 inch tall scaling on the night at 12 stone 4lb. He was on the victory trail having beaten Harry Fellowes at Sheffield on his last run out in a fight with a £50 aside stake and a purse of £80 for the winner. The financial stakes for this fight was £25 a side and a purse of £50 which was donated by a Mr Bridgewater. The winner and his backer would walk away with £75.

Around 400 fans turned up in support of Iron. However, this was dwarfed by the number of followers of Dick Parkes. He was very popular and half of Goldthorpe had turned out in support.

The evening's entertainment commenced at 8pm with an eight round fight between Billy O'Brien of Mexborough and Ted Shillitto of Doncaster. They were fighting for

£3 a side and a £4 purse. (O'Brien won with a knockout in the fourth round).

Also on the bill was Tommy Stokes against Milsey Parkes of Bolton on Dearne. This fight was for £5 a side and a £4 purse. Tom Stokes boxed very well knocking his man out in the eighth round.

As time came for the big fight, tensions and spirits were running high. When the fighters entered the arena, the atmosphere was electric. The noise became ear splitting as each side, up on their feet, cheered for their man. The anticipation was for a battle royal and they weren't to be disappointed.

The fighters both adopted the same strategy for the contest; to try and place as many body slams to weaken the opponent before finally finishing him off, being somewhat in a weakened condition. This tactic went on round after round. In the seventh round, Parkes landed one particular full chest blow, a real rib bender, on his opponent. It was a blow whose effects Iron felt for several weeks afterwards. Iron rallied and still the strategies continued. Parkes, being the older of the two showed some signs of tiredness by the fourteenth round and Iron managed to capitalise on this, delivering a killer punch. Parkes was knocked out. The timing of this was fortuitous as it was just at the same time when Iron felt he couldn't hit the man anymore, it was his last slug. The background noise in the arena up to this point was deafening. The crowd had been trying with vigour to incite the fighters. With Parkes down on the canvas, Iron threw his arms up in the air. He was the new heavyweight champion of Yorkshire. Come on!

Iron Hague in fighting pose.

Back in Mexborough, Iron's celebrity status and popularity increased. The town all felt they had a real star in their midst's.

Frank, as manager, waned to keep up this momentum and now had to secure even better fights to keep on the trail for champion status. Frank used to try and set aside an hour each day in his office for management duties. He used the time to think things through, write off letters to other managers and promoters. It was hard work but someone had to do it. You had to keep working at it or it wouldn't happen.

The next organised professional fight manifested itself in a bout against Albert Rodgers of Sheffield. The deal, finalised in the first week of July was for twenty, two minute rounds. The purse was again to be £25 a side with an additional £50 being donated to the prize money by the mysterious Mr Bridgewater of Doncaster. (Mr Bridgewater may well have been connected with the venue and chucked the purse in to up the fight status.) This meant, of course, the admission monies received would also rise. Bridgewater had a long association with boxing promotion. Rodgers was 30 years old and a well experienced pro. He was 5 feet 7 inches tall weighing in at 12 stones 7 pounds.

The venue was once again to be at the Doncaster Drill Hall. The fight was billed as "The Defence of the Yorkshire Heavyweight Title". Ever since the fight was announced it had been the talk of South Yorkshire boxing circles. Rodgers was considered by many to be the finest heavyweight around. Hague was still classed as a youngster and still needed to prove himself in their eyes.

Iron's got into serious training for the ensuing fight and Frank Law even shelled out for Iron to go to Blackpool for a spell away from the Mexborough maddening crowd. Here, Iron undertook a lot of roadwork each day for fitness. He was still only 19 years of age, he was 5 feet 11 inches tall and fighting at a weight of 11 stones. He would certainly have the advantage of height and reach on the night but would that be enough?

The 4th August 1905 saw a sell out crowd of supporters. The proceedings commenced at 8pm with an opening boxing exhibition by Iron's younger brother Johnnie Hague and young Frank Ogley of Denaby. The prize for the best style shown for this three round melee was a silver medal. It went to Johnny Hague.

The referee for the contest was Tom Gamble of Manchester and was to be fought with two minute rounds. For the first three rounds of the fight, Rodgers showed the judges what boxing was all about. He managed to get under Iron's longer reach and score points. That was what the game was all about. He came out top on points for all three rounds.

By the fourth round, Iron's' corner were getting frustrated and were telling him to "get in and stop the runt". Iron responded and started to land one or two hard blows. Rodgers, knowing that these would finish him off if connected, ran round the ring leaving no square inch untouched. Iron kept the pressure on into the fifth and 6th round by landing of one or two rights and lefts.

It was clear that by round six, Rodgers was no match for Iron and his corner threw the sponge into the ring to end it, fearing permanent damage to Rodgers could occur. That was now another professional fight and win. So, where next? Not where Iron thought.

Chapter 7
The Dreaded 'Lurghie' and Bad Days at the Office

After the last fight, Iron planned a short rest and then intended to restart his training schedules. Unfortunately, this did not go to plan. He felt very unwell and was laid low with a severe cold that seemed to transgress to a flu leaving him with a very bad chest infection. He could not get his stamina back. The weeks dragged into months as the winter of 1906 started to fold back in readiness for spring to arrive. This was very bad news for Iron indeed. Although he had started to feel well again, as soon as he was put under any pressure, his lungs would let him down and he would be stood panting like an old horse pulling a load uphill. It was to be many months before he started to return to anything like his former self. He probably had dipped into a mild pneumonia that only time could heal.

As the summer came towards a close, Iron did manage to up the training ante to make a meaningful start back towards being in a peak condition.

One frequent visitor to Iron over the months was Tom Stokes who though a friend, was still very sore about the past performances between them. He still felt he had the ability to oust this young pretender. After discussions with Frank Law and some pleading, it was decided that Iron would once more accept a challenge from Stokes. As this was an initiation fight back after Iron's illness, it was made clear it was not a Yorkshire Title Fight, just a contest between two men. This was not an ordinary fight. As Iron had been the victor twice before, the contest was varied from the normal twenty rounds to be one of only eight rounds. Many viewed that this should have been sufficient for Iron to overcome Stokes. The agreement to win within a certain distance or be classed as the loser was quite a common occurrence in the boxing booths.

The fight was arranged to take place in Mexborough in September 1906. It was not on the circuit as such, it did command a good Mexborough audience though, the skating rink venue was packed to the roof. The fight set off quite vigorously but then steadied down. Stokes was certainly "on guard" and proffered a defence which Iron found tough to break through. Round by round, the fight went on. The crowd sat expecting at any moment that a huge right and a left would swing into action, putting Stokes down but it did not happen. After the end of round eight, the contest had run out of steam and ceased. Stokes team claimed that Iron had not stopped his man as he stated so he had lost. This decision was upheld. It was not a nice taste but one Iron had to accept. It certainly put a smile on Tom Stokes face.

Whilst Iron had been incapacitated, Frank Law still kept up his search for the next career fight. It was never easy as the purse had to be attractive. The answer to these efforts came by a letter, from London, addressed to Frank at the Montagu Arms. It was from the manager of London boxer, Charlie Knock. He was prepared to travel north to fight and had excellent credentials. He was 26 years of age and even though he conceded a few stones in weight to Iron, he was hungry and had a backer.

Charlie was not on a winning streak but desperate to carry on his career. He had lost five of his last six fights, the last being the 10th November 1906 .This was against Sailor Curley Watson of the Royal Navy, Chatham and was fought at Wonderland, White Chapel Road, Mile End, London. (Note - Watson's birth name was Robert Bertram Watson being born in 1883 at Barrow in Furniss). The majority of bouts held at Wonderland were only two minute rounds. Knock had in fact, the previous May, claimed the English crown from Watson, (fighting at 144 pounds) in a bout at the N.S.C. The later loss at Wonderland was not recognised as a title fight as it was not staged over three minute rounds. Despite the recent losses, Knock was still keen and was very well respected for his ring craft.

Iron's trainers believed that Iron's size advantage and well known capacity for taking the punishment would obviate any advantage that Knock may gain. Iron started a strict training campaign in readiness. As in the past, Frank Law sent him away from Mexborough, back to Wickersley, to avoid unnecessary distractions. The training was interrupted abruptly however when a family tragedy suddenly occurred.

Charlie Knock of London – opponent and later on trainer.

Irons' 8 year old cousin, Vicky Bennett, the daughter of Mickey Bennett, was run over by a pony and trap travelling through the town. She was killed outright. Her father, Mickey, Iron's' uncle, was by now playing for Sheffield Wednesday as well as working. He was very close to Iron, proving to be his sounding board for his woes. The trauma of it all understandably halted the pre fight training schedule, which was not ideal. Vicky had been living with her family at

12 Charles Street, Mexborough at the time. She had three brothers and a sister. Her father, Mickey, and elder brother were working at the Phoenix glassworks in town at the time. The December 6th issue of the Mexborough and Swinton Times ran the headline:-

"The Dangers of the Street"

To make matters worse, the driver of the horse drawn vehicle was none other than Iron's friend, John Law, the son of his manager. At the Coroner's hearing miner and citizen, Eli Webster, related as to how he saw the accident at 12-10pm on the Wednesday previous.

He saw Vicky running down Sarah Street and then onto the adjoining High Street. As the street sloped downwards, she was running at some speed. She then continued on straight into the road without stopping, straight into the path of the oncoming vehicle. The two wheeled light trap was being driven along High Street six feet from the roadside. The child, oblivious to it all, ran straight into the horse where she impacted with its shoulder. The impact knocked her down onto the road where the carriage wheel then ran over her. The driver was exonerated from any blame. It was stated he had no time to react or prevent the impact with the child. Criticism was made as to some stone pillars which stood at the junction of High Street and Sarah Street which probably, for a passing second, obscured the child's view of the street she was running onto. The child's mother, Annie, confirmed she did not blame the driver at all. There was nothing he could have done to prevent the accident. She pointed out

View of High street, Mexborough. To the left hand side can be seen the stone post which obscured the view of Irons niece resulting in her death. The post was removed shortly after this picture.

that a couple of years ago, her daughter had suffered another accident in the same spot when another vehicle ended up running over her toes.

The verdict of the jury at the inquest was Accidental Death. A recommendation was also made to the men of Mexborough to remove the stone pillars from that location. Despite being on private property, the Coroner commented that "What I know of Mexborough men, the matter of private ownership of the stone pillars will not stop their will being imposed."

Another controversial subject that was flagged up at the Coroner's hearing was the fact that Jury had to view the body. A member of the jury had found the experience mortifying and written to the coroner questioning its meaningfulness. The Coroner, whilst sympathetic, explained that it was the lawful procedure all over Great Britain and viewed as a necessary requisite of all Coroners juries.

Mickey Bennett sent word to Iron to continue his training in earnest. There was nothing he could do by travelling back to town. The Hague flag of sorrow would be carried by his mother and father. It helped but it didn't make it any easier.

Vicky's funeral was on the following Sunday afternoon. Iron's mother, father and siblings were present. Also included within the mourners was poor John Law, the driver. A wreath was also sent bearing the message "with deepest sympathy" from Mr and Mrs F Law and famiiy, Montagu Arms. Everyone knew John law was blameless for this tragedy.

The fight with Charlie Knock was at the Doncaster Victoria Drill Hall on the 8th

The old Sarah Street sign still hangs today, marking the original exit way from the post office square. The street was demolished in the 1960's.

December 1906. A fair few fans had travelled into the town from Mexborough including Iron's father and brother. Iron had not seen them since the news of young Vicky's death. Several fights were on the bill that night but Iron was headlining. One match that many had come to see was a fifteen round contest between S Price and W Rodway. This fight was the continuation of serious goading that had occurred by miners at different collieries as to which pit had the best man. This fight was met to great crowd heckling. Rodway eventually took the bout winning in the eighth round.

The Doncaster Watch Committee afterwards stated they would not allow such local fused rivalry fights of this calibre to be fought in the town in the future. After the fight, the supportive victorious miners went on into the town centre drinking beer, being a nuisance and not unsurprisingly, skirmishes broke out. That was boxing with passion.

There had been some light heartedness on the evening when two ten year olds billed as the "Mexborough Midgets" boxed a three round exhibition fight. They were billed as the champions of the future.

Tom Stokes was also on the bill facing Mike Riley of Liverpool.

Iron and Charlie Knock's headlining fight soon seemed to come round. Knock had little support from the crowd which was not unsurprising given his distance from home.

As the fight progressed, Irons physical size, that was believed to be his saviour, ended up being a disadvantage. Ring wise, Knock bobbed and weaved and showed great speed in dodging irons punches. Iron was starting to get a little frustrated when in the third round, from nowhere, a right hand from Knock hit Iron straight on the chin and down he went. This was a rarity. The punch not only took him by surprise, it showed his Achilles Heel. Iron was out for the count. A loss that was totally unexpected now necessitated some careful future planning.

Charlie Knock and Iron actually became good friends despite the events of the evening. He was to feature in Iron's life again.

The year of 1906 was as a nightmare year. Not the kind of year anyone expected at its outset, the like of which Iron never wanted to experience again. After this last fight, his backers had lost money and his rating as a star attraction had took a tumble.

After some soul searching and consolation talks from Frank, Iron was persuaded all was not in vain and he could learn by it and became an even more determined fighter. He still had youth on his side and the fight game was all about taking knocks on the way but learning from them. He would build up on his weak spots, strengthening them and improving further his strong points.

Chapter 8
A Military Call Up

The Army had provided a steady stream of boxers over the years. Boxing was always a great pastime amongst the troops. Plenty of the fighters around were of a military background. Army boxing fell between amateur and professional. It had encouraged boxing as a recreation since the early 1890's and instituted its own championships in 1892. The fact that boxing made for the improvement of the soldier was recognized by all those of authority in the Army. General and Commanding Officers alike were most zealous in promoting boxing clubs, tournaments and championships within their commands. The controlling body of armed service boxing was "The Royal Navy and Army Boxing Association". It had, for its president, His Majesty the King, and for its vice-presidents, five naval Commander's-in-Chief and eight military General Officers. Each service and each regiment all had its boxing stars.

The best boxers within the services were held in very high esteem. Competitions took place, from regimental novice's right up to being the Army Champion. It then went on to inter service championships. The great majority of the audience were the serving soldiers and sailors and they appreciated the fighters who could deliver the punch, and those with the ability to counter punch and show off tricky little bits of ring-craft.

Many boxing competitions were run with great zest, lower ranks and privates competing on a regular basis. The officers competed at their own level. It would not do for officers to get involved fighting the privates, particularly as it could affect the discipline of the regiment. The Officers Championships became part of the 'Army and Navy' championships from 1894. The Regimental Officers took great interest in finding the boxers in their midst's. They all looked for the potential rising stars, to extol and bring honour to the colours. As there was only small money prizes, the Regimental trophies were often magnificent and far outshone the prizes won in civvy street bouts. It was a world within a world.

The next series of fights Frank Law arranged crossed into the military world. The New Year celebrations, seeing in 1907, were only just days behind them when a hand delivered letter arrived at the Montagu Arms. A motorcyclist despatch rider had driven down especially from York. The letter confirmed all the arrangements for Iron to fight two of their chosen soldiers.

At Fulford Barracks in York were a couple of very handy up and coming heavyweights, Shoeing Smith Sergeant Randall and Trooper Fred Gibson. These two soldiers had defeated all comers including some very respected fighters. Their officers in charge, on hearing of Iron's success, decided with no more ado to write to Frank suggesting a contest. Fulford Barracks was built between 1877 and 1880 at a cost of £15,000, housing the Prince of Wales own WestYorkshire Regiment. The barracks were home over 1250 officers and men.

This was an unusual fight request, being asked to train to fight two people. After negotiations between all parties, it was agreed the strategy would be to go to York and Iron would fight each man but on consecutive Mondays, a hard task for any professional.

After more discreet enquiries, Frank found out that Gibson was supposed to be the slightly better man of the two. Training was intense and nothing was spared in the preparations for these ensuing battles.

On the 9th January 1907 Iron, Frank and two of his trainers slipped down a darkening Station Road and caught the late afternoon train to Doncaster and then another onto York. They were met at the York Station by a chauffeur driven staff car. Once at Fulford, they were given a whistle stop tour of the barracks before being shown their changing room, which was a store at the end of the mess hall where the fight was to take place. They found out that the first fight was to be against Randall. He was supposedly the less able of the two.

The crowds of squaddies piled into the Mess Hall which was set out with compact seating surrounding the first class ring. You couldn't have possibly fit in one more

Iron Hague and Frank Law making their way down Station Road for the train to York in readiness for the fights at Fulford Barracks.

seat anywhere. The atmosphere around the barracks was quite electric with great excitement and anticipation as to the fights outcome. As Iron entered the arena, stripped down and ready, there was a civilised applause but the crowd went rapturous when Shoeing Smith Sergeant Randall came in.

Not unsurprisingly, Iron soon showed the crowd the make of a true professional. In the first round, Iron landed a hard left that sent Randall scuttling to the floor.

He hit the canvas and took a count of seven. In the second round, Iron knocked Randall down twice, both to counts of nine. In the third round, Randall managed to stay on his feet but you could see his head was down. The fourth round saw the contest ended. After three hardy blows, Randall's legs went from under him. He collapsed down in a heap and was counted out by the referee. It was a great contrast to the last victory against Parkes in that the lack of Iron supporters present meant the victory was met with a silence.

The officer in command of Fulford sat alongside his fellow officers on a table at the ringside. He addressed the crowd by congratulating Iron on an excellent showing and said he was equally looking forward to the next contest. In the audience watching with great intensity was Trooper Gibson. He reassured all he wouldn't be caught out like his fellow had been.

The following Monday, the 16th January, soon came round. Fortunately, the recovery period for Iron from his bout with Randall was only short as he was not taxed greatly. At the barracks, psychology was applied and everyone the visitors came into contact with commented that Iron would be in for a pounding tonight, they goaded that the ambulance men were on standby. These adversities all went over Iron's head.

Iron had not really seen his opponent before and when Trooper Fred Gibson climbed into the ring, did think to himself, "This boy looks like he has a bit more about him." He certainly looked the business. As the bell for the first round sounded, the crowd cheered on their man as he rushed forward and nearly planted a left on Iron's chin. Iron responded with a left which hurt Gibson as he immediately fell into a clinch. Breaking away, Iron landed a left and a terrific full right. Gibson momentarily looked into the air and then down he went. Oblivious to the world, he lay stretched across the canvas. The atmosphere took on that similar to one found in a mortuary. That had been a very easy payday. Triumphantly, the Mexborough contingent left the sullen Fulford barracks and headed back to town.

After some three weeks, an official letter was again delivered by hand to Frank Law at the Montagu Arms. It was from the officer in charge of training back at Fulford barracks. The letter informed Frank that the Regiment had a third fighter who they would like to arrange a match for with Iron. A purse would be provided as before and the fight would be back at the Mess Hall at Fulford.

Frank Law was a little reluctant this time as he was talking to others in Sheffield and London and didn't want anything upsetting the apple-cart.

Iron though, quite fancied the prospect. It was agreed this fight would go ahead on the 30th January 1907. It turned out the fighter they had in mind was not a recruit but a local York boy. He was called Tom Horridge and was a 14 stone 7 pounds rugby football player. The fight was again on a Monday evening and the stake was £50 a side plus the purse. It was a bit of a no-fight as Iron managed to have his man on the deck within seconds. As the bell went, Iron had charged at his man unleasing several connecting punches. A huge right punch stopped the challenger in his tracks and he was out for the count.

All in all, it had took Iron fourteen minutes to demolish all three of the best fighters from Fulford. What a result.

Chapter 9
A Dispute Over a Purse Leads to Better Things

Following the fast action at Fulford, events took a bit of a lull. Franks talks had not turned up anything positive. Talks continued however throughout spring and summer and a contest was eventually organised for the autumn. It was to be back at the Carver Street Arena in Sheffield on the 28th October 1907.

This time it was to be more challenging. It was to be against Jack Scales of Bethnall Green, London. Scales was a former claimant of the heavyweight English title back in 1902. It was believed that this contest tonight would give Iron a chance to demonstrate what he was all about, against this ring wise veteran. Unfortunately, although the deal had been struck beforehand between Frank Law and Scale's manager, it became disputed on the night. Whether this emanated from a dispute between Scales and his manager or that the manager had had further thoughts, Frank was unsure but the fight suddenly became in jeopardy. The Scales camp suddenly demanded more of the purse. Frank Law stood his ground on the matter. He was too astute a businessman to be hoodwinked. The crowd awaited unaware that there was any dispute or that the negotiations were continuing. The crowd started slow handclapping as their patience wore. The referee and the officials were starting to scream at the men, "Get in the ring or the bout is off." So not to disappoint the crowd, it was speedily agreed that the fight would start but it would now be over six rounds only, not the scheduled twenty.

Jack Scales in a fighting pose.

The fight that went ahead appeared to have been effected by the impasse of the managers. The six rounds passed and no one boxer really got on top of the fight. At the end of the sixth round, the referee announced to the eager crowd that the result was clearly a draw. This was booed at by the fight goers, who felt somewhat cheated.

Back in the changing rooms, Frank Law was fuming. "You would have knocked the crap out of Scales if it was the proper

Fred Drummond in a fighting pose.

Iron Hague with his trainers, George Law to the left and Charlie Bolton to the right. The Picture was taken at the Montagu Arms.

fight" he shouted. "Who do they think they are? Well whatever they are clinging onto, they had better have a good grip because we are going to snatch it." Iron was very confident that over twenty rounds, he would definitely come out top dog. Frank stormed out of the changing room and went next door to where Scales and his manager were sat talking. There were a few harsh words and bluffs called but the upshot was that an announcement would to be made to the fight fans.

"Gentlemen, following discussions between the two managers it has been agreed that there will be a rematch and Jack Scales will fight Iron Hague here again in Sheffield." This pleased the crowd greatly.

(Jack Scales unfortunately gained a bad reputation for "throwing fights" during his career. It was believed he was a lot better than his record shows).

Frank Law arranged the next fight against heavyweight Fred Drummond of Lambeth, London. The purse was to be £50 a side and would take place on Boxing Day, 26th December 1907. The fight was to take place at Carver Street in Sheffield. Fred, who was aged 32, had started his career in 1901 and was a N.S.C Novice competitor in 1903. He had notched up some twenty four fights to date. His brother was also on the boxing circuit.

The preparatory training was stepped up for this contest and Iron was said to be in the pink of condition, possibly the fittest of his career. This had been a telling time for Iron as it meant he had to resist the temptation of the Christmas festivities and treats.

As far as boxing was concerned, Iron's major advantage in the ring was having great strength behind his left hand punches. A lot of boxers are substantially weakened on their left punches so to have one with a killer blow strength was a bonus. At the Montagu Arms gym, to assist in developing the punching power, two doors were hung and Iron used to hit them alternatively for a minute ending with a full flurry. To do this he needed a supply of doors as they used to split open, submitting to the battering. New sparring partners were always being sought to draw him on.

On a personal note, one thing that Frank Law insisted on for his protégé was the opening of a bank account for his winnings to be deposited in. He had noticed that Iron was a soft touch when it came to money and that if he had 10 shillings in his pocket, it may as well have been everyone's. Any poor soul in need making a representation would be the recipient of something, even if it was the last coin in his pocket.

On the Boxing Day evening of the 26th December 1907, Tommy Stokes and Iron shared a taxi to Sheffield. Stokes was first on the bill.

A good crowd from Mexborough got the train from Mexborough to Sheffield Victoria station and filled up the arena. The fight had become part of the festive celebrations. Unfortunately, they were not treated to a long drawn out battle royal on various counts that night.

Iron sat with a cheque for his bank account.

Tommy Stokes faced Enoch Clarke, a well known middleweight. The bout was hyped up with allegations of a personal South Yorkshire grudge that was to be settled by this fight. Strangely, Stokes was in the ring waiting for about twenty minutes before his opponent appeared. This angered Stokes, who shot out like a bat out of hell as the opening round started. Stokes weighed into his opponent and delivered a first round knockout.

The last contest of the night was the one most eagerly awaited for. Iron's fight was top of the bill. The crowd were chanting loudly as the fighters entered the ring. Iron was the first in and strutted up and down as if extending his warming up exercises.

The opening round showed great promise of a good contest as both men fought warily but at a fast pace. Iron was the main aggressor but the round finished with Drummond landing several left hand punches, albeit they were not backed by great strength.

Just into the second round, Iron delivered a huge right that smashed into Drummond and down he went. He tried to get up several times but that was the end of him. A clean knock out for Iron; another victory under the belt.

For this bout, the press also confirmed that Iron was in the best condition of his entire career to date.

Fred Drummond gave a very average showing that night considering his past. Perhaps he had too much Christmas pudding? He was clearly outclassed by the youngster, perhaps he was having an off day.

After the fight, Drummond's manager sought Frank Law out seeking a rematch over twenty rounds for £20 a side. His man was not happy at the bout and felt that Iron had robbed him. Frank could not believe his audacity.

Opponent – Fred Drummond .

Chapter 9
London's Calling

The National Sporting Club was founded on the 5th March 1891 as a gentleman's club with a main purpose of running Monday evening boxing shows for members and their guests. The idea behind it all was Arthur Frederick (Peggy) Bettinson who knew and understood boxing very well. He had been the amateur Lightweight and Middleweight Champion of England in his youth. He was a very eccentric character, said to be very forceful in his nature. The premises were situate at number 43 King Street, Covent Garden, London and could accommodate about 1300 spectators. It attained the honour of being a "Sporting Institute" by enrolling members of the Amateur Boxing Association. It was being run exclusively for members only and their guests and was very bohemian in its style. The first President was none other than Hugh Lowther, the 5th Earl of Lonsdale. The rules were that both the fighters and the crowd had to be on the very best behaviour. Spectators had to wear full evening dress and bouts would only start after the dinner was cleared away. You had to sit there in some silence as no cheering was allowed during the rounds. The fights took place in an eerie silence, all you could hear was the squash of the gloves and of leather hitting flesh and bone.

The fighters had to abide by the Queensbury Rules and this went a long way to improving the integrity of the sport. The National Sporting Club did more to establish the sport of boxing in Great Britain than any other organisation.

Boxing scene at the National Sporting Club, London . This was a little different on standards compared to the likes of "Wonderland"

One of the problems the Club had to cope with was the smaller purses it offered fighters. With only 1300 spectators, it could not compete with the 6 penny seats at the "stack em" high venues like Wonderland in the Whitechapel Road or the Cosmopolitan in Plymouth. The NSC maintained and it was almost universally accepted that English Boxing titles could only be fought for in the Covent Garden clubhouse. With the image it portrayed, many boxers agreed that it was indeed special and it was an honour to be called up to fight there.

Thomas Weston was one of the 1300 national members of the NSC. A regular competition hosted there was the "Novices Heavyweight" competition. Thomas suggested to Iron's team that they should enter although strictly speaking, Iron was far from being a novice.

He used his influence with "Peggy" Bettinson to try and persuade him that the winner of the next competition should perhaps having the opportunity to fight Gunner Moir, the current English Heavyweight titleholder. Peggy did not dismiss the idea. Frank Law, ceasing the opportunity, duly applied for an entry into the competition for Mexborough's Iron.

The fight night was scheduled for the 13th January 1908. There were thirty two competitors all hoping to lift the coveted prize. The Mexborough party that day travelled to Doncaster and then took the train on to London, Iron carrying his customary leather medicine bag. Despite the distance, Iron preferred to travel and then fight as opposed to travelling down days before to acclimatise. Unlike now, the journey to London, then from Mexborough, gave the traveller two choices; travel to Doncaster then onto King's Cross, or to travel to Sheffield Victoria for travel to Marleybone Station. On this occasion, they took the Doncaster service so arriving in King's Cross.

Once at the Sporting club, Iron found out that he had to box a trial bout first against Seaman Arthur "Spoff" Drummond, the brother of Fred Drummond, who Iron had pulverised only weeks before. This fight was scheduled for three rounds. It proved to be a good opening tester, with Iron doing well. It was a 'no decision' trial bout to check that Iron was good enough to appear at the N.S.C. At the end of the three rounds, an extra round was ordered by the officials.

The Heavyweight Novice Competition was organised around a series of three round fights. By shortening the length of a contest, it should leave the successors able to fight a few bouts on the same evening's bill.

The first night fight of the novice competition was set for the Thursday 16th January with Iron being matched against local boy Tom King of Southwark. Iron found it very strange boxing in the National Sporting Club. It was not like other venues where your fans would all come in and heckle you in support all the way through. The audience here sat silent, bolt upright and were dressed to the nine pins. Amongst

Wonderland Stadium, London with a large crowd in attendance.

them was Thomas Weston, he was in silent support for Iron.

Iron boxed his first three rounds and won with a knock out in the second round. A great start. Annoyingly, the Sporting Life reported the wrong result in their paper the next day but then subsequently corrected it.

The next fight was against George Turner of Bromley by Bow, London. Iron continued his winning form and again effected a knockout in the first round after having had his man down for a count just beforehand.

The next fight was against Londoner Jack Gibson of Bow. This was a steady fight for Iron and once more he showed his metal. He knocked his man out in the second round.

The next three rounder, which was classed as a semi-final bout, was to prove more difficult. It was against Harry Croxon of West Drayton, London. He was one of six brothers of whom four where on the boxing circuit. The fight was very closely run and the judges were unable to make a clear decision. The fighters were ordered to fight a further round, which they did. After this the judges were still indecisive and so the referee's casting vote came into play. He though, had no doubts about it and awarded the point to Iron. He was the winner.

Now all that stood in front of the Mexborough contingent was this last fight, the final of the Novice Heavyweight Competition. Even Frank Law could not resist putting on the pressure. "There is now only this fight to win and we are on our way. Glory awaits." The words kept reverberating around Iron's head as he got into the ring. He was now facing Alf Pearson of Barnsbury, Islington, London. The number of rounds had now been extended to six to make the fight more practical. Iron became conscious more than ever of the audience sat donning black jackets, white silk shirts with glittering diamond pins. As the bell rang for round one, he charged out and was like the furious wind that comes from nowhere. He was obviously overbearing as he knocked his man clean out, still in the first round.

He had now just won this latest N.S.C Novice Heavyweight Competition. The crowd sat there clapping very politely. One of them though was clapping just that bit harder and louder, Thomas Weston.

Iron now felt he had won something of worth in this pugilistic world. Telegrams were sent rattling up the wires to Mexborough to tell the town," Your man has won." He had beaten five men inside ten rounds and four of them inside six rounds, what an achievement. His explosive punching had made short work of them all and now the door of opportunity was well and truly opened. It must be stated that in fairness, Iron was far from being a novice and his five opponents were all proper novices at the game.

As the steam train pulled into Mexborough station, Iron was taken aback by the large number of family and friends there to greet him and help him share his success. He

Shot of Montague square Mexborough, with the Montague Arms to the right and side and the Prince of Wales Theatre to the right.

was hot property. A few journalists were amongst them all vying to get the better story out first. Frank Law was very professional making a formal statement that they were all highly delighted with Iron's achievements and that it only reflected the hard work that Iron had put into it all. There were now several opportunities which they would be considering over the ensuing weeks while Iron had some well earned rest. Iron amused the crowd by interrupting saying "I don't need that much rest." From there, it was up to the Montagu Arms for the celebrations to continue.

A famous pugilist once said, "A measure of how good you are performing in the ring is by the number of children who just follow you around." Around Mexborough town, Iron now knew what the author meant. Little kids would follow him about and point at him to others. There was a truth in this statement.

CHAPTER 9
THE HARLEM COFFEE COOLER

Whether a boxer was black or white made no difference to Iron Hague.

Frank Craig in bare knuckle pose.

Irons next fight was to be on the 16th March 1908 against Frank "The Coffee Cooler" Craig. He was a coloured fighter who had come over here from the USA to box as in the UK, there was no colour bar in operation. In the US, fights between "whites" and "coloureds" were discouraged. Titles were protected to ensure they were held by white boxers only. This meant that some excellent legendary boxers were denied that coveted World Title they justly deserved. Many of them came over to Europe, to fight fair and squarely in our boxing rings.

Frank Craig was born 1st April 1870 in Columbus, Georgia. He boxed out of New York. He was some 5 feet 10 inches high and weighed around 11 stones 7 pounds. As a boxer, he was quick and clever but he was now some 37 years of age. He had fought as a middleweight and light heavyweight but tangled with a number of heavier men. He had been fighting since the late 1880's. In the past, he had defeated the likes of Joe Butler, Charlie Knock, Charlie Allum, Denis Haugh, Fred Woods and Joe Ellingworth. He claimed the World Middleweight Title in 1894 after a fight against Pritchard on 17th December.

In 1899 he fought for the World Middleweight Championship but lost to Tommy Ryan by a K.O.in round 10.

Craig had beaten all the respected middleweights in the US and once more returned back to England for pastures new. He had won the Middleweight English title from George Crisp in 1898.

Punch magazine cover depicting Frank "Coffee Colour" Craig on the left hand side.

On the 4th January 1894, Mark Twain witnessed Frank Craig in action. In a letter to his wife Olivia Clemens he wrote:-

"Mr Archbold of the Standard Oil company got tickets for us and he and Mr Rogers and Dr Rice. We went to the Athletic Club last Saturday night and saw The Coffee Cooler" dress off another prize fighter in great style. There were ten rounds; but at the end of the fifth The Coffee Cooler knocked the white man down and he couldn't get up any more. A round consists of three minutes; then the men retire to their corners and sit down and lean their heads back against a post and gasp and pant like fishes, while one man fans them with a fan, and another with a table cloth, another rubs their legs and sponges off their faces and shoulders and blows sprays of water in their faces from his own mouth. Only one minute is allowed for this; then time is called and they jump up and go fighting again. It is absorbingly interesting."

The press started running a build up, listing it as Hague's most important match of his career to date, The Coffee Cooler was a very worthy opponent.

The top of the bill fight was listed as being at Catchweight (non matching weights) and was staged at the Carver Street Drill Hall in Sheffield. The fight was a sell out. Iron's fans packed the 6-15pm train from Mexborough to Sheffield's Victoria Station.

The fight kicked off with great enthusiasm from Iron who couldn't wait to get started. Iron managed to knock Craig down in each round to the rapturous applause from the crowd. He was just saved by the bell in the second round. During the fourth, Craig was down again and this time, his seconds carried him back to his corner fearing his own safety. A knock out was awarded to Iron.

If ever a sight conjures up feelings of sympathy and sorrow it is that of a former champion trying to relive his glory days wearing the same suit of yesteryear which is now unfortunately tattered and torn. Frank Craig probably conjured up the same sentiment amongst the crowd that night. His past had lifted the audience with expectations but his body now tiring could not nearly deliver.

Iron was now back on winning form but life takes many a twist and a dark sceptre was just round the corner.

Frank Craig in fighting pose

Chapter 11
Pits and Fatalities - I'll Miss You Uncle Walter.

Iron was out running around the three village route of, High Melton, Barnburgh and Adwick on Dearne that he often started the day with. The win over Frank Craig was to be his stimulant for better things to come. By the time he was running back into Mexborough it was 9.30am. He had just got back into the gym when a young boy appeared with a note. "This is for Iron Haigh" the young messenger said. Iron glanced over and thought nothing of it, his mind was on other things. Tom Stokes took the note off the boy and read out the written message. "Iron, this note says you have to go home immediately" cried Tom. Iron somewhat puzzled asked him to repeat it. As Iron scratched his head he asked, "Who is it from?" "Your mother" was the reply.

As Iron turned onto Woodruff Row, he could hear a wailing sound emanating from near his house. As he opened the door he saw his mother slouched over the settee, her face was red from crying. "James," she shouted "Uncle Cocky is dead". Iron stood in disbelief and listened whilst his father, John, explained what had happened that terrible early morning at Denaby Colliery.

A lump came in Iron's throat but he was too hard to cry. It didn't mean he didn't hurt inside though.

William "Cocky" Bennett.

He was at first very angry and then became very protective towards Cocky's widows and his cousins. "I will make sure they are looked after. It's the least I can do," he retorted. The whole family were momentarily glued together inside the small front room.

The rest of training was cancelled that day. Iron not unnaturally thought about events over the years with Cocky. He always seemed to understand Iron's plight. He was at his level. That was a level his father could never seem to bend down to. When in trouble, Cocky was always there if he needed someone to talk to. He was worldly wise as far as Iron's sporting career went and a proper rock. Even when Cocky was playing football for Bristol Rovers, weekly

Williams "Fatty" Foulke, Sheffield United goalkeeper and Walter Bennett in Sheffield United strip.

letters were sent to him and Iron's mother would include a special bit in the letter, a message or question from Iron.

It was always kept as sacred and private. His mother would read out Cocky's reply and treat it as if she was oblivious to it.

Since the Hague family came to Mexborough, they had become a part of the mining community. Each of the towns and villages of South Yorkshire were dominated by a colliery complex producing the endless stream of black gold. Serving the collieries was a whole host of other industries, all employers in their own rights. It was hard to get away from the grips the coal industry had. Every family had someone within who worked in a mine or a related industry. The dangerous nature of the work underground often exposed the miners to a high risk of injuries which had to be accepted. Just occasionally these injuries, once sustained, were so severe, the fatality of the worker occurred. It then became a time for the whole community to lament and mourn the loss of another dear brother.

On the 6th April 1908 Sunday evening, the men queued up as usual to enter the cage at Denaby Colliery to be wound down to the pit bottom . They were the first production shift of the week. It was 9.30pm and this was an early draw for what was an unpopular shift. It signalled the end of the weekend beer break and heads down now for the week. Amongst them was 33 years old Walter (Cocky) Bennett. He had recently retired from football at the highest level and was now working as a miner.

The wages paid to the professional footballers of the day nowhere near provided a means for retirement and continuing working was a necessity. When aged only 16, scouts had seen his ability with the Mexborough Town Football Club, playing at Hampden Road. He was offered a contract with Derby County F.C. The offer was a very good one but Walters father insisted that his son should continue at the glassworks and get a trade under his belt. Other offers materialised including Newton Heath (today's Manchester United) but all were turned down. One that came though and appealed, even to Walter's father, was an offer from Sheffield United F.C. He got

Mexborough Town Football Club.

a high wage for the times of £40 per annum.

In the 1905/06 season, Walter was SUFC's leading goal scorer with a total of eighty two goals. He was a first class winger and his career was eagerly followed by the town's citizens. Many of them started to attend SUFC games just to watch him. In his first season with the club, they won the League Championship. He was very highly regarded by both the club and fans alike.

In 1901, he was called to play for the England Squad on two occasions. He played against Wales at Newcastle's ground which was like a mud bath. He also played at Crystal Palace's ground against Scotland. Although the game was a draw, he was credited with playing well on the wing. He was known for his sharp temper and lack of patience. He took no prisoners but underneath it all, was a man of great heart. His football career had spanned fifteen years.

In the 1904-05 season, he was transferred to Bristol Rovers who were floundering near the bottom of the second division. His arrival acted as a catalyst and the team started to perform. He saw them get promoted into the first division. He was never happy living around Bristol and wished to return back home. He had offers from many southern clubs to play for them, including one to play cricket for Gloucestershire (he was a good all-rounder). He turned them all down to return and play for Denaby United with a job at the colliery. A lot of his fellows thought him mad but it was what he wanted to do; back to where all his family were.

As the chain link door was pulled up on the pit cage, Benjamin Gethen and Cocky stepped aboard loading some essential tools and materials they needed. Benjamin

The England Football Squad, including Walter Bennett who can be found sat down to the far left.

was in his late 60's and already had clocked up fifty six years working in the mines. The two of them were paired up to drive a new Passover Passageway in the pit bottom. This was to construct a new engine house. They had been engaged on this for about a month. They had given a price to the Denaby Main Colliery Company for the job and were to be paid on results at the end of the construction, not per shift.

At 5.15am, the Deputy Joe White, was just finishing his night shift and paused to talk to them about the job they were doing. He watched them filling off dirt then they had a break for ten minutes. There wasn't ever a shift go by in the pit without discussing the rudiments of football. Probably tiring of the constant banter, Cocky ended the conversation to say he was going to fill another tub so he could clear the face for a last fill and then they were done for the night. If there is a thing called "Sods Law" then it operated in the Denaby mine that night. While the two talked on, Cocky walked back into the heading and picked up a pick some sixteen yards from the heading face. At that very second, a large ten ton stone dislodged itself from the roof and came crashing down, right on the spot where Cocky was standing. He was crushed in an instant. His head and shoulders were buried out of sight. Cries of "help" rang out from his colleagues whilst they feverishly tried to prise Cocky out from under the rock.

Help soon came and it was decided the only way to get him out was to break up the rock into a smaller manageable piece. Furiously hammers and picks were engaged. The miners worked nonstop smashing down on picks held in place by volunteers, all in all this took forty five minutes. During this time, Cocky never moved or spoke.

The medical attendant attended to Cocky as soon as practical but confirmed all was in vein. Cocky was dead.

The roof, at that point, was unsupported but deemed to have been firm and solid. Ben Gethen blamed himself though in reality there was nothing he could have done. The weight had obviously come on at that part of the mine, just at that time.

The Coroner after examining all the facts gave a verdict of "Accidental Death".

The funeral was one of the biggest the town had seen. It was on a Thursday afternoon and the town's citizens lined the streets as the procession passed through winding its way up to the Mexborough cemetery. The weather became very atmospheric as it darkened the sky with black rain bearing clouds. Rows of sombre clad men stood in a respectable silence.

The coffin bore a man who was sadly missed by many. His grave was flanked by twenty nine wreaths from all walks of life. They included his widow, brother George, his sister Lillie, uncle Tottie, aunt Hannah Knowles and cousins, Mr and Mrs William Biggs (Bulls Head), Mr and Mrs Story, Tommy Hakin, Grimsby, Mr and Mrs Soar (Commercial Hotel), Montagu Arms barmen, Mr and Mrs Thomas Weston (Reresby Arms), Mr and Mrs Turner-Sheffield, William (Fatty) Foulkes and Mr J Banner (Sheffield United F.C), Mr J Banner, Sheffield; Mr John Artindale, Sheffield, Mr Peters, Mr Soar , Mr and Mrs Wilde (Rock Tavern Dixon Lane Sheffield), The Don Working Men's Club, the committee of Mexborough Town Football Club, Conisborough Cricket Club, the directors of Sheffield United F.C., Mexborough Cricket and Athletic Club, Henry Thickett and Bristol City F.C., Swinton Cricket Club, Constitutional Club, The Sheffield United Players, regulars of the Bull's Head, Royal Oak, Denaby United F.C. Plant Hotel and the Sheffield Wednesday players.

The pall bearers were players of Denaby United whom Cocky had played with the Saturday before in the Midland League. Inside the chapel, the vicar gave a kind testimony as to how Cocky had reached so many people and affected their lives. He went on to say that he who was returning to earth had been conspicuous in his lifetime as witnessed by the large crowd gathered to pay their respects today.

William Fatty Foulkes was a very interesting character. Born in 1874, he is believed to have been the heaviest goalkeeper of all time. He weighed some 25 stones. Once he sat down to lunch early, devouring the food that was intended for the whole team. That is where the expression "who ate all the pies" often sung on the football stadium terraces originated from. He wore shirts with a twenty four inch collar and could punch a ball off the goal line to the halfway line. After leaving Sheffield United, he played for Chelsea. Whilst there, in one game, he picked up a Port Vale forward and threw him into the back of the goal. He once collided with his own goalpost and snapped it in two. If he was injured, it needed six stretcher bearers to carry him off the field.

Walter Bennett's gravestone lays in Mexborough cemetery.

Sheffield United rallied to the plight of their former player's family and held a benefit match for them the following Easter Monday. A match was arranged between Sheffield United Reserves and Mexborough Town, to be played at the S.U.F.C home ground at Bramhall Lane, Sheffield. This was a great gesture by Sheffield United and appreciated by everyone. The crowd of 9000 generated some £100 gate money for the widow and children.

Chapter 12
"Scaling" the Heights Again So the Sunshine Was Outshone

Following the previous fight with Jack Scales back on the 28th October 1907, Scales' manager had been keen to organise a return bout to appease Scales' conscience. Frank Law and Scales' manager finally agreed terms of a twenty round contest with a total value of £275, £50 a side with £175 purse given. Frank made sure every detail was listed down and signed for this time following the problems of the past. The day for the contest was set as Monday 11th May 1908 and was to be at Carver Street, Sheffield.

Despite regular training, what was apparent was that Iron was gradually gaining weight. Was some of this down to his reduction of the punishing training schedules or was it because of the fact he was filling out? For the fight, Iron weighed in at 13 stones 2 pounds. Jack Scales had the weight advantage being 13 stone 8 pounds. The bookies slightly favoured Iron in the fight and the odds were set at 7 to 4 on in his favour. The fight commenced to great cheering from the Mexborough contingent of spectators. After an initial fast flurry, the fight settled down but Iron clearly established a points lead during the first round.

The second round again set off with great vigour but Iron was soon clearly in charge. Then suddenly, Scales dropped his guard and from nowhere Iron delivered one of his famous left punches. Scales never stood a chance and he was knocked clean out. So another victory for the records.

Afterwards, back in the changing rooms, a whole host of fans queued to congratulate Iron on his victory and wish him well for his next fight. He was now increasingly good to know and apparently everyone's mate.

The year of 1908 was proving to be a busy year for the Mexborough pugilist. Iron was invited to return to the National Sporting Club to once again fight under the auspices of the people that counted as far as boxing was concerned. Frank Law would have liked to have had more time to prepare but this wasn't possible so training had to be intense.

Monday morning of the 1st June 1908 saw Iron and his seconds and manager trudging down Station Road to catch the train to Doncaster and then onwards again to King's Cross.

The opponent nominated by the N.S.C was Corporal Sunshine, who served with the Dublin Fusiliers. He was the Army and Navy Heavyweight Champion for 1905, 1906 and 1907. There was no doubt that with this call up that Iron was being groomed towards a shot at the Heavyweight title but this obstacle (ie Sunshine) had to be put away first. Sunshine was no ageing veteran or green novice. A hard fight awaited.

Corporal and later Sergeant Sunshine stands in fighting pose.

The fight was set to be over ten rounds only which would dictate that a lively performance was needed. The Corporal had the height and weight advantage of the two fighters. Iron was in superb physical condition for the contest, his hard concentrated training paying off.

Sunshine showed off his superior ring craft once the fight started. He dodged and weaved out of distance from the many punches thrown by Iron. In the second round however, he was caught off guard and Iron planted a good left to the face, quickly followed by a right to the cheek. Down went Sunshine onto the canvas where he took a count. On rising he clinched Iron so to recover his stance and stamina.

In the third round, Iron sent out strong body language of an impending attack that Sunshine easily detected. He side stepped it and retaliated with a right hand blow to the head. Down went Iron onto the canvas. Iron got to his feet and delivered a hard right body slam.

Unfortunately, Iron was too winded to follow it up and like his counterpart relied on clinching for the rest of the round to aid his recovery. The referee cautioned Iron for infringing the holding rules.

This angered Iron and at the sound of the bell, he came out very determined. He laid into Sunshine and hit him five times without a return punch being thrown. The fifth punch sent his opponent reeling backwards and down Sunshine went. Although exhausted, he got up on the count of nine. Iron again launched himself at his opponent and another punch laid him out once more. This time, Sunshine had a seven count. Iron immediately attacked with a hard right which did the trick. Sunshine was down and out not making the count. Iron had won by a knockout in four rounds. The victory was met with the usual polite applause. This restraint wasn't shared by Iron and his team who all jumped up and down screaming and hugging in front of the moribund crowd. Moribund that is, except for Thomas Weston, who was clapping more vigorous than the rest. It was his money that provided the purse so he had a double celebration.

After the fight, Sunshine approached Iron's father and mother who were both in the audience and commented "You have got a future world champion here."

With a win for the protégée and a cash return on the night, Peggy Bettinson was delighted with the Mexborough man's performance and he promised he would find another career fighter to for him to challenge.

The following August, a reporter stopped by at Mexborough to interview Iron and his manager. The rumours going around were that he may be being lined up for a fight against Gunner Moir, the current English Heavyweight champion. The interview went well and Frank Law, with great bravado, put out a message Iron would fight any Heavyweight in the interim who fancied their chances – bar Gunner Moir. The article went out in commentary of the August 5th 1908 edition of Sporting Life.

Interestingly, one fighter did respond to the challenge. It was Jack Costello of Birmingham. The only issue was the fight would be a Catchweight bout which is not what the article was really about.

Chapter 13
Onwards Ever Onwards and Back to London We Go

Peggy Bettinson was as good as his word. A letter was despatched to Frank Law in September, inviting Iron to fight Charlie Wilson of Notting Hill at the NSC on the 10th October 1908. The fight was again to be over ten rounds. The purse was set at £50 a side with a £75 purse added. This was not the biggest purse Iron had fought for but the intrinsic value of the fight was immense. The bout was listed as being at Catchweight as Wilson was a Middleweight weighing 11 stone 4 pounds whereas Iron was 13 stone 7 pounds.

Once a fight was arranged, Iron went into his serious training mode. One of the ongoing arguments though between Frank Law and Iron was that Iron let himself go in these interim waiting periods. Having the gymnasium at the Montagu Arms probably didn't help. Like any young person, Iron extolled in engaging in frivolity and drinking bouts with his friends. Frank's view was that this was fine within reason, say just after a win, but should not be become a norm. As an athlete, Iron had to have different disciplinary codes to normal people his age. The effect of prolonged partying was that it did impair the fitness of the fighter. This meant that training was harder and needed to be more prolonged. The gay abandonment of youth made Iron feel some invincibility and that he was made of superhuman stuff. Training was a necessary evil more needed by others than by him.

Johnny Hague, Iron's Brother. They were very close.

For five weeks, Iron's trainers worked hard with him. Each morning, it was up early and off, now power walking, as opposed to jogging round the villages of High Melton, Barnburgh, Harlington and Adwick on Dearne before returning back to the Montagu Arms Gym. The afternoons were taken up with "ball" exercises and sandbag punching. The evenings were taken up with sparring sessions. These sessions invariably were witnessed by countless of the locals who came to watch the young man do his stuff. The area had not enjoyed this much success in the boxing world before and

Iron Hague (right) with his sparring partners - note Charlie Bolton, trainer in the middle. The picture was once again at the Montagu Arms.

there was a novelty attachment to it.

Frank's son, John, was by now, heavily involved in the training routines. One aspect of the training that was lacking and badly needed was some decent talent to spar with. To make up for this, Frank Law introduced a system whereby Iron boxed, taking on two fighters for each round. Halfway through, out would step one boxer and another would step in. This gave a freshness to each of the sparrer's which meant Iron needed that bit extra stamina to keep up. Local fighters O'Brien, Parkes and Iron's brother, Johnny, were recruited to add to the sparring quality.

The pace was gradually eased upwards each day. On the Thursday before the fight, each of the men then boxed one minute of a three minute round. This meant he had three fresher men to box each round. This was kept up for a full eight rounds. At the end of it, Iron was puffing and blowing but managed to keep up the whole distance. The training now brought to a head, London now awaited.

Charlie Wilson was believed to be a potential new Middleweight champion. He had beaten Gunner Moir previously in a straight competition It appeared this fight was going to be a particularly hard one.

On the Thursday evening of the fight, Iron's bout was listed as third on the programme and it was midnight before they entered the ring. Wilson had weighed in at 11 stone 4 pounds. Iron weighed in at 13 stones 7 pounds.

During round one, Wilson tried showing off scientific boxing flourishes, exhibiting classic moves but Iron was having none of it and punched at every opportunity. In the second round, Iron rushed in and planted two straight lefts but in doing so, caught a right on the side of his head that sent him into a spin. Wilson missed a golden opportunity as Iron's dropped guard exposed his jaw completely. The third round saw Iron take a hit again which sent him staggering into the ropes. Quickly recovering, Iron evaded further damage for the rest of the round. Iron's corner had to have very sharp words, the fight needed Iron to now get a grip and take control.

Come the fourth round, Iron came racing out looking like a new man, boxing like a man with energy. He managed to break through Wilson's defence late on in the round with a right hand jab that hurt. Iron seized this opportunity and went in for the finish. Punch after punch was delivered with points being scored. Wilson took the punishment but then collapsed to the canvas for a count of eight. He was still groggy when he rose and Iron despatched him again. This time he had a count of six. The bell rang, which for Wilson, saved him the day.

In the fifth round, Wilson, somewhat wary of further damage dodged and weaved round the ring. Iron deciding enough was enough, launched a further attack delivering a huge right to Wilson's head followed by a left to the jaw. He went down for the count. His seconds were screaming at him to get up. He started to rise, staggered and fell back down. He was out.

The press of the day were not overly kind to Iron, comments were:-

"Hague looked fat and flabby"

"Hague is a young man and strong too, but can be greatly improved in good hands"

"He is too excitable and requires steadying down and until this is taught him, he can never be champion."

One lasting memory of the fight was that Iron's nose had been broken. It was his first serious fight injury.

Chapter 13
Towards The Championship and a Big Mistake

After the fight, a lot of straight talking was done in Iron's camp. Though victorious, there was clearly a lot of work to be done. Frank Law and Thomas Weston were both of the same opinion. Iron didn't share their sentiment but agreed to go along with their wishes. Frank believed Iron needed even more experience before taking on Gunner Moir for the title. To quote him, he stated "Iron needs a final canter before the big race."

Peggy Bettinson at the N.S.C agreed that another fight would be preferential. This was because Bettinson was under some pressure to allow Ben Taylor, who was known as the Woolwich Infant, to have an opportunity for the title also. The ideal solution to this problem was to host a contender fight between the two of them. This bout was billed as an eliminator as Taylor, like Jack Scales, had at one time, claimed the English title. The fight was scheduled for the 14th December 1908 along with two other scheduled bouts, all being over ten rounds. This night was to be used to also promote one of the regular 'annual benefit raisers' for Mr Bettinson himself. He always held one each December having done so right from the start of the club. These were with the full ratification of the members who probably felt he earned it.

Ben Taylor

Considering the adverse press comments about Iron, training commenced in earnest. Taylor was some five years older than Iron and been on the circuit longer. He had, in the past, defeated Corporal Sunshine and boxed eight rounds with World Contender Jack Johnson. They fought at the Cosmopolitan club at Plymouth. The fight was memorable for the courage of Ben Taylor despite being well outclassed and being hit all over the ring. Johnson took the World Heavyweight title that year from Tommy Burns in Australia.

Taylor was 6 feet 2 inches tall and the hype stated he weighed a colossal 22 stone. He wasn't known as "Woolwich Giant" for nothing. The reality was that he was nearer 14 stones 10 pounds but it sounded good in the media. Taylor was classed as being in the top bracket of available boxers. He was another known beer drinking man who apparently disliked training even more than Iron did.

He was born at Arundel in Sussex in 1880. Ben Taylor was a man who knew what it meant to be poor. His father had died while Ben was just a child and his mother, to keep the family going, relocated them to Woolwich, south east London, where she worked washing dishes for the officers of the ships at the local dockyard. Tragically, when Ben was 14, his mother drowned after falling between a ship and the quay, leaving the youngster to fend for himself.

At 17, he joined a boxing booth and toured London and the Home Counties, before signing up as a fighter for 'Skipper' Jim Hulls (so called because he often wore a yachting cap), who ran boxing shows at the Woolwich Drill Hall.

Attendance at the N.S.C was now becoming a formality for Iron. On the night, the referee was Mr J H Douglas. Iron's corner consisted of Dick Parkes, George Law (Iron's brother in law) and brother, Johnnie Hague. The hype issued by the papers was ignored by the Mexborough contingent. It went over their heads, they were here to do a job. Taylor was just like any other boxer, there to be beat.

As the first round started, both fighters cautiously measured each other up. After thirty seconds, Iron broke through Taylor's guard and landed some quick left body slams followed up with a hard right. Taylor stumbled with the impact. As soon as he recovered, a huge right hand smashed into him sending him down on the canvas. He was down for a count of seven. He rose up again and Iron attacked once more. This time Taylor was knocked through the ropes into the crowd. The bell then rang coming to his salvation.

With the start of the second round, Taylor told it all in his eyes. He was clearly not with it. Iron capitalised on this and hit him with three lefts followed up by a right. Taylor went down for the count and never got up. The Woolwich Giant was firmly defeated.

Back to Mexborough, the hero returned once more. Frank Law did his customary thing. He put some money into Iron's bank account and handed him a packet with spendable cash in for the rest of his cut.

One of Iron's problems was that he listened to the Town's bar room lawyers, of which there were plenty. In a packed house at the Montagu Arms just a week after the last fight, Iron was buying people drinks like they were going out of fashion. He eventually became embarrassed as he had run out of ready cash. He looked around the room to try and find Frank to get some more money from him but Frank was not there. Iron quickly established he was in one of the 'Snug's' with a couple of friends. Iron left the lounge and shoved the Snug door open with some force. He apologised to the people sat inside and asked to talk to Frank in private.

The picture was dubbed "Iron's team" . It includes Frank Law at the top right, Johnny Hague at the side of Iron and Dick Parks at bottom right.

Frank excused himself from his company and took Iron into the corridor. He asked for some cash until tomorrow when presumably he would get some funds out of the bank.

Frank had tried to put a business head onto Iron but it just would not fit. Frank tried to reason that Iron needed to preserve his funds, not splash them around on people hell bent on spending his money for him.

He had seen this coming for some time and it needed bringing to a head. Frank's good advice went way over Iron's head and they parted that night not the best of friends.

Back in the lounge, the bar fly's eagerly awaiting another free fill, realised it wasn't going to happen. So the comments started to roll:-

"Where's all that prize money gone? With all them fights behind you it is you that should own this place."

"You are being had for a mug, all that money. How much do they cream off?"

"You need to get a grasp of things, they are taking you for their own ends."

"Ditch them while you can still earn something lad."

These thoughts all rattled through Iron's head that night as he lay in bed. The next morning, he decided that he needed to sort this out once and for all. He called at the Montagu Arms and told Frank he wanted to meet about his management. Frank postponed this meeting to the next day as he needed Thomas Weston to be there after all, he was the other financial backer.

At 7pm on the Tuesday night, Iron was summoned into Frank's office at the Montagu. It had a large mahogany partner's desk, various accounting ledgers were at one end. The whole room was eclipsed in shelving weighed down by files. Parts of beer hand pumps were discarded down in one corner.

Thomas Weston greeted Iron on his entering the room but you could tell the atmosphere was frosty. He was invited to sit down but he declined the offer, so standing before the two seated men, his peers of the ring.

Iron started the dialogue "I am not happy with our arrangement. I deserve a bigger slice of the cake. I have made you two gentlemen plenty of money and now it has to be my turn. Everyone is telling me the same."

Frank was clearly quite annoyed at this but Thomas Weston calmed him down. Thomas went on to explain that the basis of their agreement was in line with all the other boxers on the circuit. He needed men round him who believed in him. Men who would put up a king's ransom to enable his fights to go ahead, using money they could equally lose at any time, money that was beyond the reach of most men. It would not be Iron doing the crying then if the money is lost. He was provided with a training gym and equipment, he had trainers who all had to be paid for their services. Has he thought about all of that?

Frank interrupted by saying he was deeply offended by this insinuation that he was being mistreated, he had looked after him like a son. The looking after his protégé had gone far past the boundaries of any normal boxer/manager relationship. He had been looked after like a prince. Frank had always looked after his finances. He only allowed him a few pounds at a time as Iron's skills on money management were terrible, he had now got a good balance in the bank, away from the vultures. What was wrong in that?

Iron struggled to put up any arguments, he was lost in this kind of situation and he simply stuck to his script . He asked again if they would alter the arrangements in his favour. The joint answer was a definite no.

Iron stood his ground and said it was a hard decision but he was going to terminate their relationship and look for other backers.

He thanked them for all they had done and left the stony, silent room.

In later years, Iron, upon reminiscing about his boxing career, said that walking out on Frank Law and Thomas Weston was the biggest mistake of his life. I tend to agree. After he left Frank's supervision, money just went through his hands to anyone who asked for it and there were plenty of them that did.

He certainly threw his money about. The bank balance so carefully stacked away dwindled to nothing. Iron recalled that after leaving Frank, there were times when he didn't even have the fare to get him to the venue where he was fighting.

As far as Iron was now concerned, it was the start of a new era. The press on getting the story lamented that they were sure Iron would get a new backer but he would struggle to find anyone in the same league as Frank Law.

One stroke of luck was an enquiry sent to Frank Law that he sent onto Iron for him at his house. There was an enquiry for him to appear at the Sheffield Hippodrome to do a sparring exhibition with the old Cornish Champion Bob Fitzsimmons.

Fitzsimmons was a name very well known in the world of the pugilists. He was born in 1863, his trade was that of a blacksmith. He received some fight training from the last Bare Knuckle World Champion, Jem Mace, who helped him develop a certain technique which he further developed over the years. Bob commenced his boxing career in 1883. During the years following, he beat some of the greatest fighters around like, Gentleman Jim Corbett, Jack Dempsey and sailor Tom Sharkey (this fight was refereed by the legendary lawman Wyatt Earp). All these three boxers were Irish born.

Bob Fitzsimmons depicted in this print fighting Peter Maher.

In his career, he held the World Title at Middleweight, Light Heavyweight and Heavyweight. His official fight record shows he had 82 professional fights of which he won 51 (44 of these by knockout) and drew 5. Bob maintains he had more like 350 fights under his belt. He was probably right as the records then were very poorly kept.

The show at the Sheffield Hippodrome on the 11th February 1909 was billed as "The past and the future". Iron was down to box three rounds of two minutes. The show was a sell out with a crowd of 4000. The exhibition was very professional and well received. At the end, Bob addressed the crowd to tell them that "Iron had boxed exceptionally well and that here is a coming champion". He told the Hippodrome manager afterwards that "if he could have Iron for a month, I could make him into a real good man". He had identified a rough fighter who needed some polish.

Many however believed that Iron had not performed at his best as he had been on the beer trail since winning Ben Taylor.

Chapter 14
The British Heavyweight Title is at Stake

As news got round that Iron was looking for new management, one local businessman was very interested in the job. He was William Biggs (known as Billy), the landlord of the Bulls Head on Mexborough High Street. He was known to Iron very well and Iron's dad did drink in the Bull's Head as a regular. He was also the gentleman who put up the purse to allow Iron to fight in the first place for the Pitman's Championship.

Billy Biggs was born in Bedworth in Warwickshire in 1870. His father, also called William, had come to Denaby in the 1890's and they resided at the Reresby Cottage, The Mission Church, Pit Row Denaby. William Senior did not engage in pit work, he specialised in bar management taking on bar work. They later took over the New Masons Arms on Doncaster Road, Mexborough.

As a young man, son Billy excelled as a footballer, playing for Mexborough Town FC. He was well known in the area for his sporting prowess.

Following in his father's footsteps, he also went into the licensed trade and took over the tenancy of the Bull's Head on the High Street at Mexborough. His wife, whom he married in 1898, was Lily who came from Ferrybridge, West Yorkshire. The Bulls Head was run as a family affair with assistance from his brother John Henry and his sister Letty. Two live in servants also resided at the Bull.

As news of Iron's arguments with Frank Law circulated around the town, it pricked up the ears of Billy. A great sports lover, he was prepared to take Iron on and manage him if he was willing. He knew he wasn't in the same league as Law and Weston but he had other qualities and great bravado to push Iron onwards.

Charles Bigg's of the Bull's Head – Iron Hague's second manager .

The Bulls Head, High Street, Mexborough.

Iron had a meeting with Billy and they agreed a deal between them. So now Iron had a new manager. There were some interim problems to sort out, like somewhere to train. Some space was made at the Bull's Head but it wasn't adequate and the search went on for somewhere more appropriate.

Iron actually went to see Frank Law to tell him what he was doing. They had a long standing friendship which continued despite events. Frank's view was that he was making a mistake but the door was always open for him if he ever wanted to return.

Unfortunately, after Billy was in place as manager, things seemed to then drag on a bit. Billy was concentrating his efforts on the new partnership going forwards, ensuring sufficient funds were in place for future contests, writing letters here, there and everywhere.

One observation at this time was that with Frank Law's watchful eye no longer fixed on Iron, he was throwing his money around even more than before. This was another of Iron's later regrets. He lacked any financial skills whatsoever.

At the end of the first week in February 1909, Harry Jacobs of Wonderland made contact. His 2000 seater venue situate on Whitechapel Road , Mile End in the East End of London, was staging an increasing number of top fights with great purses as the incentive. He told Billy he could get a fight at Wonderland with Gunner Moir with a purse of £500 if he was interested. Billy showed the businessman within him by rejecting this offer. He pointed out that recently, a Lightweight's title fight at the National Sporting Club had a purse of £900. The sum of £500 for the English Heavyweight title was completely inadequate; it was worth a lot more than that.

It was also the unwritten law that to be an undisputed British title (English title had been changed to British by the N.S.C in February 1909), it had to be at the N.S.C and be three minute rounds, not Wonderlands two minutes.

Gunner Moir then got involved directly and said that each side should put up £500 which would then make it very worthwhile. Iron was delighted with this and wanted to accept straight away. Billy though, needed to talk to others, he would not be able to pledge this amount without additional backers. The situation was becoming more public in that two new rival boxing magazines had been set up in addition to The Sporting Life and their journalists were competing for news and Iron was hot property. The magazines were the Illustrated Sporting Budget and Boxing World.

The papers ran the headline on the 11th February 1909 "Gunner Moir to defend his title, probable match with Ian Hague". Billy contacted the newspapers to confirm he had contacted Moir and was willing to take up Moirs' offer but for £200 aside and the best purse to be offered. The journalists said in their article they thought the N.S.C would be the preferred venue but it was the size of the purse being offered that would dictate the show in the end.

These articles were read by Frank Law with great interest. Obviously, Billy had bit off more than he could chew financially. Frank and Thomas Weston could have pledged that quite easily. They decided to sit the situation out.

Peggy Bettison was keen to have the fight at the N.S.C and speedily came up with an offer of a purse of £900. Billy and Moir's manager met Bettison and sealed the deal.

There would be £200 a side put up, the fight would be over two three minute rounds and six ounce gloves were to be used. The £200 a side incidentally, was the lowest amount that could be put up under the N.S.C rules for a Heavyweight bout and had been for several years, the title had almost slipped into abeyance due to the poor quality of English/British heavyweights throughout the 1890's and early 1900's. The majority of those claiming it being classed as 'third raters' that is, until Jack Palmer and Gunner Moir came on the scene. The winner was to take £650 and £25 a side was to be paid towards training costs. The date for the fight was set as Monday April 19th 1909.

Gunner James Moir was born 17th April 1879 in London, making him some six years older than Iron. He resided in Lambeth. He was considered to be the great hope of the British people capable of winning the coveted Heavyweight Championship of the world. In 1907, he became the first Englishman to contest for the title since Bob Fitzsimmons lost the belt to Jim Jeffries some eight years earlier.

Previously a sailor by trade, he had turned to boxing whilst serving in the Navy. Moir was covered in tattoos, which made him a strange sight in the ring. He had won the Army champion in the Indian Heavyweight Championships in 1902 against Gypsy Smith of the Lincolnshire Regiment at Poona. His first known professional fight was in 1903, which was a first round victory of the otherwise forgotten Fred Barrett. He had had to retire with an injured hand. This was followed by three consecutive losses by Moir, one of these was to American Charlie Haugh of Boston, Massachusetts, Charlie "Slounch" Dixon of Stepney and other was when the referee had stopped the contest. All were equally forgettable opponents. Despite the rocky start, he went onto Australia where he made his debut in December 1904 in Sydney winning in the sixth round against Bill Smith.

Moir then secured himself a bout in with the veteran coloured boxer Peter Felix, the former heavyweight champion of Australia. This was on the 14th February 1905, also in Sydney. Moir flattened Felix inside of two rounds and earned himself his first real notoriety in sporting circles.

Moir's newfound fame allowed him to enter a tournament to determine the Heavyweight Championship of England the following year. After knocking out Irish born Jim Casey (also known in the U.S.A as 'Young Fitzsimmons') in an elimination bout, he faced the reigning British titleholder, Jack Palmer (real surname Liddell, born in Newcastle on Tyne) at the National Sporting Club on the 29th October, 1906, taking the title via a ninth round disqualification in just his fourteenth bout.

Gunner James Moir , the then Heavyweight champion of England.

Four months later, Gunner destroyed challenger Tiger James Smith of Merthyr, South Wales (he was actually born James Addis 27th July 1875 in Yorkshire) in the very first round and became the new sensation, loved by the British sporting press. Up to this point, Smith (Addis) was considered at the N.S.C as being their 'blue eyed boy' who, with a powerful big punch, could do no wrong. In reality, weight wise, he was a middleweight.

When world Heavyweight Champion, Tommy Burns, travelled to England looking for credible challengers, Moir was first on his list, this being his sixteenth traced bout. He cut such an intimidating figure with his greater size and colourful tattoos. Betting placed Gunner as the favourite to take the championship. But when the two actually met in the ring, on December 2 1907, the smaller but faster Burns was clearly Moir's master. Burns scored a knockdown in the first round and another in the second. In order to give the audience its money's worth, he carried his opponent for nine rounds before laying him low in the tenth.

As news of the impending fight spread, a great deal of excitement went around South Yorkshire. Some were still of the opinion that Iron should engage in more fights to gain experience, despite the fact that Iron had engaged in more bouts than Moir. Iron's view was that he was well ready and itching to go.

Back at Mexborough, Billy called a meeting of everyone involved in the team. A careful training programme was devised for this "the big one". They discussed previous reports on Moir, trying to identify his strong points and more importantly, his weaknesses. Ideas were muted as to the ideal training areas and programmes of fitness.

Iron Hague being ticked off by manager Chas Biggs

The training routine involved a power walk of four or five miles at 7am, returning for breakfast. This always consisted of poached eggs on dry toast.

After a short rest, Iron would then do a daily run for ten to twelve miles around the outlying villages. This was varied sometimes by alternating between a walk, a trot and a sprint, which made it really hard. With several weeks to go, it was decided that Iron needed taking away from Mexborough. To get him away from the increasing number of well wishers interrupting schedules so to concentrate more heavily on boxing skills

The Pier Hotel, Withernsea, East Yorkshire - Iron's training head quarters for the big title fight.

and the fight itself.

Billy arranged for them all to go to the Pier Hotel at Withernsea, East Yorkshire on the coast, some eighteen miles from Hull. The training team staying there consisted of Tom Stokes, now Pitman's Champion, Dick Parkes of Goldthorpe, a French pugilist, a runner called Pierre Bousquet and Iron's brother, Johnnie.

Billy was also there to oversee proceedings. Bousquet had been fetched in to help strengthen the team. He was a very capable amateur middleweight who himself was competing for the Amateur Championship of England. He would accompany Iron on all the runs, etc.

Whilst at Withernsea, they were approached to take a break in the training and attend a show at nearby Hull. They wanted Iron to appear at the Empire Theatre in a series of exhibition fights. These were designed to let Iron show off to the crowd the up and coming stallions ring craft and ability. Three exhibition fights took place on the 6th March 1909, the first against Charlie Cannon, the second against "Young" Walker and the third against his brother, Johnnie. The crowd were very appreciative. At the end, Iron was wished well in his championship endeavours the applause and cheering nearly lifted the roof off.

The Withernsea training routine still involved Iron out on the road at 7am, now for a twelve mile run, returning for breakfast. Dick Parkes took control of the training and supervised the events. After breakfast, they would have a game of billiards and chill out generally. After a light lunch, the afternoon would see a variety of gym work including skipping, shadow boxing, ball punching. Two punch bags were used, one was the free swinging 'bob and weave 'traditional bag that Iron used to pummel with enthusiasm and the other was fixed to the floor and ceiling by a wire. After this, sparring sessions would take place involving them all.

The Frenchman, more the runner, took some punishment from Iron but amazed everybody with his resilience of keep getting back up. After tea, it was a walk along the sands then to bed at 9.30pm. To give a bit of variety, it was arranged for some of the running to be replaced by rowing on the sea, to strengthen arms and shoulders. Iron really liked this recreational training alternative.

They kept the local cobbler busy in repeatedly stitching up the split punch bags damaged in training. On the 25th March, the pressure from the locals at Withernsea was for Iron to do a little exhibition for them.

Billy gracefully agreed and a three round exhibition fight was staged at the Assembly Rooms against Tom Stokes. The grateful citizens combined the night with other entertainment and donated the whole proceeds to Iron's benefit fund. This was used to offset some of the training costs being run up. Iron commented later in life that the training at Withernsea was one of his happiest times ever. Everyone got on and the comradeship between all was excellent, it was like one big happy family.

During all this time, Gunner Moir had been training at Whetstone under the supervision of Dai Dollings. Whetstone was a wealthy suburb of North London.

A week before the big fight on 12th April, Iron's contingent returned back to Mexborough. Although the tactic was to ease the training schedule and let Iron rest up somewhat so he was fresh for the onslaught, it was not to be. As in Withernsea, local pressures prevailed to see the man and become a part of what was happening. On the Saturday morning, Iron appeared on the High Street outside the Bulls Head along with Billy and Dick Parkes to participate in a run. The streets were lined with well wishers keen to see Iron. Even they were taken aback at the amount of support.

Further crowd participation took place on the 16th April 1909 when that night, Iron boxed three round matches against the three best men of the Dearne Valley district. These were his compatriots' Dick Parkes, Harry Fellowes and Tommy Stokes. The fights were to follow on with no breaks, testing fitness to the limits. It was like fighting three fresh men. This spectacle took part in the local Mexborough Hippodrome theatre. It was a sell out and could have been sold out even yet again. As the rounds were boxed, a narrator called out a commentary to the watching audience. When Iron initially entered the ring, there were calls for him to take off his sweater, to which he obliged. He revealed his leaner frame and bulk to the audience for their approval. This met rapturous applause. These fights were not for him to show his smashing right and left sledgehammer punches but for him to manage the endurance that this placed him under.

Despite all the training, there was an opinion though that Iron was still carrying a little too much weight.

Chapter 15
The Day of the Contest

It was 7.30am, 19th April 1909 and at the Hague residence at Woodruff Row, Iron was already dressed and sat in the front lounge. He was already in his black suit and shirt and tie which was early for anyone so attired. Some of the superstitious said it was a bad omen to dress in black beforehand.

Irons response was that if there was an unlucky omen, it was not for him. His father, John, was upstairs getting dressed whilst his mother prepared breakfast for them all. Iron's brother, Johnnie, suddenly entered the house, "Well, are we all ready our kid?" was his opening question. Iron slouched down on the settee replied to the positive, he was ready. Unusually, Mrs Hague was dressed in her Sunday best outfit, anticipating a constant stream of close family and friends as well wishers. She wasn't disappointed. Iron's aunts, uncles, cousins friends and neighbours all came to pay homage to this king in the making.

So engrossed was everyone that the appointed hour of 9.00am departure soon came round. The outside door of the house was propped open, letting in the fresh spring air. Suddenly, the room darkened as a group of men filled the recess. It was Billy Biggs, Dick Parkes, Tom Stokes and helper Bill Baxter. They had previously assembled at the Bulls Head some sixty minutes earlier to pack up the tackle they would need in the forthcoming fight, towels, sponges, lotions, bandages, wraps and some medical items all were packed into the bag. Also travelling to London for his first ever visit was Iron's father, John. He was as proud as proud could ever be. Iron's brother, John, was also to travel with them. The party was swelled by backers C H Evans, C H Athron, A Winter, D Dalton and Mr C Dunham. They would all be taking seats in the area specially reserved for them in National Sporting Club.

"Right lad" Billy's voice boomed out,"we are going to set off and Iron, you are in front with me and the others will follow a couple of steps behind" were his instructions. Iron protested "But we are only walking for the bloody train." Billy lowered his head to be straight in eye level with Iron "Listen son, your public await." The party were to briefly stop off at the Bull's Head en-route to pick up the equipment bags. Iron knew there were people out there to give him a send off but he didn't realise that thousands of well wishers had appeared and were lining the streets, all the way along High Street and right down to the railway station. As they went into the Bull, they were given red and blue rosettes to wear, being the colours of Mexborough Town Football club. When they re-emerged, the crowd had shuffled up and a roar rang along the street , renewed again and again as they ventured along. The atmosphere was electric, caps were flung high in the air. Scores of rough hands were thrust out, hands that told of a long association with hard work, hoping for a friendly shake

Iron Hague is pictured and captioned as being "A promising heavyweight".

from the terrible right, from which so much was expected in the forthcoming contest.

There were people hanging out of windows and the cheers were as if the King himself was progressing down the streets. Some people had been there hours to get a great viewing position. The elderly had chairs carried down for them, they were flanked by their grandchildren whilst their sons and daughters towered above, standing behind them. People were furiously waving their arms and supporting banners, all wishing Iron good luck.

The adoration even spilled onto the railway station itself, the police restricted the access to the platform so people were not endangered with the crush. The passenger footbridge over the lines was like a world record attempt to see how many people could be mounted on it.

The fight party awaited only momentarily before their train arrived. Iron stood there, towering above the crowd posing for the press photographers who had been allowed access to the would be hero.

Crowd on Station Road off to see Iron Hague departing for the title contest – 19th April 1909.

Further picture on Station Road.

The crowd cheers increased as the train pulled in and arms again started waving everywhere. Quite emotional,they all mounted the 10.09am steam train heading for Sheffield Victoria Station for their onward route to Marleybone Station, London. Iron said that if it were not for the police's intervention, he would never have fought Moir as he would have been pulled to pieces by the crowd's enthusiasm. Also boarding the train were a collection of journalists

At 2.30pm, they arrived at London. The Mexborough contingent hoped to become absorbed into the anonymity of the busy London streets. It wasn't to be however. As hardy northerners wearing the trademark flat cap, they certainly stood out. The journalist from the Star noted that Iron looked to be in remarkable health and condition. He was described as having a bronze look, effected by the Yorkshire sea breezes.

Iron and Johnny Hague waiting to alight the train for their journey to London.

They made their way to Anderton's Hotel at 162-164 Fleet Street, where the plan was to settle down and relax for four or five hours before the off. The hotel was well known and associated with sports. It was here that the inaugural meeting was held for creating the Southern Football Leagues, countless boxers had stayed there on the English title trails. It was here that 'Jack the Ripper' suspect "Alonzo Maduro" stayed, disappearing into the night in 1888, never to be seen again.

Iron, after checking in, simply went to bed to enjoy an idle hour.

Contrary to the report done by the Star's journalist, London reporters had been circulating adverse comments that afternoon regarding Iron's physical condition indicating that he had neglected his training during the previous week and was a stone above his best weight. This swung the bookmakers to change the odds into Moir's favour of 6 to 4. There was an intimation this false rumour was fuelled by the Yorkshire crowd to get better odds on their man. One of the waiting journalists collared Iron in the hotel lounge and asked him what he had to say about the impending fight. Iron replied he didn't have anything to say about it, he didn't need to!

At 8.00pm prompt, a fleet of taxis arrived amid pouring rain and the Mexborough party made their way to Covent Garden. Strangely enough, a journey through rain was superstitiously thought of for would be fighters at the N.S.C to be an ill omen.

The fighting was to commence at 9.15pm prompt just as the diners had finished their meal. The first contest of ten rounds was between Sam light of Marleybone and Young Sharkey of Notting Hill, both local London boys.

The contest proved to be a hard fight which lasted for eight rounds when the referee stopped the fight. Light was considered too badly beaten to continue so Sharkey took the honours.

The next fight on the bill was between Driver Himpfen and Wally Pickard, again a ten round contest. The fighters were very evenly matched and both fought hard every round. The referee at the end, was very hard pressed to differentiate in favour of either fighter and announced a draw.

Next on the bill were two exhibition fights. The first three rounder was between Jim Driscoll of Cardiff and George Moore of Barking. Driscoll, the Featherweight Champion, received what could be described as, for the N.S.C, a flattering reception.

The second exhibition bout was between Johnny Summers of Canning Town and Joe Bowker of Salford, Manchester. His birth name was actually Thomas Mahon. They boxed well and received the crowd's approval at the end.

Whilst all this was going on, Iron and his seconds were in the changing room. He had stripped down and changed into his boxing shorts some thirty minutes before the appointed starting time. Pacing up and down, the tension was running high. "For God's sake, sit down and relax" cried Iron to Billy Biggs who was driving everyone mad. "Go back to your seat and leave me to it" Iron requested. He readily agreed and made his way back. Iron was engrossed in his steady warming up exercises. Stretching his arm joints one by one, standing on one leg while retracting his knees, bending down and standing up. He launched into punching flurries into fresh air. He stood there with his boots tied up tight and all gloved up.

At 10.35pm, the crowd were introduced to the legendary Bob Fitzsimmons who was there for the spectacle. At 10.40pm, Gunner Moir made his entrance into the ring. It was not until 10.50pm when came the call Iron had been waiting for, "Please enter the ring."

Moir stood in the corner nearest Tattersall's, donning his heavy dressing gown, trying not to be seen to be taking notice of the audacious young challenger. Moir was being attended for this fight by Dai Dollings, Jim Walsh, Arthur Gutteridge and Charley Moir.

As Iron and his party came in making his way through the gangway, he noticed the place was fuller than usual. To make the cash purse up, Peggy had certainly beaten the drum and packed them in. There were even dinner suited spectators standing on the spiral staircases and walkways.

Iron looked at Moir as he entered the ring. He thought the Gunner looked a trifle nervous. With all his big fight experience of the past, Iron thought this unusual. Iron himself was by now focussed on one thing only – the man in front of him whom he was to now fight.

The referee for the fight was Tom Scott and the timekeeper was Mr E Terega. Moir was very heavily tattooed and when the fighters were called to the centre of the ring, a Yorkshire voice unceremoniously boomed out "Get in there and hit him, don't stand around looking at all the pictures."

The fight commentary, written by the late Harry Carpenter, is now used to illustrate the fight's events. (Harry did this in the 1970's for the BBC who were doing a radio tribute to Iron Hague.)

"As you join me at the National Sporting Club, it's the Champion, Jim Moir, who's first into the ring for this contest to decide the Heavyweight Championship of England.

This is only the second time the Gunner will have defended the title since he beat Jack Palmer here two and a half years ago and that fight didn't prove much, with Tiger Smith going down in one.

Still, there's no doubt who's the favourite here tonight, there must have been a lot of money that's gone on Gunner Moir. The odds have shortened from 5/1 to 5/4 in the last few days but one thing's certain, young Iron Hague will have to go some to put Jim Moir down.

Well now, a word or two about the challenger. He's 23 years old, he's not had a great deal of professional experience, although what fights he has had show he's not a fighter to be dismissed too easily. He seems to specialise in the quick knock-out, and from the weight he's carrying, I'm sure that's what he'll be going for tonight.

Well now, Iron Hague just climbing into the ring now and if first impressions are anything to go by, he is carrying just a bit too much weight I think, particularly if this fight should go the distance.

Well both men now together in the ring, and any moment now, this Championship fight will be underway.

And there goes the bell for round one.

And it's the Champion, Gunner Moir, who's on the move first. Circling round Hague, looking for that opening.

But it's first blood to Hague with a left to the jaw.

A very fast left jab, it takes Moir a little by surprise, he moves away.

Hague's after him, they clinch, Hague pushes the Champion away.

I think the Gunner's a little wary of that left now. He's keeping well clear.

It's Hague, he's dropped his guard.

Right to the body from the Champion.

Another left from Hague, this time a bit too high. I think it connected up on the Gunner's cheekbone. Moir, keeps his distance now.

This is amazing, after less than a minute, this Yorkshire youngster's got the Champion on the run. Hague's refusing to go after him, he's sticking to the centre of the ring.

In comes Moir, and he's down, he's down, Moir is down!

A right from Iron Hague puts Gunner Moir down in round one of this Heavyweight title fight.

The Champion, not waiting for the count, he's up at two.

And another right from Hague puts him straight back down again. This is fantastic!

Moir is back on his feet, he's heading for his corner, he's turned his back on Hague.

And he's down again! This time a body blow, almost from behind.

The Gunner's not getting up – I don't think he's gonna get up.

He's lying against the ropes, 5, 6 - Moir's second's tugging at the ropes, urging him to get up – 9, 10, he's out! He's out!

Moir is out, in what I make, two minutes and forty seven seconds of round one.

Iron Hague has taken the title from Gunner Jim Moir.

And only now is he getting to his feet after taking that terrific punishment from the

Lord Lonsdale – initiator of the Lonsdale Belt.

Picture taken of Iron Hague after he had won the heavyweight title. Note the intimidating haircut.

Iron fists of young Hague.

Well, no wonder they call him Iron.

And on this showing, it'll be a good man who'll take the title from Iron Hague.

Heavyweight Champion of England, in just two minutes and forty seven seconds.

And that has made boxing history here at the National Sporting Club tonight."

The "Iron" supporters in the watching crowd could not restrain themselves and they jumped up and burst into a very loud cheering and applause. Tom Stokes and Billy jumped into the ring and hugged and kissed Iron. Iron's father and his brother, Johnny, hung through the ropes reaching out into the ring. Meanwhile, the Gunner was being revived. Twice Iron went over to reassure him and shake his hand.

Lord Lonsdale himself entered the ring and congratulated the Mexborough man on becoming the Heavyweight Champion of England.

This was quite an honour. Iron although not used to etiquette and formality, thanked his Lordship with a modest dignity. John Hague was overcome with emotion. He rushed up to Iron and said with tears in his eyes "Come here and shake hands with your dad." It was like a lifetime suddenly flashing by.

The Mexborough party shouted that much they all suffered with laryngitis. What a night.....

The party eventually made their way back to the hotel for a private party where the celebrations continued right into the night. The fight was talked about over and over again. Tom Stokes and Dick Parkes definitely had a good drink that night, they thought they had earned it. Talk was uppermost in many peoples minds as to who would Iron next be fighting. That decision had, unbeknown to all in the room, been tentatively already decided.

The next morning, the Mexborough party were up early to do some sightseeing. Iron was very keen to show his father some of the sights. They were all amused at breakfast when the young girl cockney waitress asked Iron if they settled the boxing championship with just one game. Everyone laughed out loud.

They all left the hotel together, returning a couple of hours later and checking out. They then got into a fleet of taxis to make their way back to the N.S.C.

At the N.S.C, a press conference had been called to witness the new English

HAGUE RECEIVING THE CHEQUE FOR £650.

The Photo. above shows Mr. Bettinson handing over the cheque for £650 to Hague on Tuesday. The figures, reading from the left, are Hague, D. Dalton, J. Hague and W. Biggs, senr.

Iron Hague receives the winners cheque from Peggy Bettinson after lifting the Heavyweight title.

Heavyweight Champion receiving his cheque.

The journalist for the "Mirror of Life" newspaper, perhaps a little shocked at the audacity of the raw Northerner, issued this rather long report the next day:-

"The contest between Hague and Moir is over, and we have a new champion of England in Ian, or "Iron" Hague of Mexborough – a big husky son of Yorkshire. The contest was a most disappointing one, as, though I never expected it to go more than six or eight rounds, I certainly did not anticipate a victory and a defeat in less that a round. I was disappointed at the showing made by Moir, and I was gratified by the display of Hague. He used his left-hand very nicely, and seldom failed to follow it instantly with a precise right – the celebrated old-time "one-two." Moir seemed to be lacking in what the old school of pugilists called "bottom spirit," which means the ability as well as the willingness to accept punishment. There are some men who are unable to take punishment, because their constitution does not admit of their quickly shaking off the effects of a hard blow, or who have not what we now call "the power of assimilating punishment." The Americans have coined an expression which partly, but not perfectly, fits the case. They say that when a man is easily dazed or knocked out he "has a glass jaw." It is the man who has not a glass jaw, "and who has a brave heart, that possesses the combination known as the "bottom spirit."

On Monday night last, Moir received a left hook on the right side of the head, which practically knocked all the fight out of him. Ten seconds after, he received this blow I said to Mr Cleveland, who sat next to me, "Harry, the Gunner's beat." I could see it in his whole demeanour, in his actions, in the motions of his arms, his head, his legs and his body. He made a half-hearted retreat, like a frightened schoolboy, and seemed overawed by the power of his rival's punching. Hague made no mistake once he got Moir going. Instead of smashing at him wielding with the right, he led time and again with a fine left, and followed it – hit or miss – with a bruising right. Moir was down twice and the third time he stayed down. I was sure he was going to get up at the point of nine, but he made no apparent effort to do so, and was counted out.

"What do you think of it?" This question was asked me at least twenty times during the first half- hour after Hague had won. I could only answer that I was not able to think just yet awhile.

I was like a man who had just swallowed a heavy meal, and was very uncomfortable, until it had at least partly digested. It took me a long time to digest the meal that I swallowed last Monday and I was uncomfortable until I had partly done so. Moir is a worse boxer than I thought he was and Hague is a much better boxer than I imagined. It may be that Moir under-rated his opponent and was anticipating meeting a raw novice who could punch if he only knew how to deliver his punch.

Suddenly Moir got one on the head, and the combination of astonishment and concussion – the mental and physical shocks – were altogether too much for his limited stock of bottom spirit, and he was a beaten man immediately on receipt of the blow.

What do you think of it? I hardly know whether to think that Hague is a champion, or think that Moir is a counterfeit. Of course, I know – we all know – that Hague is the Champion of England, but that is not what I mean. We all know when we are talking of the abilities of a boxer that when we say "He's a pretty good man, but he's not a champion," we all know, I say, that we mean he is not in the front rank of boxers and would not have much chance with the first-class men at his weight. At present I submit that we have no first-class men in the heavyweight division, and we cannot gauge a man's ability except by seeing him perform against somebody who is a leader in his class. Hague is yet, to me at least, an unknown quantity. I saw him win a novices' competition and I also saw him extended therein by an old-timer from the North. He was young then, and inexperienced, so we let that pass and do not take it as a criterion. I saw him box Charlie Wilson, Corporal Sunshine, and Ben Taylor. He beat them all – but, whilst giving him full credit for his performances and admitting that he did all that was asked of him, and also that it was a very promising series of victories for one so young in experience, I cannot hide the fact that none of these is a Jack Johnson, a Tommy Burns, or a Sam Langford. And there are others.

What do you think of it? To tell the truth, I haven't yet digested the meal, and I'm not quite decided as to what I do think of it. I have some thoughts, but if I put them on paper I might hurt somebody's feelings, and, as we know that "second thoughts are best," I'll e'en wait awhile and see what my "second thoughts" are. As regards my first thoughts – if I can dignify first impressions by that name – I may say that they were endorsed by several of the best judges in the N.S.C. – members and officials – Mr J H Douglas, Mr Tom Scott, Mr H T Brickwell, Mr George Edwards, Mr Bob Hair, Mr E Zerega, Mr Bettison and others, all of whom put the question to me, "What do you think of it?"

The very fact of this pertinent and interesting question being repeated so frequently set me thinking – no about "it," but as to why the question was put, and put so often. It might have covered or concealed the question "Do you think Hague is a world's champion?" Or it might equally have hidden the question "Do you think Moir ever could fight?"

One gentleman, who shall be nameless, made the following remark and said I might publish it and say he said so, but I won't give his name. Suffice to quote him: "Frank," said he, "I think 'Charlie Howard' would just about describe it."

What do you think of it? So far I have not committed myself to any assertion opinion, or judgement on the merits or demerits of the victory and defeat. I have not yet finished thinking of it. I have ideas , thoughts, impressions, suspicions,

As Landlord of the Bulls Head in Mexborough, he was a well known character.

hopes, and all sorts of similar things but I have not yet been able (that is up to the time of writing this, and the victory is not yet twenty-four hours old) to think collectedly and calmly and with cool judgement. It's a bit of a problem, and I'm letting it simmer in my mind for a few days. Something will happen to put my thoughts in the right direction, and perhaps next week I shall be able to give a complete and satisfactory answer to the question, "What do you think of it?"

The Editor of the "Mirror of Life" Frank J Bradley was considered one of the best, if not the best Boxing experts of the day.

The day after the fight Gunner Moir, with his manager, Major Best and his brother, Charles Moir, called at the offices of the Sporting Life newspaper. The Gunner was naturally terribly upset at the result of the contest of the previous evening. He maintained he never felt better or fitter in his life and set Hague's win down as one of those unfortunate experiences that almost every boxer experienced. He said "He did not wish in any way to decry Hague, nor to attempt to take any of the credit that is due to him but I must assert that he was very fortunate and could not repeat the Monday night's performance. I wish to challenge Hague to another match for a purse of between £100 to £500 aside dependent on him to be fought out as early as Hague wants but the sooner the better. I can box at once. I will be pleased to hear from Hague if he will accept this challenge."

Billy Biggs, in defending his man, told the Sporting Life "It may be easier for the Gunner not to refer to last night as a contest but perhaps as six lucky blows." The offer was noted but there were bigger fish to fry.

Portrait of Iron Hague, commissioned by The National Sporting Association after his new title victory.

Chapter 17
The Sam Langford Contract Affair

The immediate offshoot of the fight's success was an offer of another lucrative purse. This offer was finalised at the N.S.C after the handing over the winner's cheque. The deal was arranged quite hastily while all parties were still riding high on the victory wave.

There had been some politics building up in the wings before this offer which Iron was not fully aware of.

Jack Johnson had been helped financially from London so enabling him to travel to Australia to meet Canadian Tommy Burns for the world title. This was on the understanding that if he won, he would return to London and defend the title at the N.S.C against Sam Langford. Johnson won the World Heavyweight title on December 26 1908, when he fought Burns in Sydney. The fight had been long coming in that Johnson had followed Burns around the world for two years, taunting

Sam Langford with outstretched arms showing the length of his reach.

him through the World's press for a match. Once finally agreed, the bout lasted all of fourteen rounds before unusually it was stopped by the local police in front of over 20,000 spectators. The title was awarded to Johnson on a referee's decision of a technical knockout, the award was misleading anyway as Johnson had clearly beaten the champion.

Johnson then reneged on his promise. The N.S.C said they would not recognise Johnson as Champion. They then planned to match Iron against Sam Langford and would bill it as for the vacant World Heavyweight title, although no one took this seriously.

After Johnson's victory over Burns, racial animosity in the USA was fuelled, resentment ran deep amongst the white population. So much so that author Jack London called out for a search to commence to find the "Great White Hope" to take the title away from Johnson. As the world title holder, Johnson was then pitched mainly in a series of exhibition fights against a variety of "great white hopes". In 1909, he did however beat Frank Moran in what was only an exhibition bout of four rounds, Tony Ross. Fights with Al Kaufman and the Middleweight Champion, Stanley Ketchel, were no decision verdicts, with Johnson getting the newspaper decision. The latter fight with Ketchel was keenly fought by both men right until the twelfth and last round, when Ketchel threw a right to Johnson's head, knocking him down.

Slowly regaining his feet, Johnson threw a straight right to Ketchel's jaw, knocking him out, along with some of his teeth, several of which "supposedly" were embedded in Johnson's glove. Johnson's fight with Philadelphia Jack O'Brien was a disappointing one for Johnson. He was much heavier, weighing some 205 pounds compared to O'Brien's who weighed in at 161 pounds. The result was only a six-round draw – that was the newspaper decision as it was a no decision bout.

Johnson, to his credit, would not bow down to white American public opinion which meant the finding of proper suitors for the World Crown became more restricted. One of the obstacles cited was the level of purses demanded by Johnson, which scarcely anyone could match.

Johnson had fought Sam Langford in Paris back in April 1906 and won but times had moved on from then. There were growing calls for him to have a rematch. Langford had since then improved and notched up a series of convincing victories. There was however sensed to be some reluctance on Johnson's behalf to meet Langford again. One reason cited was that a fight by two coloured boxers would not generate sufficient interest to warrant the total cash needed to meet Johnson's requirements.

Langford was now over in England and stalking Johnson for a fight. England did not display the prejudices that held him back in the USA. Bettinson thought it a good idea to match the newly crowned English Heavyweight Champion against Sam

Langford and in the meantime took advantage of the day in hand.

Just before the title fight, Bettinson told both Hague and Moir that the winners would have a contract to fight Langford. A deal would be on offer for the winner to take on Langford in a fight of twenty, three minute rounds. The purse was to be £200 a side topped up with £400 from the N.S.C. Moir said that he wasn't interested as he wanted to support the colour ban on black fighters. Iron stressed he had no objection to fighting any man, be he black or white.

The Mexborough crew were still on a high and it was viewed as part of the success of it all. A copy contract was given to Billy so that the party could get on their way back home to sunny South Yorkshire.

Sam Langford was born 4th March 1883 and was some five years older than Iron. He was a Canadian by nationality. He was headlined as the "Greatest Fighter Nobody Knows". He was rated as number two by the Ring Magazine on their list of "the 100 greatest punchers of all time". Langford was originally from Weymouth Falls, a small town in the province of Nova Scotia.

He acquired various nicknames over the years being known as the "Boston Bonecrusher", the "Boston Terror" and the "Boston Tar Baby,".

In stature, Langford was only short standing only some 5 ft 6½ in but he weighed in at 185lb (13 stones 3 pounds). He actually started out as a lightweight. He was a powerhouse. Johnson's refusal to fight Langford was viewed as because he saw him as the greatest danger to toppling his crown. In later years, Langford was rated as one of the ten best heavyweights of all time.

Some of Langford's most memorable fights were his numerous encounters against fellow black boxers Sam Mcvey, Jim Johnson and Joe Jeanette. These coloured boxers all suffered from the prejudices of the day. In later years, Heavyweight Champion Jack Dempsey said "The hell I feared no man. There was one man I wouldn't fight because I knew he would flatten me.

I was afraid of Sam Langford."

The agreement by Iron to fight Langford was not in his interest in reality, the time was too short and he was walking into something blind, hindsight is the most wonderful sight ever, as the old saying goes.

Iron was approached by a syndicate to fight Jack Johnson for £5000 at the Stadium Shepherds Bush, London. This was just after he had signed to fight Sam Langford and so was contractually impossible. This would technically have given him a shot at the World Title. Though very likely to lose, Iron said it would have at least given him the career high of having fought at this level. He held this to be another of his great regrets in life. The offer still hung though if Iron managed to beat Langford.

Chapter 17
The Hero's Grand Return

The news of the victory had travelled around the area even quicker than the news of Queen Victoria's death. News of the win was the night before portrayed to some two thousand people who had gathered outside the Bank Street office of the "Sheffield Telegraph". A notice was pinned in the window as soon as the telegraph message arrived. Shouts immediately rang out "Three cheers for the new champion of England" to which the crowd reacted whole heartedly. Some 2000 envoys then dispersed spreading the news and preparing for the hero's return.

Iron the champion

On the Tuesday evening at approx 7.30pm on the 20th April 1909, the Sheffield to Doncaster train pulled into the station. If the trip down to London had been a big eye opener with the number of well wishers, the return trip was about to blow their minds. Some seven years previous, a large crowd had gathered to see the return of the Boer War Volunteers but it was nothing compared to this. As the train crossed over the bridge at Swinton Road, a large flag could be seen flying from the South Yorkshire Hotel. This was most unusual and signalled something was afoot. The police were clearly struggling to hold the crowds back, becoming more physical after seeing the train appear from around the Swinton curve. The cheering commenced before the train had even stopped.

The station master, Mr A Dickinson, had reserved a space on the platform for the travellers to pause in after alighting the train. Members of the Mexborough Orchestra, conducted by Mr A Beal, were seated at the ready with their instruments. As the train pulled in, they could hardly be heard above the cheers as they thumped out "The Conquering Hero" .

The crowd sang;

"Oh He's a Yorkshire lad,

Oh he's a grand un,

Oh he's a Yorkshire lad,

Iron's a champion."

The station was absolutely crammed with people all straining their necks to get a view of the new English Champion. Some had been there for four hours in order to get a good view point.

Iron dressed in a pin stripe suit and wearing a matching flat cap had descended from the carriage the last, being behind Billy and the team. The roars went up and flags were being waved all around.

Leader of the Town Council, Thomas Chambers, made a quick speech praising Iron's great achievement emphasising he was a son of Mexborough and as town envoy had, represented everyone that day.

Police cries of "Make way, make way!" could only just be heard from the police officers as they forced an exit route through the throng for Iron and the party.

Outside the station, a wagonette awaited, it was all dressed up. It had been pulled by two horses but because of the crowds, the horses could not be led through. The horses were detatched from the wagonette and instead, it was pulled by bystanders. Iron was beckoned to the vehicle, duly climbing on its back. Once aboard the wagonette, his youngest brother, George, was passed up and he sat the nine year old on his knee. Iron was then asked to stand up, to give people a better view to which he did, waving to everyone all around. The noise was deafening. Some 40,000 extra people had come into Mexborough that night to witness the spectacle. They were here on mass from Sheffield as well as all the surrounding towns and villages.

The champion returns – this scene sketched in the 1960's recreating Irons triumphant journey back into Mexborough.

Slowly progressing through the parting crowds, the carriage made its way up Station Road.

There were mothers with babes and young children who would all, in later years, tell of the momentous day Iron Hague came back after wining the English Heavyweight Title. Many of these people had seen Iron a thousand times before but this was now an essential sighting. As the wagonette approached the Montagu Arms, Iron saw Frank Law. He had stood on the doorstep to gain some height. Iron had the carriage stopped while he shook Frank's hand furiously. Frank had a large lump in his throat. He had launched Iron's career, took him nearly all the way and it should have been Tommy Weston and he who took the praise for this achievement.

Ever the professional, Frank never showed this, it was Iron's day. The wagonette was led down the Low Road then back round into the town centre.

The town's public houses were packed to the rafters and entry into the Bull's Head was impossible. It was only as night drew in that the crowds started to disperse.

The victory tour finished by about 8.30pm and Iron was then taken, not unsurprisingly, to the Bull's Head. The pub was absolutely packed with invited customers packed in like sardines in a can. There were calls for Iron to mount the platform in the singing room to address the crowd. "Well lads, I've worked very hard but I never thought I should get as far as this. I've allus tried my best and that has a lot to do with it. When I saw Gunner Moir sparring round me, I said to myself, if this is the champion of England he's the funniest champion I've ever seen. Why lads, I'd only to punch him just where I wanted." There were still thousands on the street outside and there were calls for him to make an appearance at the window. He did a few times then latterly telling them "You've all seen me now – goodnight." The crowd answered back "Good night" in a unified reply. They then all dispersed.

It was a day never forgotten by thousands and talked about for years.

WELCOME HOME.

GREAT RECEPTION.

EXTRAORDINARY OUTBURST OF PUBLIC FEELING.

MEXBORO' OUT OF BOUNDS.

South Yorkshire Times headline.

ENGLAND'S NEW CHAMPION

"Iron" Hague's Great Boxing Victory.

MEXBORO'S WILD DELIGHT.

SHORT WORK OF THE GUNNER.

THREE HISTORIC PUNCHES.

GREAT ENTHUSIASM.

(BY OUR OWN REPORTER.)

South Yorkshire Times headline.

Chapter 19
Dissension in the Ranks

No matter how well you do, there is always some dissension in the ranks. Somebody somewhere is not happy. It's called human nature!

Billy Biggs was fuming after he read a report about the fight which quoted that Mr Tom Weston was very proud of bringing Iron to the front and so winning the title. He issued his own reply that he disputed the claim made by Mr Weston and that the honour for bringing Iron to the championship rested with himself. He went on to say he had organised the financial backing and training for the fight and was proud to have affected the result. Mr Weston had nothing to do with it. Billy was very ruffled and obviously very sensitive to anything being attributed to Frank Law's era. Iron didn't quite share the same sentiment.

MR. ALF. LIVERSIDGE, OF SWINTON RELATES HIS EXPERIENCE.

Veteran's Views on Present Day Boxing

BARE KNUCKLES VERSUS GLOVES.

MR. ALF. LIVERSIDGE.

In the cosy little cottage, No. 58, Middleton's Villas, Swinton, lives Mr. Alf. Liversidge, who, half-a-century ago, was the

Alfred Liversidge, former trainer of Jem Mace.

One old character the local newspapers used to often consult on boxing matters was Alfred Liversidge of Swinton. Alf was some character. In his youth, he had been a prolific runner and held the title "England's Fastest Man". He once raced a cavalry officer on his horse through the streets of Norwich and won. In the late 1850's, he went on the road helping to train the legendary future World Heavyweight bare knuckle champion, Jem Mace. After Mace lost a bout, Alfred took him under his wing. He helped steer Mace through a series of victories against the likes of Sam Hurst, Bob Brettle, Joe Coburn, Ned Obaldwin – the Irish Giant and the legendary Tom King.

Amusingly, he told the South Yorkshire Times after Iron's success that "the modern style of prize fighting was like "going pleasuring" compared to his own days in the sport. Now, after a fight, if you go into the room where the men have a wash down you will find everyone smoking cigarettes and you wonder who it is that had been fighting. In my day, the men who had been at it with bare knuckles had nowhere left to put the cigarette".

A bare knuckle fight to which Alfred Liversidge related with his statement on present day boxing.

One obligation the Champion had to endure was that the N.S.C commissioned a portrait to be painted of him in victorious pose.

The fight with Sam Langford was set to be on Tuesday the 25th May 1909 so time for training was getting quite short.

Since the return from London, Iron had been involved in one huge round of celebrations, which he duly loved. Hard work though would now have to be the order of the day, he was weighing almost 15 stones and needed to get back to 13 stones 10 pounds at least.

One topic of conversation around the town was how much money Iron got out of it all. The actual amount was wildly speculated on, people viewed him as if he was now a millionaire in their presence. This meant many took advantage of Iron's good nature, cadging bits here and there. In reality, Billy was not that forthcoming in his accounting and his explanations seemed a little vague as to how Iron's cut was worked out. This banter though did not always go down well. Dick Parkes, also drinking in the Bulls Head, vented his anger a few times when asked his opinion about the cash winnings. He was clearly very unhappy and discontented.

He told Iron that Tom Stokes and he were very unhappy about how things were all worked out and asked him to go to speak to Billy about it. As much as Iron did, it fell on deaf ears. Billy did not give them much credit for their input intimating that it was he, Iron, who had pulled it off and they were riding on his back. Iron was not influential in the relationship and Billy dominated him intellectually. What really rubbed up though was that Billy bad mouthed Parkes off to anyone who brought up the subject.

It was announced that following the success of training at Withernsea, a return to Mr Ramster's Pier Hotel was urgently needed to accelerate the training process. Dick Parkes thought that enough was enough and he wasn't going to be taken for a mug again. He confirmed that he would not be going. Along with Tom Stokes, he wrote a detailed letter to the South Yorkshire Times setting out the grievance and their position.

Dear Sirs

We, the undersigned, have noticed in the papers during the last few days several letters and comments in connection with our leaving the above England's "champion at Withernsea and refusing to go on training him, and we think it is only fair to the British sport-loving fraternity, as well as ourselves, to give the exact state of affairs as they stood and the cause of our suddenly, as was stated, throwing him up, and leave others to judge whether we have been fairly and honestly dealt with by the champion and his "backers."

As to Parkes, he was with him about a month doing his level best and giving the benefit of his experience to get his man in the pink to face what everyone thought would be a long and keen punishing contest.

He was allowed 25s per week and his keep and out of that he had to keep a wife and three children and also to stand a somewhat severe knocking about as sparring partner to "Iron".

It is now a matter of history how the fight went on – how Hague and his backers received that winning end of the purse and the bets, but it is not recorded how they treated Parkes and Stokes after the victory. Neither Stokes nor Parkes have been given a penny out of the winnings and as the champion and his backers refuse to give them anything, well – that's the "hitch" that is reported in the papers, and what we have stated are the true facts.

We ask all the sporting public straight: "Have we been honestly dealt with? Can anyone imagine such a case as this? Does anyone know of a case where two trainers and seconders in the ring have been treated so shabbily and not been granted at least £25 to £50 out of the purse and stakes in a contest of less importance that the "Championship of England."

Parkes and Stokes are men who have been in the pugilistic arena for ten and five years respectively and have had the benefit and advice, as well as training, of one of the finest trainers in England, namely Sam Hayden of Eckington, and they both made good use of their knowledge in training the present champion – and all this for "nothing." We know of even local contests where the only stake was a score or so of pounds, the trainer receiving a fair satisfactory proportion for himself in addition to extra gifts by the friends of the victor and himself also. Of course, one is bound to admit that neither Mr Biggs and the others interested with him, nor even "Iron" himself, have any idea as to the methods to be adopted in a strict training to fit the man under their charge for a strong, tough contest, but we have gone through the mill ourselves, and have always had to pay for it, and in expecting a decent gift out of the winnings we are doing nothing wrong, but only what any right-minded man would expect. Those who ought to, should give them at least £25.

Briefly summed up, the facts are:

Parkes trained Hague "on appointment," at a nominal sum per week for four weeks, and expected a handsome donation out of the stakes after the contest; went with "Iron" to London and seconded him; came back. Result, got nothing but weekly wage.

Dick Parkes   Tom Stokes

Tommy Stokes – felt very agrieved.

In the following week's South Yorkshire Times, Billy's reply was printed. He wanted the general public to be aware that neither of them were employed as "trainers" and that only Parkes was guaranteed a regular wage in the role of an "assistant" to Iron Hague. Biggs said he felt that it was his duty to see that Iron's parents should benefit from any monies earned by the champion. He pointed out that Parkes and Stokes had both had their expenses fully paid. It was not stated what money was paid to Iron's father. Strangely, it was an odd thing to do as Iron was beyond the age of consent and would be expected to look after his own affairs. His record in the past on financial dealings had not been great, perhaps Billy was attempting to assist Iron indirectly. The whole affair caused much bitterness and Parkes and Stokes received plenty of sympathy. If Parkes was not a trainer who then was? Somebody had to do it. Was the whole affair just an example that Billy was a little over zealous as regards his hands being on the money?

Charlie Bolton – Hagues trainer.

Just before the party left for Withernsea, it was announced that Charlie Knock, whom Iron had fought previously, was to act as trainer. They were also to be assisted by Charlie Bolton who, because of his background, was known to his fellows as "the plough Boy from Barnburgh".

The differing trainers' styles were considered to be a good tactic for Iron. William Biggs junior went with them to oversee the management of the trip, no doubt under strict orders from his father.

The difference this time in using the Withernsea venue for training was the national press and a large group of supporters, followed them up there. This was a distraction they had to put up with.

Langford did not arrive in the country until the 7th May, which some boxing critics thought was too short a time for him to properly prepare. He arrived at Plymouth on the Hamburg-American Liner "The Deutschland". He was accompanied by his manager, Mr Joe A Woodman, another boxer Jimmy Walsh, Mr Edward Keevan and his trainer, Mr John D Davis. In an interview, he told journalists he was delighted to be back in England again. During the journey up to London, he enquired what weight the Mexborough boxer was? He was told Iron would enter the ring at about 14 stones. Langford's trainer interjected that he, Langford, would be conceding a couple of stones. "Well" remarked Langford "it's very few men I have conceded less to." Langford also went onto say "Hague must be a fine young fellow, I have every respect for the Yorkshireman so readily agreeing to fight me."

Langfords Manager confirmed that from what they had heard of Iron, they expected it to be a good fight.

Langford's training camp was set up at the Coach and Horses Inn at Stonebridge Park, London, he had only 18 days to go. People should not have worried about Langford's fitness as he had last fought in Boston on the 27th April and was still in very good shape. He had fought every fortnight previous for months.

The Press reported that training at the Pier Hotel at Withernsea was progressing very well. Iron and Knock got on very well and in a press release Knock stated he was astounded how much Iron had come on since he last met him in the ring.

Knock trained Iron hard but complained about being heavily interrupted with the resident press and ever present spectators. One observation made by one of the journalists was that Iron worked hard but was always glad to see the end of the session. Was there anything wrong in this?

One visitor to Withernsea to watch proceedings was "Peggy" Bettinson himself. When Peggy arrived, it was at night and he found Iron and his entourage indulging in fish and chips and skittles, washed down by beer. He told Iron that he had better pay attention to his condition with this fight, any weakness in it would be exploited by Langford. Iron questioned him "Why is that? He doesn't weigh 12 stones, whatever chance has a man of that weight got against me? " Peggy confirmed that if Iron beat Langford, the NSC committee had decided to award him a valuable Championship belt. Iron told Peggy that he was confident of a victory so tell them to start making that belt now.

Another offer that landed firmly on Iron's door meant he would have to cut his training short. They wanted him go to London a week earlier to appear on the London music hall stage performing a few bouts of exhibition boxing. This offer was declined, there was a lot of work still to do. The champagne lifestyle of the weeks previous had taken its toll on Iron and he still appeared a little unfit, which his camp were conscious of.

Sam Langford

One strange incident involved the former opponent Frank "the Coffee Cooler" Craig. Following his defeat by Iron back in march 1908, they had remained good friends. Frank had even attended some of Iron's training sessions. Frank was lined up to fight three exhibition rounds against Sam Langford on the 20th May 1909. This was in reality a public sparring session. The rumour circulating round was that Craig had been hired by Iron's manager to act as a spy on Langford. "All's fair in love and war" as the old Shakespearian saying goes. After his bout with Langford, he was to

Part of the watch presented to Iron Hague by Kimberworth Cricket Club after winning the heavyweight title

return straight back to Iron's camp to pass on information as to the boxing styles and approach used.

He was to reproduce these in sparring sessions with Iron. Langford learned of the scam and ensured he gave Craig a good drubbing. "Something proper for him to take back to Yorkshire" commented Langford.

In the 26th April 1909 "Sporting Life", a reader signing himself 'Amateur' stated "Hague was being rushed and the bout with Langford was a mismatch that would ruin Hague". This reflected the general feelings at the time.

Most of the press were not as convinced by Iron's bravado and thought that Langford would win by a margin. They felt that Langford's greater experience and superior ring craft would prevail over the Mexborough man. They commented that it was only a little time back that Hague was at the foot of the ladder.

This was, to all intent a real mismatch, Langford having had at least eighty eight previous professional bouts against some of the world's best fighters from lightweight up to heavyweight, losing only seven of them.

Not everyone was on Iron's case though, he did receive plenty of invitations to attend functions and events. Kimberworth Cricket Club had a collection and bought Iron a gold watch and chain with attachments as a token of their pride in his achievements.

The watch presented to Iron Hague by Kimberwork Cricket Club.

Chapter 20
25th May 1909 the Hague v Langford Fight

As the day progressed, the betting odds swung from Langford being a clear winner to the more sober odds of 60 to 40 as Iron's chances were talked up a little. One party who welcomed this odds change towards Hague's was Joe Woodman, Langford's manager. He knew his man and viewed it as a way of making more money. He slipped a bet on, just minutes before the fight, being on Langford to win. The bet was so large that the bookmakers had to rush around like fury to lay it off over several other bookies.

Iron's contingent all left together again from their London hotel base in a fleet of taxis having arrived there that day. The format had been as previous, arriving there mid afternoon, chilling out for a few hours then off for the fight.

Such was the interest in it all, the crowds arrived a little earlier than usual. The ticket men controlling the entrants to the N.S.C had their work cut out as there were many trying to get in unlawfully to see the spectacle. Many "Iron following" Yorkshiremen had been allocated tickets and could be easily distinguished with their accents. There were many of the top sportsmen of the day represented including once again, Bob Fitzsimmons. The 46 year old was immaculately attired and still looking very fit.

Johnny Hague

Despite the previous dispute between Dick Parkes and Iron over the title money split, Parkes had come along to London to support him.

The first fight of the night, after the evening dinner, was scheduled for 9pm. This fight was between Iron's younger brother, Johnny Hague, and Tom Woodford of Hull.

It was billed as the Yorkshire Derby. Johnny was deemed to be a pocketbook version of his older brother. They were boxing at Catchweight for £25 a side and the club purse. It was Johnny's debut at the N.S.C and he wanted to impress.

Boxing Referee , Eugene Corri

The referee was Mr Eugene Corri.

As the bell sounded, Johnnie rushed his taller opponent and caught him in a barrage of punches. Twice Woodford was on the canvas and took a count. As he rose, Johnnie started again and once more, his opponent teetered to look like he was again going to go fully down. So bad were the damages inflicted that just after he rose, referee Corri stopped the fight to protect the boxer. What a great introduction to the NSC for Johnny winning in the first round. Strangely enough, Tom Woodford had also trained at Withernsea with Iron's camp.

This was then followed by an international bout, Digger Stanley of the UK (Fulham) and Jimmy Walsh of the USA. The purse was £350, the contest for twenty rounds. It was listed as being for the World Bantamweight title. This proved to be quite a fight with both fighters being well matched. In the end, the referee announced a draw.

The Hague-Langford fight had caused quite a stir in the country, being whipped up by the press with all sorts of stories. There was a lot of varied public opinion as to what the final outcome would be.

One very interested party was John McCormack, the Irish tenor who was appearing in Rigoletto at Covent Garden where he was singing the main role as leading tenor. He dearly wanted to attend the N.S.C but the opera company would not accept his "stand in" when he was actually physically fit. The best McCormack could do was organise the theatre fireman to receive telegraph messages sent from the N.S.C so to relay him the information, round by round from the theatre wings.

Just before 11pm, Iron made his way into the ring wearing purple shorts with narrow Cambridge blue trimmings. He was accompanied by Charlie Knock, Bill Baxter, John Law junior and Billy Biggs junior.

Opera singer tenor John McCormack was a keen follower of Iron's career.

Langford was already there sitting in his corner. Iron was, in reality, a long way from being fully fit. As he stepped into the ring, the thought flashed through his head, the thought that many a boxer has had previously and will no doubt have in the future – perhaps I ought to have trained harder. The reality was that it was far too soon for Iron to be getting back into the ring for such a top class fight. Conversely however Langford, since the 17th March, had six bouts against good class men. The last was a draw over twelve rounds with Canada's Sandy Ferguson who but for his love of the beer, could beat any other white Heavyweight around. Langford though, was a different breed.

Iron noticed Langford's physical appearance which epitomised fitness. He was like a bronze statue. Iron was impressed with his big shoulders, tapering waste and very lean legs, he was tailor-made for the fight game. Strangely though, Iron wasn't daunted in the least. Few men had ever stopped him in his track and this was just another fight.

The press recorded that the crowd were disappointed at Iron's appearance.

As Iron limbered up, Langford rose up and wandered over to Iron's corner and raised an objection to the bandaging used around Iron's hands. This dispute took several minutes to sort out and it seemed to all that Langford was being petty minded.

Scene from the fight between Iron and Langford at the National Sporting Club.

The weights of the fighters were given as Iron at 14 stone and Langford at 11 stone 4 pounds, although Langford looked heavier. The referee was Eugene Corri, who brought the fighters to order and then the contest started.

The first round was a bit like a tug of war with the fighters jostling each other. Langford was dancing around as fast as a bantam weight. Iron managed to land a light left to the face but it seemed to go unnoticed.

Iron was then forced into a neutral corner and subjected to a tirade of blows which ended when Iron launched a good right hander that hit home. Iron was then on the attack, all of a sudden the gong sounded. The end of round one.

During the break, Iron thought things out. He thought it was no good trying to box the fellow as he was very sharp and would amass points against him. There was only one solution, calculated heavy smashes to wear his opponent down.

As round two started, Langford came rushing out like a hurricane. He landed several blows on Iron but he responded with a hard left to the face forcing Langford's head back. This was followed by a full right smash that could be heard all over the arena. Langford shot backwards and bounced down on the canvas. The blow ricocheting down Langford's face nearly ripped his ear off. Blood was spurting out. Iron thought he had near on killed his opponent. The force of the punch had fractured three of Iron's knuckles. The referee counted as Langford lay there. Unbelievably, he rose on the eight count and stood up. He was very wobbly and looking into space. Iron with his right hand in severe pain just looked at him bewildered. Responding to his screaming second's, Iron threw another right but missed his target and hit the top rope so exacerbating the hand injury. If only Iron had not have been hurt the fight could have been over. The gong sounded and Langford had survived the attack. Back in his corner, Langford told his manager "There ain't going to be no pictures."

The blow had really hurt Langford and he was responding to the fact they were told the fight was to be filmed to make a movie story out of it. He was worried he may not see the next round and that wouldn't make much of a fight.

As the third round commenced, Iron had been told to concentrate on Langford's left ear injury but with his badly injured hand, this proved almost impossible. Langford's recovery rate was excellent and he was ready to do battle once again. As they jostled, Iron raised his right arm to block a punch when Langford hit out again, catching Iron's glove and his damaged hand. He landed another which also caused Iron's nose to bleed. Iron did manage to land a right on the squidgy ear which caused blood to spurt out but what was apparent was that Iron was struggling. The bell rang and saved the day.

The fourth round saw Langford eagerly walking out ready to finish his damaged opponent. Punch after punch was landed and Iron could feel himself slipping away, down he went. In his own words he said he could feel himself falling into a beautiful sleep in which he had a dream. As the seconds tried to revive him, Langford leaned over and with a big grin said "That baby's out for keeps." Iron dreamed he had knocked Langford all round the ring. He remained very groggy and was going to be carried off on a stretcher.

After what seemed like hours, but was only minutes, Iron aroused and sat there a little confused, thinking hard about what had happened. Dick Parkes appeared to console his old friend. Iron asked him what had happened and Dick explained to him that he had been knocked out by a fine punch that no one could have stood up to. Iron looked at him and said "Well that's a first for me and by a black man as well." He couldn't understand how this smaller man had beaten him. Langford had proven that strength and straight punching was not enough. The crowd felt Iron had not disgraced himself and then responded by carrying Iron above their heads and shoulders cheering him.

Back in the changing room, a doctor examined Iron and attended to his injured right hand. Just before Iron was ready to leave, Langford entered the changing room. His head was heavily swathed in bandages. He went up to Iron and took his hand and said "Hard luck Hague, you gave me the greatest fright I ever had in my life. I remembered nothing after receiving that blow in the second round until the commencement of the third." Iron showed him his damaged hand to which he was not surprised. Langford wished Iron the best of luck for his future contests. Before departing he said "If it's any consolation to you Hague, I can say you are the only white man in the world who has ever put me down". He then put his hand to his heavily bandaged face and said " but worse luck, you have left me with a beastly souvenir" referring to his cauliflower ear.

Sam Langford landing a punch on Iron.

In later years, when Langford was narrating his life story, he stated that the hardest he ever got hit was against Iron Hague of Mexborough, fighting in London. So at least Iron made an impression. He also reconfirmed his statement to Iron that "the only white man to ever put him down on the canvas in all his years of boxing was Iron Hague." Putting him down however, was no consolation to Iron.

Iron felt awful for his fans. He thought that he had let them down. He was obviously very crestfallen in realising that he had met a better man. He was unable to understand how such a lighter man (almost three stones less) could have inflicted a knock out result on him. Langford, the next day in his press call, told the English press that Hague was a good fighter and with more experience, would take a lot of beating. The reality was that Iron had put up a great performance against a very experienced World Champion in the making. Langford had fought many hardened fighters over the years, proper battling men. On the odd occasion he lost, he made sure he learned by it. Iron had done plenty of fighting but not against men of a similar high calibre. Iron had nothing to be ashamed of.

Iron and his entourage set off for home the very next day being Wednesday, 26th May 1909. He was so down, he had planned on getting the 6am early morning train to slip back into Mexborough unnoticed but Billy was having none of it.

Iron did not go to the N.S.C to collect his losers cheque, Billy saw to that. It was early evening by the time the steam train pulled into the station. Although the rain was falling hard, a good crowd had assembled to demonstrate that although beaten, Iron was still held in high esteem by his townsfolk. They were quickly ushered into a waiting wagonette and transported up Station Road to the Bull's Head. Voices shouted out "Better luck next time." Iron was visibly moved by this Mexborough show of affection for him in a time of crisis. He was still well respected.

On the 31st May 1909 (Whit Monday), Iron travelled to Wombwell then walked over to Darfield to open a new sports ground on School Street for Darfield Cricket Club. He made a speech in front of a large throng, promising the crowd there was better to come of him. The Houghton Main Colliery band then boomed out some of their repertoire while Iron cut the ribbon on the new ground. Thereafter followed two days of sports contests and merriment. In a way, this booking was good for him. He had made the commitment the month previous as a champion and was in some trepidation as to people's reaction to him. It couldn't have been any better. A great warm welcome awaited him, as if a returning King to his people.

Chapter 21
Home, Death and Marriage

As the days passed by, the agony of losing waned but Iron had to face his peers. He went to see Frank Law, who was very critical. "Iron" he said, "it was the greatest mistake of your career undertaking that fight. If you had still been under me, that fight would not have taken place. If I had my way, black and white would not meet in the ring. A white man is at a great disadvantage as a black man is impervious to blows on the head. If you can't hurt them, how can you defeat them?" Iron listened but was not convinced. Frank Law finished by stating that there ought to be separate champions, a black one and a white one.

Iron replied "If a black man can't fight a white man, how can you have a world champion?" Frank answered by saying "If his rule had been carried out, Tommy Burns and Jack Johnson would never have met for the title and Burn's would still be champion." Iron finished the discussion by jokingly stating that if he should ever be matched against a black man again, he would take along a coke hammer to hit him with. Iron confirmed that as far as he was concerned, he had no animosity towards Sam Langford. He was one of the nicest men he ever met outside the ring. The problem was that he met him inside it.

Retired athlete, Alfred Liversidge, was once again approached by the newspapers for his opinion on the fight. Alfred told them "Iron Hague was all right amongst his own class but he must not get amongst the darkies. He should be able for any white man, but I wouldn't if I were he, go for Sam Langford, Jack Johnson, Joe Jeanette or Sam McVea. I don't think there is a white man could get near any of them. If Langford and Johnson got matched, it would be a big fight. Langford is the younger man by five years and Johnson is 34 and you don't get better as a boxer after that age but Langford is a wonderful man and he will improve a little more." His opinion was what a lot of people believed.

One regretful thing that Iron started indulging in once again was spending his hard won money on what he called "good times". Beer flowed lavishly for all in his company. The number of hangers-on and leaches grew by the week. Down town Mexborough was his territory where he was "the King" with his followers in tow. Drinks in the Montagu Arms, The Bulls Head, The Albion, The South Yorkshire and the Red Lion became a regular run round.

On Saturday 12th June 1909, a visitor to the town was none other than Major Best, Gunner Moir's manager. He travelled up by train and was met at the station in a carriage by Billy Biggs and a driver. The purpose of the visit was to try and arrange a re-match between Iron and Moir. The only way Best believed for Moir's career to be put back on track was to once more fight Iron Hague but this time, beat him.

The Major stayed whilst 9pm before getting a late train back to London. No deal was done. Moir had already contracted to fight young Johnson on the 3rd July and Billy wanted to wait for the outcome of that fight first. He didn't want Iron fighting a loser.

Billy and Iron were hatching much grander plans. They were hoping to capitalise on the American market which was opening itself up to fashionable British fighters, for serious money. In any case, Iron was not in training and a fight at short notice would be bad news, with all to lose and little to gain.

A further approach was made to Iron and Billy on the 24th July 1909. A letter adorned with very fancy postage stamps was delivered to the Bulls Head:-

Dear Sirs

I am writing on behalf of Sidney Russell, professional and esteemed boxer of South Australia, I am his manager. We have been following your progress in the press and note that you are the current Heavyweight champion of England. Sidney has fought very well over the last few years with many wins under his belt and is a national title holder. He is very well respected in the Australian boxing circles. We believe that he is well qualified to fight you for the title and throw out a challenge to you accordingly.

We are aware that they don't like foreigners interloping into English boxing but as we are part of the Commonwealth we feel this should be allowable. If it isn't we want to speak to the King. We can offer a sizeable purse for any contest. You tell us where and when.

Yours sincerely

Duke Mullers.

Manager

Iron and Billy decided, for whatever reason, against this challenge also and Billy wrote back to inform them of their decision. The Australians, not to be deterred then concentrated on arranging a fight with Moir. There was a belief that England's more liberal boxing stance on colour had brought it to the forefront in the world of boxing. Eyes were on it and its fighters came from all corners of the world. Hence Australia's great interest.

The 9th September 1909 seemed like a typical late summer day in Mexborough. Iron arrived at the Bull's Head for his regular meeting with Billy but was told he was in bed as he was not too well. Iron thought no more ado and returned home. Later that day the news filtered out. Billy's condition had deteriorated and sadly he had passed away, he was affected by a failing heart.

At the age of 66, William Clews Biggs was no more. Iron was quite badly affected by Billy's demise, all the town seemed to stand still until after the funeral.

So where did Iron now go from here? Manager-less and under pressure to get back in the ring, Iron had to contemplate his fate. He wasn't left to himself for long. A message was sent to Woodruff Row for Iron to go and see Frank Law at the Montagu Arms. Iron kept the meeting, a long dialogue took place, the two shook hands and were re-united. Frank Law was back in control.

One of the first things that Frank did was to get the Low Drop Gymnasium back in shape and get Iron back into training. The training was again to be under the supervision of Charlie Bolton, assisted by George Law. The hanging doors were again set up for Iron to hit to get the right hand strengthened, following the injury against Langford. To show the boxing world that Mexborough was alive and kicking, Frank issued out a challenge on behalf of his man, addressed to any white man in England. For a contest purse of between £100 and £200 pounds, Iron will fight over twenty rounds at a venue to be arranged. This would hopefully be the N.S.C. The response was not what Frank anticipated. Only further coloured American boxers answered the challenge. These were all declined.

Advert for the Montague Arms – the building to left hand side housed the low drop bar and training Gymnasium.

Charlie Bolton with bag packed ready for contest.

Meanwhile, Iron continued training. As previous, he was to become a spectacle that attracted a crowd to watch him. This was good business for Frank as he used to send his barmaid down with trays of beer for purchase by the thirsty observers. Frank's niece was Lucy, who acted as cook for the Hotel. Visitors used to stay at the hotel from all over and it was often full. Often there would be a request for food to be sent down to the gym, Lucy would prepare it but not take it down, which was accepted. It was not in her remit. She couldn't stand Iron claiming he was "brussen and pig headed".On this occasion, the barmaid who was asked to take the food down didn't show and the food was going cold. Frank told Lucy that there was no one else to deliver the meal so she would have to do it.

The journey down to the gym from the bar was a bit higgledy piggledy, up and down stairs. Iron, taking a toilet break, met Lucy at the top of the main stairs from the bar. He moved from side to side blocking her way not letting her through. She protested and tried to move round him. He continued to block her way. Iron had not really had much time for women in his life before as the rigours of training and his lifestyle where not conducive for a settled relationship.

Following his return this time though, Iron's eye had been focussing on her closely as she ran about the place. Iron, still blocking her way, asked her to meet him after training so they could go for a walk together. She pointed out she was engaged already and her fiancé wouldn't be happy. Iron reassured her that would definitely not be a problem. She reluctantly agreed to meet him if he would now let her by. He did but as soon as training was over, he waited for Lucy to finish her shift. 6pm saw them walking down Station Road and sitting on a form while the trains went by. Lucy realised that Iron was a gentleman and that her previous perception of him was ill found. They established they had a great deal in common and could laugh together.

The next month could only be described as whirlwind as within this short time, there had been a marriage proposal and a lightening wedding organised. Iron went over to Wath on Dearne to seek permission first from Edward Law, who was Lucy's father. He was a miner and apparently, was as taken aback as everyone else, nonetheless, he

Iron's wedding portrait

Lucy's wedding portrait

consented. Iron and Lucy went to see the Reverend W.H.F Bateman wishing to get married as soon as possible but he pointed out that there had to be a reading of the marriage bans over the next three Sundays. There was also a wedding booked to take place on the 30th October.

Mr & Mrs James William Hague pose for the camera.

Wednesday the 27th October 1909 saw the wedding of 23 years old James William Hague and 23 years old Lucy Law at the St John's Parish Church, Church Street, Mexborough. The bride was given away by her father. The service was carried out by the Reverend Bateman duly helped by the Assistant Clergyman, Reverend S. H. S Spooner. A wedding feast was engaged in afterwards at the Montagu Arms. It now seemed that boxing was going to have to take a back seat for awhile. After the wedding, they stayed at 2 Sarah Street where the Hague family had recently moved to from Woodruff Row. Iron soon sorted out a house for them to live in, this was at nearby 22 Orchard Street, still in Mexborough.

After a two week break, which served as a honeymoon, mid November saw Iron back into training.

Peggy Bettinson contacted Frank Law in early December. He was putting on another show and wanted Iron to appear on the bill. The week before Christmas saw Iron travel to London to once more visit the N.S.C. As he entered the doors, thoughts flashed back through his mind to his last fight here with Sam Langford. Psychologically, he needed a successful fight to free his demons. It was only an exhibition fight but nonetheless, was still a fight of sorts. The three round bout was against J W Douglas. This exhibition night was part of Peggy Bettinson's 'Annual benefit'.

Douglas was born 3rd September 1882 in Middlesex, being christened John William Henry Taylor. He was some three years older than Iron. His father was an N.S.C referee. In addition to boxing, he was a top class cricketer captaining England. His initials, JWHT, got him the nickname "Johnny-wont-hit-today" due to his stonewalling style. In 1901, he won the public school's middleweight title. He won the A.B.A Middleweight title in 1905 and the Olympic middleweight title in 1908.

Iron kept his cool during the bout. The press reported that Iron could have easily embarrassed the young boxer but chose not to do so, he did not show off. Murmurs did go round the N.S.C that Iron did not look to be in great physical condition, he was carrying too much weight. Other reports were more blunt and stated "the fat and flabby Hague was pathetic and couldn't prevent Douglas from hitting him."

Johnny W.H.T Douglas – boxer and International Cricketer.

The exhibition behind him, Iron returned to Mexborough to spend his first Christmas at home with his new wife.

Chapter 22
Pressures and Crisis

The New Year started with a damning article in the "Boxing" magazine. It put out a headline;

"Wanted a champion who will defend his title"

The accompanying article commented about Iron that a period of ease and contentment is about the worst thing that could happen to the man. With the experience he had gained and in the knowledge that he had a lot to learn before he could be considered to be a "World Beater", Boxing felt that Iron Hague should have made efforts to gain polish and further improve his skills.

It went on "Recent challenges would appear to have fallen on deaf ears." The magazine felt Hague was only coming up with vague promises that he might get himself into condition, sometime about the end of February.

It speculated that Boxing voiced that Iron had lost his ambition and preferred to live on the winners and losers purses from the Moir and Langford fights and that a return to the ring would only be prompted when the ready cash had been got rid of.

The article was as a result of widespread mutterings in the boxing world. Clearly, Iron needed to get back in the ring as soon as possible if he was to continue to be taken seriously. There is no doubt that he had never had any real money before, the cash received had deflected his eye away from the game. These views were shared also by Frank Law.

The article obviously caused a stir in the Mexborough camp as arguments prevailed. One person who had read the article with great interest was Harry Marks of Cardiff. He was the manager of a few boxers in South Wales who believed he could help Iron out of this predicament. He caught the train up from Marleybone for a secret meeting with Iron. The meeting obviously opened Iron's eyes with all the promises he made. Without further ado, he agreed he would sack Frank Law once more and sign up with Welshman Harry Marks using for his trainer British and European Lightweight champion, Freddie Welsh.

Marks himself was the first Welsh amateur to win an A.B.A title ,winning the lightweight division in 1898. Trainer Welsh (born Frederick Hall Thomas) was a keen vegetarian and strict task master. One thing for certain was that he would be pressured into hard physical training.

Frank was not best too pleased with this decision but had to accept the situation. He didn't want to fall out. He thought Iron was a "bloody fool" taking the word of someone he didn't know as literal. They parted company on the basis that "Frank and

This cartoon surely requires no explanation of any kind.

This cartoon needs no explaining . Iron came under a lot of criticism from the Press.

son John are always hear if ever needed". John and Iron were very good friends and their alienation was the last thing anyone wanted.

Harry Marks put out a press release the following week that Iron was in serious training and that they were to leave for a year's tour of America, sailing on the Cunard liner Lusitania from Liverpool on the 9th February 1910. When asked about the English Title Iron answered that they would have to wait while he got back.

This change of life plan had not gone down too well with Lucy. She was expecting their first child and her husband wouldn't even be there for the birth of their child. Harry Marks talked a good game and persuaded her it would bring them life changing wealth. He told her that there were bags of money in America waiting to be put up for heavyweights .She very reluctantly agreed to her husband's absence.

Just before he left Iron went to watch brother, Johnnie, fight Alf Senior at Cleethorpes in Lincolnshire.

It may have been an omen as Johnnie lost his fight. Iron boxed a few rounds there in an exhibition bout for the fight crowd.

Iron left for Cardiff and got into serious training the first week of February. One disappointed party to this was George Law who had organised a boxing fundraiser at the next door Prince of Wales Theatre. On the bill were Tom Stokes who was accompanied by other local boxers; George Thompson of Swinton, Arthur Marks of Kilnhurst, Bert Lynch from Denaby and Fred Denham from Mexborough. This was just one week after Iron had gone. Before the proceedings, Tom Weston took to the stage and read a wire from Cardiff. It announced that at short notice there was to be a boxing match on the 11th February 1910 in Plymouth whereby Iron was to fight Petty Officer Curran. It also mentioned probable future fights at Paris and Sheffield. Frank Law and Tom Weston were in some disbelief as to these unfolding events.

It was decided that Iron should at least have one last fight before he left these hallowed shores. Although classed as a championship fight this was repudiated by the N.S.C who stated that only bouts held there could in value be for the British title (formerly English) , which was a long established precedent.

Petty Officer Matthew Curran was listed as belonging to the company of HMS Mars. He was a hard hitting Irishman from County Clare but raised in Plymouth who could both give and take punishment .He did have a big weakness in that he didn't like to train. He was a natural fighter but didn't enjoy that part of it. Some of his training had to be at sea which had its limits. Like Iron he was often criticised for carrying too much flab. His nickname was "Nutty". This was on account of the fact he always rushed out every fight regardless. This was because he needed quick action. He wasn't for long fights if they could possibly be avoided. The longer the fight went on the harder it was carrying all those extra pounds. He was conspicuous for losing most of his fights on fouls, than for any sporting merits in the ring. He picked up the name "Foul collector" but in reality was as much sinned against as sinner. He was certainly a formidable fearless challenger.

Petty Office Curran

The fight was set to be at the Cosmopolitan Gymnasium, lymouth on the 11th February 1910. Curran fought most of his fights there and was immensely popular with the fight fans.

On the 10th February, Iron travelled down to Plymouth with his new team, Freddie Welsh, John Leonard, Jack Davis and Tom Bridgeman. Iron convinced himself that he was in fit condition but even he was a little worried about his damaged right hand.

There was a large attendance on the night. Curran received the louder applause because of the large naval presence.

The fight started and the first two rounds went very steadily as each man got a feel for each other. Iron just about claimed the third round. The fourth round saw a lot of action. Curran was downed twice but Iron had three short counts against him. Iron thought that in this one round, Curran has had me down more times than in all my career. In the fifth round, Iron emerged refreshed and boxed Curran into a corner but once more, as with Langford, Iron didn't go for the killer punch when he could have, he let the opportunity drift by – again. The next few rounds were tightly matched with Curran just inching ahead. Iron was still biding his chances to deliver that fatal right hand. An opportunity arose in the twelfth round but Curran managed to just side step it. The fight continued into the thirteenth and fourteenth rounds with Iron again missing opportunities. As the fifteenth round started, Curran rushed out and delivered a full right smash to the jaw that knocked Iron clean out. It was yet another defeat.

Back in the changing room after the doctor had satisfied himself Iron had suffered nothing serious, Iron and his team sat in deliberation.

The problem was, as Iron saw it, his huge right smash had lost its impetus following the damage sustained against Langford. Iron's timing was also poor as he had slowed down. His eye could see the opportunity but his body wouldn't deliver it fast enough.

The Western Daily Mercury and the Western Evening Herald had almost identical headlines, "ENGLISH CHAMPION DEFEATED".

There were more calls to make Curran the new champion but that was very quickly nipped in the bud. To take that honour, Curran would first have to beat Iron at the N.S.C . Under the N.S.C rules, if a title holder was fighting away from home (ie the N.S.C) and he lost, it did not count for title purposes.

What Iron needed was a couple of months of hard training and professional assistance to repair the damage. He was still only 24 years old and had a long career ahead of him. Instead though, the new manager, Harry Marks, had Iron fighting again the following Monday, the 21st February in Sheffield against Jewey Smith.

Marks told Iron he was satisfied with his performance. He reminded him that "He had not had the gloves on for nine months and had been partying all that time. You lasted fifteen rounds it was just very unlucky for you." There was scarcely sufficient time for a full recovery by Iron and the next fight was definitely ill timed.

Leaving Portsmouth the following day, the troop returned to Cardiff where a few days training were undertaken. Then, on the Sunday following, Iron travelled up to South Yorkshire to pay a quick visit home. Here, he shut the door and spent time alone with his expectant wife. News of the impending Sheffield fight had gone all

Picture depicts Tommy Burns knock out of Jewey Smith. Smith actually fought well he had little preparation time for the contest.

around the town, a few of the townsfolk wanted to support Iron on the night.

The bout against heavyweight Jewey Smith was at the City Boxing Club, Sheffield. As an opponent, perhaps Marks had not done his homework. Jewey Smith had previously boxed for the World Title against Tommy Burns in Paris. This fight was arranged with only ten days notice and Jewey was to be remunerated by a percentage of the gate money. The deal was arranged by Wonderland promoter, Harry Jacobs. Jewey only got £20 for the fight and Jacobs got substantially more. Remarkably, at this time, Smith had only had about nine bouts including six service bouts while he was stationed in South Africa.

Jewey Smith in fighting pose.

Smith looked far from the type cast Middle Eastern Jew Iron expected. He was robust with a square jaw, a mop of auburn/red hair, bushy eyebrows and the appearance of having a tucked in chin and no neck. Smith was popular with the crowds, not particularly a hard hitter for a 13 stone fighter. He was renowned for mixing boxing styles and could take a punch. His great physical appearance Iron thought, made him muscle bound. He was covered in tattoos and Iron was trying to read their script as they stood looking at each other in the ring. Iron was heavier and some three inches taller giving him a reach advantage. He was noted as being a solid honest broker who always gave it his best.

Smith was born in 1884 at Spital Fields, London. He served in the Royal Fusiliers in 1902 and saw service in South Africa. Whilst there, he took up boxing. He left the Army in 1908 and went "professional".

As the fight got underway, Iron found Smith hard to land a punch on as he bobbed, weaved and side stepped with great speed and bounce. Iron was at times fair chasing Jewey around the ring. In the third round, Iron managed to place one of the legendary right-handers and knocked his opponent clean out of the ring. Jewey managed to get back into the ring before the count of ten. The punch seemed to wake him up as he started to box back hard. He landed a few punches which stung but were not killer blows. Iron landed a few left body smashes but they didn't bring Jewey down. The fight lumbered on for the full twenty rounds. The final decision was given to Jewey Smith. This was because of the points scored on landing the blows. At the end of the bout, Jewey's face was swollen and badly marked but Iron showed no damage.

It was the first time he had ever fought a full twenty rounds, the fact he lasted it out said something positive about his fitness. Nonetheless, Iron lost the fight and the ditch was now dug a little deeper. Unbeknown, Iron had injured his right hand again in the fourth round following a punch to the head. Iron fought the rest of the contest

The Prince of Wales Theatre (Hippodrome) where Iron fought an exhibition fight, it was sited at the side of the Montagu Arms. Many famous artists including Charlie Chaplin and Stan Laurel appeared there. Sadly it was demolished in the 1950's.

with only one good hand. The horribilis continued. Iron kept this as a secret to all except Marks.

The Press started mooting that with the outcomes of the last fights that perhaps Mr Marks should review the plan to take Iron to America.

After the fight Iron returned back to Mexborough for a few days. While there, he appeared on a boxing show at the Prince of Wales Theatre, on the 17th March 1910.

He boxed three exhibition rounds against Jim Styles of Marleybone, London. The seats were all sold out.

The third fight that Mark's had arranged for Iron was against a former opponent, the popular Corporal Sunshine. Iron knocked him out in four rounds at their last meeting. Something had changed though since then, he was now promoted to the rank of Sergeant in his regiment the Royal Dublin Fusiliers and was of a fuller build. The fight was to be in Liverpool on the 26th May 1910.The purse was set at £550.

As the fighters sat in their corners in the ring awaiting the start, a coloured fighter entered. He was Cyclone Billy Warren, an American negro who was based in Belfast but claimed to be an Australian. He threw out a challenge to fight the winner of the fight. Iron jumped right in and said he would fight him the next night regardless of tonight's result, win, lose or draw. Warren didn't expect this reply and the publicity stunt backfired on him. Warren was a real character who rarely won any of his fights and was well known for his 'tall stories'.

One thing Iron noticed about the crowd that night in Liverpool at the Arena was their multi raciality. There were Italians, Chinese and Africans there in large numbers, all rooting for Sunshine.

As the fight started, Sunshine came dashing out. Iron managed to hit him with the right and down he went. Then the lights strangely all went out. Someone in the audience also threw a bottle which just missed Iron's face. The lights were off for about for about two minutes. By then, Sunshine had staggered back onto his feet.

In the third round, a series of body slams by Iron hit home, damaging Sunshine's ribs. Iron again stood back instead of finishing his man off, again giving him time to recover. The fight then limbered on for the full twenty rounds. At the end, the fight was given on points to Corporal Sunshine. Iron and his corner were in disbelief at this result. They had the decision firmly the other way. Sunshine then collapsed from exhaustion and Iron helped carry him from the ring. He was red and marked and it was noticeable was that Iron wasn't.

According to Iron, after he had changed, he made his way out of the hall and noticed the crowd on the street was still large. Suddenly, he was recognised and the crowd surged at the taxi Iron had just jumped into. They jostled it and tried to overturn it. The driver hit the full throttle and they sped away from danger. The taxi took Iron to the railway station where he caught the train to Sheffield to make his way back to Mexborough. He didn't want to return to Liverpool again.

The only good thing to come out of it all was that the magazine Boxing World agreed the decision on the night was "bad" and Iron should have been awarded the fight. The magazines, Boxing , Sporting Life and Mirror of Life felt that although badly battered Sunshine deserved the win.

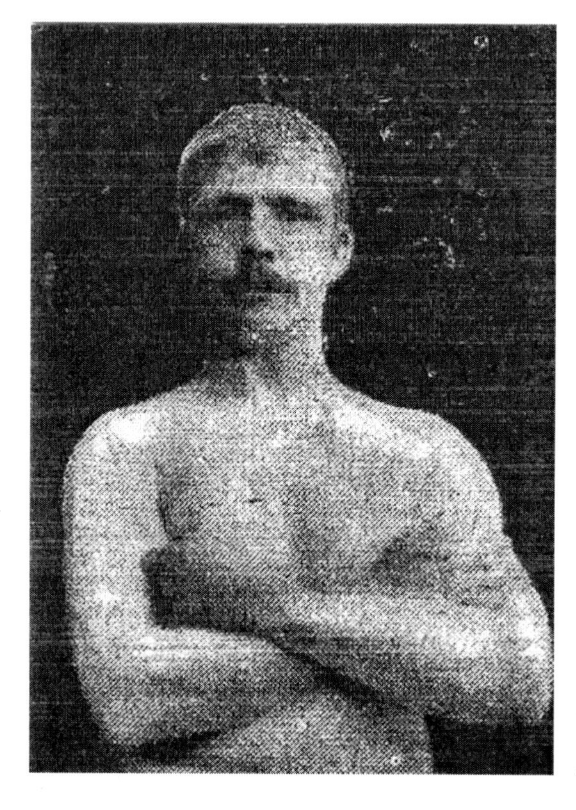

Tom Duckett riding on Iron's fame, claimed he was the first man to ever beat Hague. This was allegedly during the Boxing Booth's era. It was strongly denied and never proven.

Chapter 23
Career Overhaul

Back in Mexborough, Iron reflected on the previous six months. Not the best in his life that was for sure. Lucy was very glad to see him back once more which was a great consolation prize.

One person keen to speak to Iron was Frank Law and his son John. They talked to him quite openly. They could see what Marks was trying to do but they felt how he went about it was questionable. The men Iron had lost to were all good men in their own right and all title contenders so it wasn't as if Iron had gone down a notch or two. The reality was that he was ill prepared and unlucky. After a week at home, Marks wrote to Iron asking him to get back to Cardiff as there were more fights in the offing. He also intimated that the trip to the USA was not coming together as he hoped.

After weighing up all his options, Iron decided to take up Frank and his son John's offer and re-appoint them to take back over as manager once more. The letter informing Marks of this decision was written by Frank and signed by Iron.

This incident just highlights the infancy of boxing legal agreements as today, such changes could be resisted with law suits and compensation claims. There was not much resistance from Marks and Welsh as the dissatisfaction was mutual.

Iron, at his own doing, was not very well educated and it was known that he struggled

The Olympia, Swinton Road, Mexborough – 1911 . Boxing contests were hosted here on a regular basis.

with reading and writing. He used to sign whatever was put in front of him without much concern. He was too trusting by far.

One of the first things decided by Frank was to get the gymnasium into action at the Montagu once more and for Iron to continue his training schedule. They also had to have treatment on the injured right hand to bring it fully back into use. It was crucial to any plan going forward. Iron had been working hard but needed much more work in Frank's opinion, to lose weight and up the fitness even more.

From here on, Frank's message was forget the last six months. From now, on think positive was the message. The training started straight away and the horse and trap once more could be seen trundling around the outlying villages in the early morning with Iron running in front of it.

The first official engagement for Iron was to referee a fight in the new venue in town, The Olympia Skating Rink had now been adapted to host boxing shows.

This was to originally have been staged at Denaby Football Ground but some by-law kicked in and prevented it. Strangely enough, by-laws clicked in on this ground in the 1990's when it was decided that the long standing football club Denaby United FC could no longer play there.

The fight was between local boy Tommy Stokes and Harry Fellowes of Chesterfield. In Tommy's corner were younger brother, Arthur Stokes, Johnny Hague and Charley Hague. One can't help feel that perhaps Fellowes thought all was very incestual.

Iron wanted to follow up the challenge made by "Cyclone" Warren after he announced to the world he would fight the victor at Liverpool. Unfortunately, Warren kept his head down, never replying to letters and offers. He was probably put off by the hammering given to the victor, Sunshine.

Tom Stokes with other local boxer Dick Lawton

The first fight arranged by Frank for Iron's come back was against Private William (Brickie) Smith of the First Royal West Kent Regiment. He was the Army and Navy first ever Light Heavyweight Champion.

He had victories in the past over Jack Scales, Young Johnson, Harry Croxon, Seaman Parsons, Private Voyles and Seaman Broadbent. The fight was scheduled for the 15th August 1910 at the Attercliffe Hall, Sheffield. This was also a venue that doubled up as a skating rink as well as for boxing

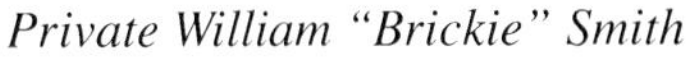

Private William "Brickie" Smith

The Smith v Drummond contest

nights. Smith, like Fred Drummond before him, was a Kent champion - this was when County titles were well thought of.

On the evening, Young Joseph was in attendance showing off his newly won Lonsdale belt as English Welterweight Champion. He boxed a three round exhibition match with Joe Goodwin. The next fight on was involving Tommy Stokes and Dick Emden of London. Stokes fought well but injured his hand and his seconds ended the fight, Stokes was not pleased about this.

The top of the bill that night was Iron Hague v Private (Brickie) Smith listed as over twenty, three minute rounds. Plenty of supporters had travelled from Mexborough on the night so there were many there to cheer Iron on.

During the first round, Iron had Smith on the canvas for a count of nine. As with other recent bouts, Iron didn't capitalise on the situation and finish the man off. He bumbled about and let him recover. Round after round passed and Iron had his opponent groggy on several occasions. In the twentieth round, Iron went out to finish Smith off. Smith ran all around the ring and was much relieved when the final bell rang. As was expected, Iron was awarded the fight with a win on points. Nonetheless, for the first time since Moir, it was "A VICTORY".

The newspapers reporting the story next day quoted Iron as being lethargic, saying he just based himself in the middle of the ring, holding his ground there, hoping to land the punches as the soldier danced around him. There was still concern over his weight.

Keeping up the comeback momentum, in September 1910, Frank visited the offices

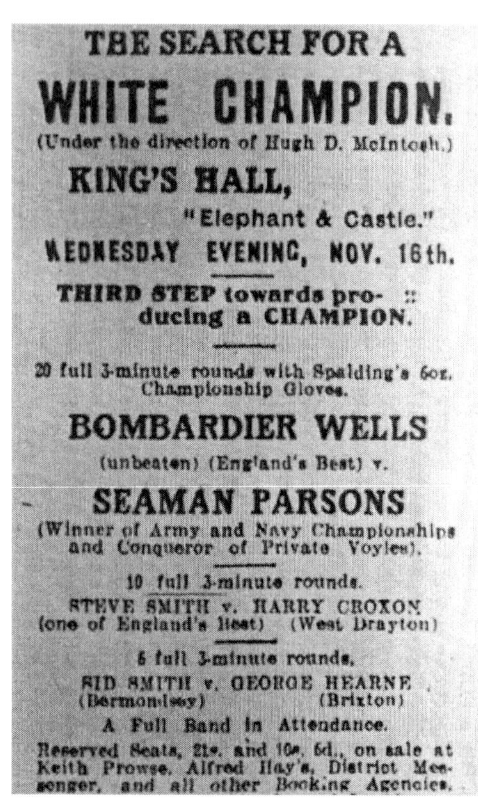

Poster looking for the "Great White Hope"

of the Sporting Life and left them a written challenge. In this document, Iron offered to fight the winner of the Wells v Sunshine bout recently announced. Derisory offers had been received by Frank for fights for the title but the money offered was only small. In one instance, as low as £25 a side purse. Frank replied that such stakes were akin to the sport of pigeon shooting and dog coursing, not for the Championship of England. In the meantime, Hugh D Mcintosh was promoting a fight between Curran and Smith and proposed the winner fight the victor of Wells v Sunshine. This would establish a new champion for the English Heavyweight, boycotting Hague.

There was a brief break from the boxing routines when on the 6th September 1910, Lucy gave birth to their first child whom they christened as Jane. Things were a little cramped in their Orchard Street home as also in residence were Iron's brother, Johnny and his sister, Lily. Iron's parents lived nearby at 2 Sarah Street, literally 100 yards away. (Orchard Street was situate near to where the entrance to Gateway Supermarket is to be found.)

Boxing promotion continued in the town when a consortium of business people put on a show at the Olympia Rink on the 12th October 1910. Some 3000 tickets were duly printed with some 2200 being sold. The star contest was a twenty rounder between Johnny Hague and Alf Senior of Doncaster. These two lightweights had met before at Cleethorpes and Sheffield.

Perhaps the mutual respect they had built up of each other made them cautious as the fight was not adventurous. The verdict was eventually given to Senior. The referee on the night was Tom Gamble of the Manchester Sporting Chronicle and Dan Dalton was timekeeper. The M.C for the night was Iron Hague. The other fighters on the bill were, Ernest Wirral v Reggie Wells(both of Mexborough), Sam Hill (Mexborough) v Laurence Craven (Denaby), Edgar Barnett (Mexborough) v Heathcote (Swinton) and Johnnie Beal (Mexborough) v Sandy Allen (Adwick on Dearne).

Johnny Hague, Reggie Wells and Edgar Barnett now all regularly trained at Frank Law's Gym at the Montagu Arms with Iron.

Corporal Brown can be seen in action on the left hand side

The next fight for Iron that materialised was against Corporal Brown of the Third Grenadier Guards on the 7th November 1910. Brown was known as a gentleman who could certainly take the punishment, he was not a hard hitter though and never knocked anyone out. The Attercliffe Boxing Hall was another sell out that night. On the same bill also was Johnny Hague fighting against Gus Platts. The fight was fought at a hurricane pace right to the end. Platts won on points.

At 10.15pm, Iron and Brown entered the ring for their top of the bill showing. During the first round, Brown danced around and landed several light blows on Iron but he didn't even feel them. He never landed one blow on Brown. The second and third round were a mirror of the first other than Iron landed one or two blows. During the fourth, Iron managed to plant a right hander that would have knocked nine out of ten men out but not Corporal Brown. He rallied from it and came back like a mad wildcat, landing one straight back on Iron. The rounds then trickled on and Brown became more bullish, moving into closer quarters to try and land punches. This was his undoing as in the eighteenth round, he got too close and was left open. Iron saw his chance and hey presto, the magic right (Iron called it Dirty Dick) smashed home. Brown was left out for the count.

Back at Mexborough, Iron's camp celebrated but not too hard. There was still a lot of work to do. After four defeats, Iron had lost some of his confidence and self esteem and he was not viewed by many fans as being any longer the "white hope". The game plan now was to revisit the men who beat him so to now beat them. To this end, a further contest was arranged with Jewey Smith on the 5th December 1910, over twenty rounds, this again to be at Sheffield.

Jewey was very confident of at the very least replicating the last fight where he went the distance, winning on points. Iron's only fear was aggravating the hand injury which was only just showing signs of proper recovery. The fight did have a lot of similarities to that previous in that it went twenty rounds being won on points. The winner this time though was Iron.

This was a little disappointing as he wanted to K.O this man to really put the record straight. Unfortunately, in the seventh round, pain twinges in his right hand told him to ease off on it. From thereon, he could only use it for defensive work. Not the hard hits and slams. Like a true professional, he gave no indications of this

Jewey Smith in fighting pose.

away. In the seventeenth round, he managed to deliver a hard left which made Smith slip down onto the canvas. Iron did deliver some good punches but lacked that finish because of his hand. At the end of the fight, Smith was clearly struggling for stamina while Iron appeared quite fresh considering. When the referee gave the decision, Iron remained calm. It was what he expected, another win.

In the Boxing Magazine, the fight report commented that "As usual, Hague was short on proper training, which is more of a misfortune than a fault, not being able to find good sparring partners down Mexborough or Sheffield way".

This was a criticism that Frank and Iron knew was true. It was certainly not for a lack of trying. There was a shortage of heavyweights around of any calibre who would come and fit the bill. When one did come along, they were subjected to some punishment by being bombarded daily in the ring.

Christmas 1910 breezed in. It was though, to be no time for relaxation as far as Iron was concerned. In order to fit in the fights, Frank had to agree to dates available for contests which didn't always suit but needed to be honoured. The next fight arranged was against Sergeant Sunshine and was set for the 2nd January 1911. Sunshine, then stationed at the Wellington Barracks, Dublin, was as keen to fight Iron again as ever. The main reason was due to the mounting pressure of Iron's Heavyweight title coming up for grabs. Another victory over Iron would be a good career move in this direction. This eagerness resulted in Sunshine agreeing to fight Iron on his home ground of Mexborough.

This was quite a turn up for Iron as he had never fought in his home town before and greatly looked forward to the pleasure. It was a great treat for the local fan base. It was the most important fight to have been held in Mexborough in the history of the town.

Iron put in a lot of effort into training and spared little in his endeavour to ensure he won this fight. Sunshine should have known by agreeing to Iron's request, he had given him all the home advantages. This demonstrates the desperateness of Sunshine to gain the opportunity to nail Iron down.

The fight was banded about that Sunshine was the enemy aggressor and Iron was out to prove he was still the Champion of England, and it was to be right on the locals' doorstep.

The fight, being on the 2nd January was so near to New Years Eve, one could expect a poor crowd. The pull of Iron and Sunshine was such that the Rink was a sell out. There were so many of the town's citizens present that Sunshine must have felt like the unwitting possum stumbling into the viper's nest. The atmosphere was electric.

As the first round started, Iron was like a man possessed. Within thirty seconds, he had put Sunshine down on the canvas. Thereafter, each round was a systematic drubbing of Sunshine, reigning down blow after blow. Finally, in the ninth, the pressure got to Sunshine and he collapsed down on the canvas and failed to get up, it was a knockout. Iron, like the King, laid himself back onto the ropes. It took a full five minutes for Sunshine to come round, he had took a fair battering. From Iron's point of view, he had wiped out the three losses, the sheet was clean again. He had showed them all. As they carried Sunshine out, Iron looked over to Frank Law and winked towards him. Frank smiled, mission accomplished.

The beer certainly flowed around the town that night. The talk was, that "Iron was definitely back".

After the news of the fight got back to the N.S.C, Peggy Bettison sent a letter instructing the defending champion his presence was required in London to defend his title. Surprisingly to the public though, the proposed challenger was to be Bill Chase, The Forrest Gate butcher.

Chapter 24
Title Defence

The date for the fight was set as the 30th January 1911. It would have been Iron's first return to the N.S.C since the defeat by Sam Langford. The speed of the request to fight, after beating Sunshine, was nothing to do with the overall confidence in the man. It was kick starting the long overdue title process. With the recent defeats at Iron's hands, the credibility of challengers waiting in the wings was suspect. There was a desire to give new blood a chance, hence the selection of Bill Chase of Forrest Green.

Chase was a stockily built boxer, being some 6 feet 2 inches tall and weighing 15 stones with a 80.5 inch reach (finger tip to finger tip). He had both a height and weight advantage. With his fight history, he was in reality, a relative novice. He had only had two professional regular bouts before winning the N.S.C Heavyweight Novice competition.

He had fought and beaten Private Smith and Private Voyles. He knocked Voyles out in the first round but his ability to take punishment was unknown. He was popular for a newcomer and was viewed as being an N.S.C. pet. He was a brilliant gym fighter who had impressed Bettinson. Unfortunately, he broke his hand in the last day of his training which considerably weakened his chances.

Bill Chase during training.

Chase's large stature gave him a reach advantage over Iron which had to be considered in tactics. The difference in approach with this fight now though was that Iron adopted a more silent and reserved exterior. He did not extol to the press and public that pre fight confidence of assured victory, that justified or not, had always been shown in the past. He was the quiet and certainly more reserved, calculated assassin.

Bill Chase with outstretched arms shows the length of his reach. He was unusually tall and towered over his trainer.

Bettinson and Lord Lonsdale had decided that the coveted Lonsdale Belt (yet uncontested for) would not be up for grabs with this fight. A poll around the N.S.C members favoured Chase to win the fight by a majority of 2 to 1.

The fight bill listing for Monday 30th January 1911 was a little disappointing in that Iron's fight did not command a top of the bill status. This honour was to Jim Driscoll who was fighting for the English Featherweight Championship of England as well as a Lonsdale Belt. Iron's fight was the fourth fight of the evening.

The first few rounds of the fight were obviously where the boxers were not adventurous, getting a feel for each other's skill level. In the fifth round, the action started proper and Iron landed a few blows to the head and Chase's eye started closing up. Realising that only a last ditch concerted effort could save the day, Chase launched himself forward landing a good punch to the head. Down went Iron for an eight count before hauling himself back onto his feet. No damage done, Iron himself now went on the offensive. Iron punched Chase with "Dirty Dick" and down he went. This brought the sprinkling of Dearne Valley fans to their feet as Chase remained down. It was a knockout, again. The title was successfully defended. Iron was a champion-still.

The day after the fight, the Mexborough fight team made their way back home to town. By the time they got there, it was early evening and the winter sun was down and darkness prevailed. The crowds were not there in the great throng as in the past but a few admirers were there to congratulate their man. Before they had left the N.S.C. after picking up the winner's cheque, Peggy Bettinson said he wanted Iron back in the ring for a further defence sooner rather than later.

They wanted to incorporate the Lonsdale Belt into the Heavyweight title and the next fight would be nominated to receive this. He also said that his committee had someone in mind and they would be in touch.

The winner's cheque was banked, at the Provincial Bank in the Montagu Square, on the Wednesday and on the following Monday, Iron went round for his cut of the winnings. Frank managed to resurrect Iron's bank account and an amount was put away from his share for a rainy day. The account had been recklessly depleted then cleaned out last year.

The month of March 1910 saw Iron in training in anticipation of the letter being delivered to the Montagu Arms from the N.S.C. It landed on the 6th March, a challenger had been identified and a title defence was arranged for 1st April 1911. The contest would be twenty rounds for £200 a side. The challenger was named as Bombardier Billy Wells.

One curious instance was that Corporal Brown, who had fought Iron originally on 7th November 1910, remained in town as his sparring partner and assistant trainer. He took up residency in the Montagu Arms. He must have liked Mexborough and its folk.

Chapter 25
Bombardier Billy Wells

Bombardier Billy Wells was born on the 31st August 1887 at 250 Cable Street, a house belonging to the East London Railway Company, near the Mile End Road.

Prior to enlisting, he had spent some time as a junior in the London Boys Boxing Club and this made him no fool in the ring. He was a non-drinker and invariably fit.

He enlisted in the military in the summer of 1906 and spent his first months at a depot in Dover, where he played centre forward in the football team and boxed in the gymnasium.

After training, he was sent to join the Royal Garrison Artillery Mountain Division, stationed in North West India. On the troop ship out there were other boxers and Wells' sparred with Gunner McMurray whom he later boxed professionally.

The Mountain Division had eight batteries and Wells joined the 6th Mountain Battery at Rawalpindi. This was a station in the Punjab, 1700 feet above sea level, being some 80 miles north of Amritsar (now in Pakistan).

Bombardier Billy Wells

Wells entered the Divisional Boxing Tournaments at Quetta, at the novice and at the open level, winning both competitions.

In one fight against Sergeant Magee, Magee went down twenty seven times in three rounds.

Wells, as holder of the Quetta Heavyweight Division, was then sent to Punar in 1909 for another tournament. Here, he beat Gunner Turner, Private Jarvis and Private Tansell to become Heavyweight Champion of all India.

The army brought in Jim Maloney from London to train the boxers. He had been in India previously as an army trainer prior to Wells going there. Wells had known him since he was twelve years old. Wells joined his army training camp at Umballa, Lucknow. By this time, Wells was allowed to box and train continuously, being excused from army duties.

Maloney himself had beaten the famous American coloured boxer Bobby Dobbs in a bout in London. The fight was given World Lightweight title billing with Dobbs as the holder it was on the 20th November 1902.

Following Maloney's advice, he bought himself out of the service for £21. Maloney identified that this young man was a force to be reckoned with and a future champion. The top brass of the army were very sorry to lose him as they had their own internal plans for him.

The Mirror of Life reporting on boxing in India commented that "Wells, without doubt, was the best and most scientific boxer of his weight, seen for many a long day".

Maloney sent a letter of introduction to Peggy Bettinson at the National Sporting Club where Wells reported upon his departure from the troop ship, "Passy".

His first job was being employed as a sparring partner to Gunner Moir who was in training for a fight against Petty Officer Matthew Curran when it was claimed Moir had K.O'd him.

Wells' first fight in his own right, was against Gunner Joe Mills, which was only a six round exhibition match. This was followed on the 22nd June 1910 with a fight against Gunner McMurray of Shoeburyness, when he knocked his opponent out in the first round.

He then embarked in a series of fights taking on, Corporal Brown, Sergeant Sunshine, Private Dan Voyles and Seaman Parsons, lasting into the autumn of 1910, winning them all on a knockout. These bouts were billed as "the search for a White Heavyweight Champion".

He lost his first fight on the 11th January 1911 to Gunner Moir at Olympia, losing in a three round shambles. Moir had spent time of late wrestling and the press reported that Moir lost the first round then used his weight to lean on Wells, throwing him down in the second round, knocking him out in the third round. The Boxing World commented "the bout was a mixture of wrestling, tumbling and wild swinging, with very little direction in the blows of either man".

It would have been better if Wells' had never spent time with Moir as a psychological barrier had seemed to build up between them in Moir's favour.

Analysing his situation, Wells decided he needed to build up his strength .To this end, he engaged the services of a certain Thomas Inch.

He was known as "the Scarborough Hercules". Inch had a 50 inch chest and operated out of a gymnasium in Fulham. Inch, born in 1882, described himself as a physical culturist. He concentrated on introducing Wells progressively to heavier weights for exercise. Dumbbells and barbells were systematically made heavier to drag out that bit of extra effort needed to do just one more repetition. The orders to Inch were to build up Wells' strength and this is what he did. It proved dividends, Inch followed Wells career and later capitalised on his fight successes to promote his own commercial activity.

The results of Inch's work were put to the test on the 8th March 1911 when Wells fought heavyweight Dan "Porky" Flynn of Boston, USA. Flynn claimed Irish birth but it was never proven. Wells won the bout on points after a full twenty rounds. Although not a knockout, it showed that Wells was fit enough to stay the pace. The win over the Bostonian allowed Wells to overstep Moir, Curran and others as challengers to Iron Hague's title.

On Monday 24th April 1911, Iron and his contingent thought they would slip out of Mexborough for the Sheffield morning train to then link up with the Victoria service to Marleybone. Unfortunately, the townsfolk had other plans.

To show their support for Iron, they gathered in great numbers to see him off and wish him well. The road down to the railway station was packed with marching crowds all wanting to see Iron once again.

The railway station itself was once again swamped and the passenger bridge was full of viewing eyes. Iron's mother was in the crowd to see her son off.

Iron and his party on arrival as previous, made their way up to the Anderton's Hotel. Iron then chilled out for a few hours before making his way in a taxi to Covent Garden and the N.S.C. arriving at 7pm.

24th April 1911 .Crowd on Station Road going to see Iron off for the defence of his heavyweight title. His trainers are to the right of him.

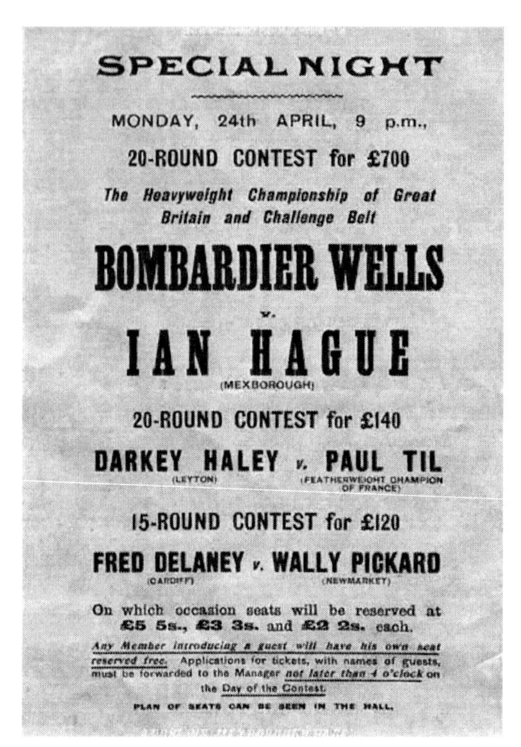

Poster advertising the forthcoming Title Fight.

Also on the bill that night was Fred Delaney (Cardiff) v Wally Pickard (Newmarket), a fifteen round contest for £120. Also Darkey Haley (Leyton) v Paul Till (Featherweight champion of France) which was a twenty round contest fighting for £140.

Seats were priced at £5 5s, £3 3s and £2 2s with tickets still being sold up to the box office closing at 4pm on the day of the contest.

At 9.05pm, Iron entered the ring. Wells was already there waiting in his corner. Iron noticed the place was packed to the rafters. The Bombardier had received a rousing cheer on his appearance, this was noticeably lower for Iron's own entrance. Iron noticed what a picture the fair haired ex soldier looked with his finely chiselled features. He had beautifully shaped limbs and body. Iron thought that he could have been easily mistaken for a champion sprinter or a rower rather than a pugilist.

In Iron's corner with him were; Corporal Brown, Jimmy Morris (a lightweight from London), Charlie Bolton, George Law (brother in law) and Iron's brother, Johnny. In the audience sat an anxious Frank Law.

The tactics discussed and agreed upon were that Iron would try and inflict hits to Wells' stomach which he was advised was a weak spot. He was told that he only had to hit him there and he would crumple like a withered leaf. Iron composed himself and stood awaiting the bell with no sign of nerves, like a war horse awaiting the bugle. The referee for the contest was Eugene Corri.

As the bell sounded Iron shot out straight into the centre, trying to force the action. Wells though was guarded and would not be goaded, he had learnt in the past not to rush things. He concentrated on using his long reach profitably.

For the first two rounds, Iron successfully delivered several blows to the stomach area but instead of crumpling up, Wells grunted, came back and returned delivering blows to Iron's head and body.

In the third round, Iron changed tactics. He decided to go at him and fight him.

Wells, the skilled boxer, just boxed around it, he would not, at this point, be drawn into a brawl.

In the fourth round, Iron adopted a "do or die" approach which left him exposed. Taking advantage of this, Wells landed a full right on Iron followed by a left. Down he went, out for a count of eight. Iron composed himself and tried to box defensively. Wells though was now on the offensive. He came in with both fists blazing and Iron went down again. He stayed down for a count of eight. Iron felt he was at his wits end then but two seconds later, the bell sounded saving his bacon. Taking stock, things didn't look good, his strength was sapped, he thought that even if he got "Dirty Dick" into position, he was lacking strength to put any real power behind it. He needed to buy time for Wells to tire.

During the fifth round, Iron put on a brave front, looked none the worse for wear and he fought a more calculated attack. Unfortunately, his rights and lefts couldn't catch Wells out. Dodging one such punch, Wells slipped and went down on the canvas. Iron went in for the finish, a hot exchange then ensued. Unfortunately, Iron's own stamina waned and he could not quite pull it off. The action of this round greatly uplifted the crowd.

The sixth round started as like the fifth with both men looking quite fresh. Iron started with a punch just missing a knockout blow to Wells' jaw. Surviving this, Wells despatched rights and lefts, he caught Iron full on the jaw, down he went for a six count. Wells, in a frenzy, continued punching while Iron was falling down. Cries of "Foul" could be heard but the referee quickly decided that question by waving Wells back. Iron recovered and arose once again. Wells then continued punching with hard rights and lefts, forcing Iron back onto the ropes. An uppercut to the throat made Iron drop his guard and Wells capitalised on the situation. A right to the jaw dropped him down once more.

Newspaper cartoon drawing of the fight which is a little unkind to Iron.

Iron could hear his seconds shouting "get up Iron, get up", but his legs felt like jelly and were paralysed. His strength was also sapped. He got one knee up but stopped hearing the count and simply rolled over. He was out

The Lonsdale Belt is won by Wells.

for the count. The fight was now well and truly over with, the title well and truly lost.

In the interviews for the press later, Iron said that before the fight he had never felt better in his life and the problem was that Wells outreached him in every instance. He also went on to say that those who believed that Wells had no strength in his punches should try and be on the receiving end of a few. He finished by predicting a great future for Wells.

Wells commented on Iron's excellent punching and great strength. He confirmed he had plenty of marks on his left side which bear testament to this. He said he was in some trepidation of Iron's qualities beforehand and adopted a strategy to not rush the fight and to keep to the script.

The next day, Iron and his party left their London hotel and made their way back to South Yorkshire. The mood was obviously somewhat sullen.

On the 29th April 1911, the Mexborough boxing fraternity, recovering from the shock of the defeat, wanted Iron to know he was a legend and was appreciated. To this end, a special presentation was arranged for him at the Montagu Hotel. This was preceded with a triumphant procession in a four horse landau around the town. Plenty of people once more lined the streets to show their appreciation of the man and his efforts, as ill fated as they may have been.

Back at the Montagu, a tea was to be had for those closest to Iron, his wife, Lucy, was with him. On behalf of "the Billiard Room Boys", a silver tea service was presented. On behalf of Lucy and himself, Iron thanked everyone for their kindness and generosity. He relived the fight in some detail for the assembled audience. He said that he would like to have a rematch but to do so would need a fair time to prepare. He now had a measure of the man and his dangerous long reach, this would need some overcoming.

Billy Wells with his trainer Jack Goodwin.

Chapter 26
Life Goes On

For a few weeks, Iron kept a low profile, spending time with Lucy and his young daughter. Frank had met with Iron the following weekend and had given him his share of the loser's purse. As with every "finance" meeting with Frank, it was always accompanied with a question "How much of this are you going to put away, you have a family now?" He never let Iron forget it, he was a constant reminder.

A further meeting was held in Frank's cluttered office on the 15th May to discuss the future. Tom Weston had come over from Denaby to have his own input. It was discussed that Iron, now as a former champion, still was attractive and most certainly his career was not over, he had choices.

Firstly, he could beat some more opponents who are the "Prince's in waiting" to force another title re-match. Secondly, he would be in demand as a defeat of him would be a good asset to a fighters C.V, this could financially be capitalised upon. There was still some good money to be earned if Iron towed the line and was prudent.

In response, Iron started to work his way back into training, with Corporal Brown still assisting.

Frank and his promotion machine went into operation. Meanwhile though, on the 20th May, Alfred Axe announced a boxing event to be staged at the Grand Rink, Mexborough. Top of the bill was to be Iron's trainer Corporal Brown.

He was matched against Jim Maher the Irish/American who recently claimed the Irish championship.

Just before the night, Maher's manager confirmed his man was struggling with an illness and would not be fit to fight. A search then went on at feverous pace to find a replacement. A fine substitute was found in Harry Croxon. He was the boxer who proved himself most troublesome when Iron won the novices Heavyweight Competition at the N.S.C.

On the night of the contest, it was plagued with heavy rain and strong wind which unfortunately impacted onto the crowd.

The meagre turnout had no bearing on the fighters who boxed for all their worth. The bout between Brown and Croxon went all the way. It was very closely fought and the only fitting verdict could be a draw. There was nothing between them you could distinguish.

After the fight, Iron entered the ring and issued a challenge to Harry Croxon for either £50 or £100 a side, the date to be set soon if an agreement can be reached. As it happened, Croxon was not keen and things seemed to go stale. With no definite fight on the horizon, the training then waned down to nothing which wasn't good.

24th June, the same week as the annual Mexborough Feast, saw boxing in the town once more. This was organised by promoter George Jones. A lot of local lads appeared on the bill, this time the Rink was full. Iron and George Law were in attendance and both were impressed at the interest generated in the town for the sport.

That same week, a letter was delivered to Frank Law at the Montagu from a potential challenger. The letter confirmed the writer was of independent means, a fellow Yorkshireman and a prize winning swimmer. He was 27 years old and weighed in at 20 stone. The letter confirmed his ambition was to take the Heavyweight title off Wells and needed to prove himself on the way up. The challenge suggested the fight was to be at Doncaster during the St Leger week in September.

The letter excited Iron and Frank replied accordingly, confirming their willingness to talk. Unfortunately, nothing then materialised. The writer was either a dreamer or a hoaxer.

After further discussions about Iron's future and some arguments, Frank Law and Iron once again parted company and Iron went "self managed". Once again, they did not let business overshadow their friendship, it was mutually agreed.

At Wombwell, a boxing show was organised and Iron was asked to go and box a three round exhibition which he had agreed to do. On this occasion, accompanying him were Lucy and his mother. It was the first time Lucy had ever seen Iron fight or ever been to a boxing match. The opponent was a giant of a man which was fine for an old war horse like Iron. As he got into the ring he was dwarfed by his big opponent. The bell rang and off the fighters went to show the crowd the skill of boxing.

Lucy, getting carried away and fearing for her man's safety jumped up onto the ring side screaming "Bill, hit him or he will kill you." In the furore of what was happening one of Iron's punches went wild and caught Lucy firmly on the chin. Down she went. That was the last time Iron ever allowed her to watch him at work.

George Law and Iron had been spending even more time together of late and had been working on a new business venture. They arranged to rent a spare piece of ground near to the Montagu Arms to open their own open air boxing arena. It was hyped up that it would provide the best in equipment and would charge sensible prices that were in reach of the working man. There was to be a weekly show, alternating between Thursday and Saturday. It was to be given the grand name "The Mexborough Stadium". It was duly constructed with the ring in the centre. Forms for seating were placed round the ring and allocated as "ring side seats". The rest was standing room only. It claimed a capacity of about 3000 spectators but for comfort 2000 was pushing it.

The opening night was set for the 11th May 1912. This was to be a busy day for Iron as Tom Cowler appeared personally in town to try and arrange a meeting between them. It was suggested that this would be in Sheffield for £50 a side. Iron rebelled by saying the purse was insufficient and he wanted the fight to be at his new stadium. The negotiations broke down.

The first show at the Stadium featured a fifteen round contest between William Gregory of Rawmarsh and Ted Vaughan, a well known Rotherham boxer. Gregory was previously the winner of the Mexborough Syndicate Welterweight Belt. Another highlight was the visit of Digger Stanley, the Bantamweight Champion who was bringing his Lonsdale Belt to show the audience. All seemed to go off well and Tom Cowler stayed to watch the proceedings. The business partnership of Hague and Law was launched.

The week after, another letter arrived at the Montagu Arms, incorrectly addressed to Frank. This time, it was from the manager of Scotsman, Jim Robb, the Heavyweight Champion of Glasgow. The challenge was for a twenty round fight. The letter was passed to Iron who was delighted at the prospect. It was agreed with the date set for the 8th July 1912. This meant Iron had to get back into training (or as he said "back into the harness") as soon as possible. This was not the easiest feat, as of late Iron had not been himself. A background illness ailment had weakened him. In reality, Robb was a rank novice more known as a wrestler than as a boxer.

In the wings, many local youngsters were all wanting to ape the success of Iron and took up boxing. Boxing had come to the forefront as a participative sport. Over the next few weeks, many promising youngsters cut their teeth at the Mexborough Stadium. These included Arthur Skelton, Sam Hill, Young Green, Johnny Beale, George Ford and Reg Wells. Iron's brother, Johnny Hague, also climbed into the ring there in the summer months. George Law was always the Master of Ceremonies and Iron acted as referee for the major bouts. For the lesser bouts, Albert Taylor of Darfield usually presided.

On the 29th June, one sell out fight was for Tommy Stokes fighting Dick Bailey of London. It was top of the bill and set for twenty rounds. The stakes were £95. Because of Iron's past relationship with Tommy, he agreed to stand down as referee and the honour went to Tom Gamble of Manchester. The fight was a gruelling contest, the type where everyone in attendance took home a special memory of what boxing was all about. An exhausting encounter took place over the first eighteen rounds. There was nothing to distinguish between the fighters. Every gain by one fighter was then wiped out by the other. For the last two rounds, Stokes, just the fresher, managed to keep ahead, narrowly, taking the fight on points.

One relative newcomer into Mexborough was "Kid" Johnson, a young boxer from London. Frank had brought him in previously to help train Iron. He was to be used again and was very key to the sparring strategy being adopted. George Law was now very much hands on with Iron's training routines.

The Monday night of the fight against Robb soon came round and a buzz was going round the town again. The fight was top of the bill and a full house of 2000 spectators, packed the Mexborough Stadium. On the programme of events were some earlier novice fights. The first was between Young Wood of Keighley who fought local Mexborough boy Young Skelton, the latter being the winner in the second round.

The next fight was between Young Littlewood of Lofthouse and Young Stanley of Huddersfield, Littlewood winning in the first round. Next was Young Horbury of Brodsworth and George Highgrove of Rotherham. This was a keen fight with Highgrove winning on points. The last novice fight was between 17 years old Herbert Oliver of Temperance Terrace, Swinton and Harry Gothard of Carbrook, Sheffield. Oliver was appearing for the third time as a novice. This fight had actually been arranged by the boxers themselves and George Law agreed to put it on the bill. It was to be over six, two minute rounds. Their fight got off on time but Oliver took a blow to the head that sent him skittling in the second round and reviving him was proving difficult. With no further ado, he was sent to the town's Montagu Hospital.

Before the top of the bill contest, Hull policeman and Heavyweight Con O'Kelly entered the ring and threw out a challenge to the winner of the next fight. This act was unarranged and done impromptu. It helped the atmosphere of the fight night but it was not a proposition that tempted Iron. He had other plans. Con O'Kelly had, in 1908, become an Olympic wrestling champion. He went on to become a good class professional boxer, boxing in the USA. His son, Young Con O'Kelly, followed in his father's footsteps and won the Northern Area boxing title then he went on to become a Catholic Priest.

Not to be outdone, Tommy Stokes then entered the ring and offered to fight any man at the weight 10 stone 10 pounds, Jerry Thompson of Grimsby being preferred.

Iron's fight prevailed on time, commencing at 9pm. Iron's corner consisted of Kid Johnson, Charlie Hague and Johnny Hague. In Robb's corner were his manager Micky Smith and stand in, Swinton's Seaman Lyalls.

The press commented how Robb looked so big and well developed with a good muscular frame and radiated the aura of toughness. They also commented that Iron looked very fit, possibly the best they had ever seen him.

The fight unfortunately never got a chance to test Iron's current stamina.

As the bell sounded both fighters came to the centre of the ring. Rob stood upright in a sparring position and proceeded to adopt a classical style. Iron responded by wading in. He sent a few lefts to the face and then a right to the head. The Glaswegian dropped to his knees with the force of the impact. Robb got up quickly on the count of two. Iron then forced him back into his corner where "Dirty Dick" then prevailed. The heavyweight Robb went straight down onto the deck. It was all over in sixty seconds. George Law, in the corner, leapt up in response to the victory and the crowd followed suit about half a second behind. The cheering being out in the open air could be heard even at the far edges of the town and into adjoining Swinton.

After Robb had been checked out medically, he took to his feet and wanted to address the crowd. He went on to say that the reason for his defeat was the ring itself, which was insubstantial. The crowd jeered him. Iron responded by saying "The new Stadium was no N.S.C but nonetheless, it wasn't the building that hit him although after being hit by Dirty Dick he may have thought so." The crowd responded with great approval and Robb stormed off. The victory put a lot of confidence back into Iron and his team.

The next morning, the great win by Iron was somewhat overshadowed by the news that Herbert Oliver had died at the hospital at 11.10pm the previous evening. He had suffered from a compression of the brain due to an internal haemorrhage. There was now the family to console and an inquest to satisfy. The town was mortified.

The inquest was at the Montagu Hospital the following night and was presided over by Solicitor Frank Allen. It was established that Herbert lived with his father and was employed as the pit bottom lad at the No 2 shaft at Manvers Main. After the fight, where he lost consciousness, he was taken to the Montagu Arms. It was at 7.30 pm and he was visited shortly afterwards by Dr John Gardener. The post mortem confirmed there was only the smallest abrasion damage and his heart was healthy and there were no other injuries.

Mr Allan asked many questions. He confirmed that the fight was to novice standard with shorter rounds, the fight was lawfully run, proper seconds were involved in both corners, the gloves had been checked, the ring floor was padded, the referee was suitably qualified, there was no previous symptoms, both were willing fighters and the blow that knocked Herbert Oliver over was only light in nature. The contributing factor was that when hit, Oliver was standing awkwardly and when he fell back he went on his head in the centre of the ring.

Being satisfied on all counts, the coroner ruled that the incident was extremely unfortunate and gave the only verdict he could that of "Accidental Death" .

Chapter 26
Even the Best Laid Plans Can Go Wrong

After the meeting with Tom Cowler had broken down, it was back to the drawing board. A further meeting was held with Cowler and his manager and the deal was finally done. In order to tempt Cowler to fight at Mexborough, Iron and George Law had offered him a large amount of money. They both showed their great inexperience as fight promoters by agreeing to the most preposterous requests. It was to be on the 5th August 1912 and was a twenty round contest. The day selected was a Bank Holiday Monday. It was in essence, a ridiculous business decision as they were paying out more than they could possibly hope to profit on the night. That though was the desperation that Iron wanted the fight to be in his home town, Mexborough. They would worry about the business side later. In the meantime, the show must go on.

Tom Cowler was a very credible heavyweight. He was known as the "Cumberland Giant". He was born in March 1892 in Hensingham, Whitehaven, and like Iron, was from a family of coal miners.

Cowler was 6 feet 2 inches high and weighed some 14 stones. He was lean and mean.

Tom Cowler "The Cumberland Giant"

There was only some five weeks before the fight against Tom Cowler. Iron knew it was going to be a tough fight and went straight into hard training. The press were confirming its belief that Cowler was well trained, coupled with a mighty physique and was the future English Heavyweight Champion in the making.

Once more, to try and up the intensity and efficiency of the training, Iron left town. This time he went to Cleethorpes in Lincolnshire, where he set up training camp at the Leeds Arms. His trainer on this occasion was Alf Wilson. Alf had been around in boxing in the Doncaster area for some years and was well respected. Iron was accompanied by his brothers and George Law.

Boxing magazine with Cowler on the front.

The training routine was very similar to Withernsea but the rowing part was less because of the tidal pull. He ran around Tetney Marsh and on the banks of the River Humber, followed by long sparring sessions in the afternoon. It was always to bed early. On the 2nd August, a huge set back arose as Iron showed all the symptoms of a summer cold/flu. It knocked him off of his feet draining his stamina accompanied by aches and pains. He laid in bed for a whole day.

Meanwhile, back at Mexborough, Tom Cowler and his entourage arrived at the Montagu Arms in readiness for tomorrows fight. Free accommodation was part of the deal. Cowler utilised Iron's gymnasium for little warm ups. As they walked around town, the visitors noticed posters everywhere advertising the event. George Law had gone mad on the order from the printer, they were displayed in most of the shop windows of all the surrounding towns.

Iron didn't return from Cleethorpes until the actual day of the fight and was still unwell, though masking it.

The train pulled into town from the Doncaster direction just after 1pm. On his way up Station Road, an interested punter asked Iron how the training at Cleethorpes had gone. Iron looked at him and said "Put it this way, I can now run faster than that tide when it comes racing in."

Cleethorpes was notorious for the speed that the high tide flooded back claiming the long flat beach. Many had been cut off and drowned over the years.

Iron went straight home to Lucy. He didn't want to bump into Cowler at the Montagu. At home, he went to lay on the bed. At 4pm, George Law came to see him to see how he was.

Lucy directed him upstairs. "I thought that I should pop round to confirm that everything is okay for tonight." Iron turned over towards George "I can't do it, I am not up to the mark. I need to be at my best for this buggar."

"But Iron, you are going to have to go on. We have promised Cowler the full purse regardless. It will cost us a bomb. We can't get anyone else as a stand in at this late stage. It will be a financial disaster."

Postcard of Cleethorpes Pier, Lincolnshire, where Iron set up his training camp.

Iron sat up on the bed and rubbed his eyes and stretched his every joint. He said nothing, he didn't need to. His body language told George okay he would do it, he would go on and do what he could. The next few hours saw Iron with a towel over his head inhaling steam from a pan of hot water. He walked around the block and backstreets taking in the air, doing everything he could to convince his body that he was fit and up to the mark. Not only was there the financial problems of a cancellation, there was the immense disappointment for the many fans who had bought tickets. Every poster he passed in the widows seemed to shout at him "Go on get out there and get on with it". As the saying goes "the show must go on".

On arrival at the Stadium, Iron had a couple of stiff rums. This was the first time ever that Iron had drank alcohol before a fight. However, he felt so ill and weak that he felt grateful for anything that would put a bit of oomph into him, if only temporarily.

In his mind, Iron knew that even if Cowler was only average with performance he would lose to him. Iron decided, for the fans sake, he would perform the best he could and do no more. It wasn't every day the promoter was the star attraction.

Iron entered the ring to great applause and cheering which contrasted greatly to the boo's and jeers Cowler received. The referee for the contest was Tom Gamble. He told the crowd to steady down as they were over boisterous.

The timekeeper, who was introduced to the crowd was Frank "Spike" Robson, the famous Featherweight of South Shields. He had been born 5th November 1877. At the age of 29, he became British Featherweight champion (1906-1907).

Iron's fight tactics were to land blows to Cowler's head early on so that it would soften him. The fight started with each getting a measure of the other. Iron's attempts to hit at the head were only feeble and easily defended by Cowler. His 4 inch height advantage and longer reach was hard to penetrate. In the fourth round, Iron landed a decent blow to the head which put the Cumbrian down. Not for long though as he sprung straight back up. Cowler, then with a new determination, administered blows to Iron in every round. Iron went down twice in the sixth round and again in the seventh round.

Iron's corner was ready to throw in the towel but hesitated. The fight continued into the eighth round when Iron was completely spent and could not put up much defence. After a series of smashes, down Iron went out for the count, the fight was over, Cowler was the victor. The one time pride of the North's sporting fraternity now lay helpless and well beaten. It became apparent that not only was Iron the loser that night. The town's appetite for the sport curtailed as well.

It was now Iron's bitterest experience and a very large pill to swallow. The losing of the title was tough but this was even tougher to handle, right on his doorstep.

To rub salt into the wounds, the whole night was a financial disaster, the admissions didn't cover the payment contracted to Cowler never mind the rest of the costs. Iron had no capital behind him and George Law had little either. There was only one thing for it. They had to sell the Stadium. To this end, it was immediately put on the market. The hunt for a buyer was now on, just to clear their debts.

Iron's loss of pride was more than he could cope with. He was in personal disarray. He made the hasty decision that he had no option other than to throw in the towel on professional boxing. Well that was that day's decision. In reality, a lot more had ended that night after the fight was over. There was a huge knock on effect right across the town's residents. Boxing had peaked and was on the wane.

Feelings and sympathy following the death of Herbert Oliver ran high around the town. As a gesture, George and Iron decided to host a benefit night on the 7th September 1912, for Oliver's family. As a young breadwinner, the loss of Herbert's income into the Swinton home was greatly felt.

The expression that "many people were only two weeks away from the Workhouse" was very true in the Dearne Valley's case. There was no Social Security available then to act as a buffer.

Despite the financial hardship felt by the "would-be" entrepreneurs, they offered the full proceeds of the night to the family. Tom Cowler had agreed to return to town to box a three round exhibition match against Iron but gave back word. He was at the N.S.C awaiting the outcome of the Curran v Moir contest in order to lodge a challenge to the victor. Instead Barney Tooley, billed as the Pitman's Champion of Yorkshire, filled the gap at Mexborough.

In the wings, negotiations to sell the stadium had continued. The unpaid creditors eagerly awaited the outcome. A buyer was found in the guise of a Mr Nathaniel Mawby of Wakefield. He had been given the attendance figures and details of the running costs for his consideration.

Mawby did his own projections and worked out that given a few tweaks and effecting some cost savings, it could be run as a worthwhile venture. A great deal of "bull" was applied as to how popular boxing was in the town. Past copies of the South Yorkshire Times were shown with a full page and a half editorial on boxing, George Law and Iron promised the new owner they would continue to support him. With nothing but good emanating out of the salesmen, there appeared to be no negatives, their word was taken literally and the deal was done, the Stadium now had a new owner.

This brought an end to the personal financial pressures of George and Iron as all the creditors were subsequently paid off and they were back level. They had however lost their initial investment in building the Stadium.

The first event at the Stadium under Mr Mawby's ownership was on Saturday, 14th September 1912. George and Iron had organised this night which unfortunately, proved to be another financial disaster. The number of paying punters turning up on the night was very disappointing. At best, the Stadium could be described as half full. In addition, matters were further compounded by the fact some boxers didn't show. The top of the bill was a fight involving Tommy Stokes. Unfortunately, on the night, his opponent declined to step into the ring unless he was "guaranteed" the negotiated purse. Considering the low attendances, Mr Mawby declined to do this. A last minute stand in was found in Jack Perry of Normanton. He was not really qualified for the fight and was knocked out in the first round. Stokes felt sorry for the man and helped carry his unconscious body back to his corner.

Mr Mawby, the very next day, reckoned he had lost about £20 on the night and decided enough was enough. If this was a sample of what was to come, he was out. The Stadium was duly closed down and put back on the market.

It was much less desirable now as there were no future plans for contests to be hosted in town.

Although Mawby was very unhappy about it all, there was nothing he could do. He must have been undercapitalised for one hit to jeopardise the whole operation

The content of the South Yorkshire Times was changing. The regular boxing headlines were now being replaced with details of the seedy goings on emerging in the town.

With the economic times as they were, crime levels were starting to rise. News headlines now included "The Red Brotherhood" and the "The Black Diamond Gang".

Gang mentality and trouble manifested itself, the town's image as a commercial centre evaporated and it became "not a nice place" to visit.

Johnny Hague became embroiled in the gang misdemeanours and found himself facing a charge of grievous bodily harm. Along with two other men, it was stated he attacked another in an unprovoked assault. At the courthouse, the police said that Hague was known to be a member of the Red Brotherhood. This was strenuously denied. The Red Brotherhood had been set up by certain criminal elements in the town with a mutual agreement to help each other out. This involved committing crimes and also providing "heavying" services and violence for punishments. A few members had been jailed but it was believed its operations continued albeit, now more under cover. All three were found guilty and they were all sentenced to two months hard labour.

Iron, claiming that his health was still not right, abstained from boxing and training altogether. He had abandoned all thoughts of a relaunch. This could have been psychological following his last defeat or more serious illness symptoms still dogging him.

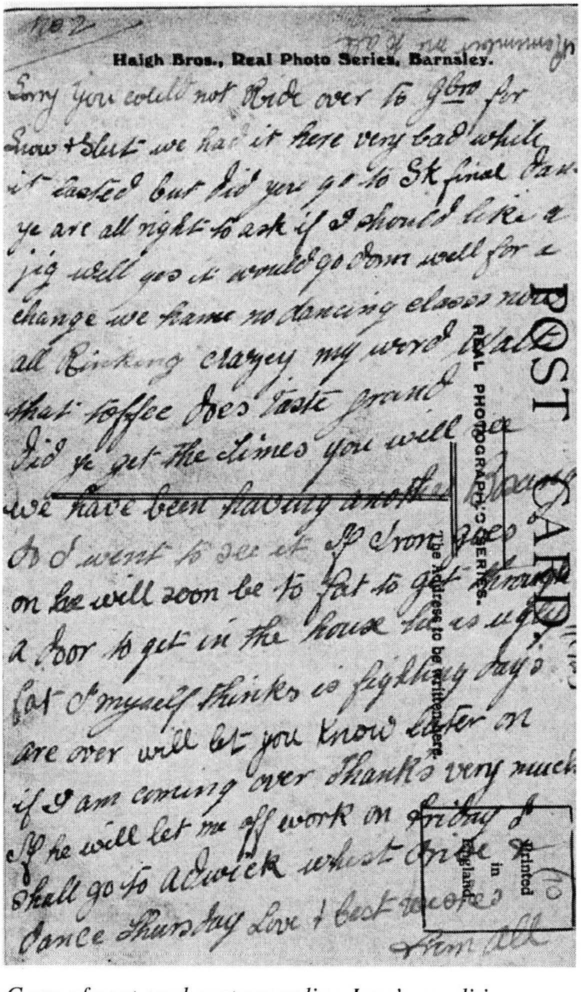

After he stopped the training, he started to pile on the weight, which wouldn't be easy to shake off. He had certainly acquired a likening for his beer and fish and chips but that's not the thing champions are made of.

A postcard sent to Ruth Hirst in Barnsley by a relative from the town in January 1913 contained the unkind lines "In the town, I bumped into Iron Hague. If he carries on like he is, he will be too fat to even get through his door never mind getting back into the ring, he looks ugly. Pat and myself think his fighting days are over."

Copy of post card sent regarding Iron's condition

As interest in boxing in the town dissipated, enthusiasts

now had to travel to The Pheasant Inn open air grounds at Carbrook, Sheffield, The Empire at Wombwell or Dillington Park in Barnsley in order to watch their sport.

For Iron, this period of his life was one for taking stock. He had a wife and a young daughter, he was 26 years of age and clearly as things stood, he could not carve out a future for them all as a pugilist of note. The money he had had gone. He could continue on the former glories, prostituting himself for purses, to fighters hoping to notch his defeat onto their fight record C.V. There was plenty of employment around in the area, he thought that seeking this out could be seen as his ultimate defeat. He worried that it would make people speak, not particularly about his past glorious achievements, but more of his demise.

Iron was a realist and after talks with his father, made a momentous decision. He decided to go back once more to the pits to secure a regular income. It was a case of needs must.

Things though were to change as the months passed by. The darkening clouds over Europe were spreading over Great Britain and circumstances beyond control meant that Iron wouldn't be left splashing about in the doldrums for long.

The assassination on the 28th June 1914 of Archduke Franz Ferdinand of Austria, the heir to the throne of Austria-Hungary, was the catalyst that triggered a series of events leading to worldwide warfare. His assassination at the hands of a Serbian nationalist, Gavrilo Princip, resulted in a Habsburg ultimatum to be made against the Kingdom of Serbia. Several alliances that had been formed over the past decades were suddenly invoked. Within a number of weeks, the major powers of Europe found themselves at war. This conflict, like no other before, escalated out to involve all the respective imperial colonies.

Countries were assembled into two opposing alliances and armies quickly mobilised. Recruiting stations were set up in most towns and posters printed to persuade the men of the town to volunteer their services. The war began with a massive and unprecedented wave of enthusiasm. At the beginning of August 1914, Parliament issued a call for an extra 500,000 soldiers. The response was overwhelming. By the end of September, over 750,000 men had enlisted. The publicity then started to state that by January 1915, a million men would be needed in total. The enthusiasm to join and fight continued, showing an "almost fanatical patriotism".

Chapter 27
The King's Shilling

Since the War broke out on the 4th August 1914, Iron had witnessed a stream of friends, relatives and other acquaintances all responding to the call and signing up for military duty.

"Kitcheners Army, join it today. Kitcheners Army, one bob a day" went the rhyme.

The newspapers of the time initially predicted that the war could be over in a matter of months, certainly by Christmas. A lot of anti-German propaganda was circulated, firing up the people to a fever pitch. The influx of volunteers up and down the country in response was overwhelming, on a scale never witnessed before. There was no conscription so reliance was on men coming forward voluntarily. Men were targeted between the ages of 19 and 30, with a height above 5 feet 3 inches and a minimum of a 34 inch chest and also medically fit.

With an average of 33,000 men joining every day, this created serious shortages of uniforms, equipment and accommodation.

Early on, some recruits were sent home and asked to come back when sent for to alleviate this.

Kitcheners message was loud and clear.

For the success of a war effort, it was not only troops that were needed. Industry needed to keep on turning its wheels. The collieries output of coal was crucial for the war's effort. To keep up production, many miners were persuaded to stay at home to continue to work the mines. That tore their loyalties as they were keen to join in what was seen as a big adventure.

There was a spirit of "Boys Own" excitement to it all. It offered a break from the hum drum life of living and working in the industrial towns.

As December 1914 came, there was another rallying call nationally to expand the number of regulars and volunteers now up to 1.1 million. More men in the town decided to rally to this call. If they had had any doubts about doing this, events were about to inflame their determinations.

A raid took place on the 16th December 1914 on Scarborough, Hartlepool and Whitby. This attack by the German Navy was carried out from ships in the North Sea. It resulted in 137 fatalities and 592 casualties, many of which were civilians.

The ships, Seydlitz, Blücher and Moltke had proceeded towards Hartlepool, while Derfflinger, Von der Tann and Kolberg approached Scarborough. At 8.00 a.m, they began shelling Scarborough Castle, the prominent Grand Hotel, three churches and various other properties. People crowded to the railway station and the roads leading out of the town. At 9.30am, the bombardment stopped and the two German battle cruisers moved on to nearby Whitby, where a coastguard station was shelled as was also Whitby Abbey and other buildings in the town.

Hartlepool was a more significant target in that it had extensive docks and factories. It was only defended by three six-inch guns on the seafront; two at Heugh Battery and one at Lighthouse Battery. The garrison of 166 Durham Light Infantrymen was warned at 4.30am of the possibility of an attack and issued live ammunition.

At 7.46am, they received word that large ships had been sighted and, at 8.10am, a bombardment of the town began. No warning was given to naval patrols in the area, which were meant to be always on duty. Unfortunately, the poor weather just before the raid meant that only four destroyers were on patrol, while two light cruisers and a submarine which might otherwise have been out at sea, remained in Hartlepool Harbour. The English destroyers at sea were armed with only torpedoes to harm the German ships but their positions were too far away to effect an attack.

Public outrage of these attacks ran high. Everyday conversations in the town's shops, streets and pubs, stemmed around this murderous act and who were the latest lads now to go. Iron was as angry as everybody else and decided that he could wait around no longer, now was the time, he must answer the call. There was a genuine fear their homes and families very survival was now under threat.

He had to then go and face the wife and his young daughter to break them the news. Lucy cried as he told her of his decision, she feared she may never see him again. He reassured her that he would be back in Orchard Street before she would know it. He said it was his duty to protect them, he would never live with himself if he didn't do his duty for the country. It was not, in reality, a great surprise to Lucy, she knew it would be a matter of time before Iron would be joining up for the cause. A lot of publicity had been directed at the womenfolk, emphasising that the safety of their home and children was dependant on the men in the armed forces. They were urged to tell their menfolk to "Go", it implied their husbands would be ostracised if they were kept at home by their womenfolk. Posters were printed of a man sat in an armchair with an audience of children around him asking the question "What did you do in the war Daddy?"

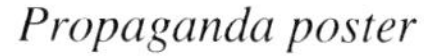

Propaganda poster

Propaganda poster

Lucy naturally was also worried as to how they would cope with Iron away what would they do for income? He was the breadwinner. Iron reassured her saying he would be sending his soldiers pay back for them. A Separation Allowance system was also introduced by the government to assist in just such situations .This would help them while the breadwinner got back. The plight Lucy Hague found herself in was far from unique to her. It was the same for all her friends and her neighbours.

Iron's brother, Johnny, announced he was also joining up so now the Hague family was well and truly "a family at war". Their father, William, with a great determination, pledged his all to assist them and keep the home fires burning. He would fight on the streets if he had to. Also joining the military ranks this time were Iron's cousins (the Bennets) and boxers, Tom Stokes and Dick Parkes.

On the 21st December 1914, as advertised, three military recruiters came to town. They were representing The King's Own Yorkshire Light Infantry, The Yorks and Lancs Regiment and then there was Sergeant Joddy representing the Grenadier Guards. As the men came in, Joddy looked every one up and down. When Iron walked in, he shot straight over to apprehend him before the others did. Because of Iron's height of 5 feet 10 3/8 inches, Joddy wanted to ensure he enlisted Iron into the Grenadier Guards. The Guards had a higher height requirement than any other regiment. At the start of the war, the elite status of the Guards Division meant they were actually inundated with recruits wanting to join their ranks. To keep the Regiment special, the Commanding Officer then increased the necessary height

Caricature of Iron Hague emphasising his thick set appearance with the heavier weight.

requirement.

The Guards regiments for new recruits now had a minimum standard of 5'8" compared to only 5 foot for infantry and 5'4" for Cyclists. The Household Cavalry maintained a standard of 5'9" compared with the line cavalry at 5'4". The minimum requirement varied for the artillery depending upon branch but was averaged at 5'7".

This meant Iron was isolated from a lot of his friends who were split more or less fifty percent into both the Yorks and Lancs Regiment and the King's Own Light Infantry.

Iron was subjected to a brief medical and had his height and weight taken. Amongst the notes, it confirms he was 29 years and 34 days old with a forty two inch chest that expanded to forty five inches when fully expanded. It anotes that Iron has a distinguishing mark in the form of a scar on his right wrist.

As part of the enlisting procedure, Iron had to take the following Oath:-

"I, James William Hague, swear by Almighty God that I will be faithful and bear true allegiance to his Majesty King George the Fifth, His Heirs and successors and that I will, as in duty bound, honestly and faithfully defend His Majesty, his Heirs, his

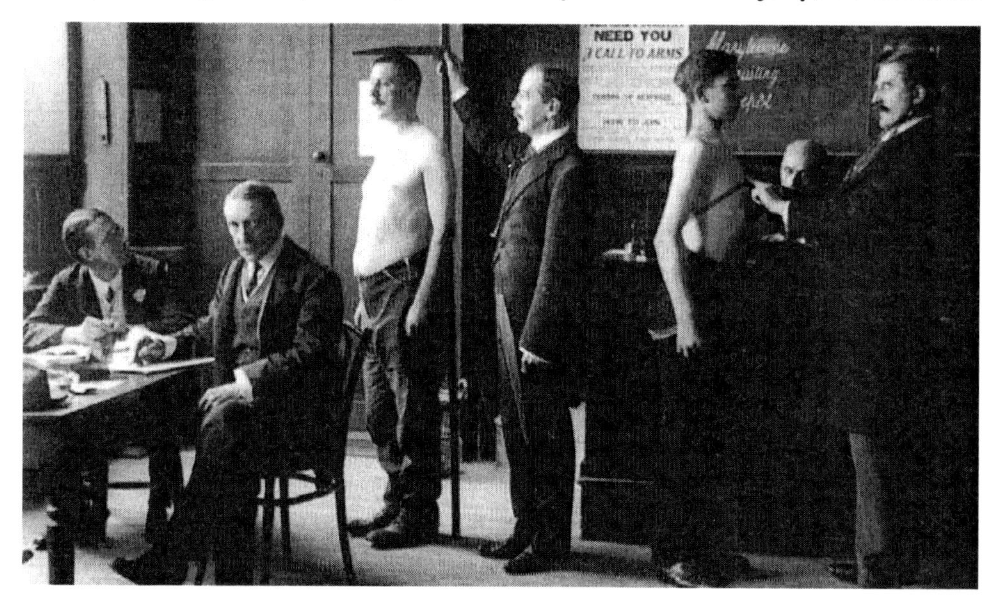

World War I joining up medical .

successors, in Person, Crown, and Dignity against all enemies, and will observe and obey all orders of his Majesty, His Heirs and Successors, and of the Generals and Officers set over me. So help me God."

The oath was sworn in front of local magistrate, Mr C Ward. He had first cautioned Iron that had he given any false answers to any of the questions on the Short Service Attestation form, he would be punished under the Army Act. The Magistrate had to also confirm that Iron clearly understood every question.

The enlistment form needed Iron to confirm details of his wife and child for his next of kin and possible pension payments. On the form Iron, is duly recorded as occupation – "Miner". No mention was made of boxing or pugilist. He was there as an equal amongst men.

With the paperwork all done, Iron was then told to return home and enjoy Christmas with his family. They would send for him soon.

After sad goodbyes to family on the morning of the 1st January 1915, Iron travelled to Pontefract. He was ordered to attend the mustering station situated there. On arrival, his particulars were checked by Major J Logan Ellis and he was confirmed as now being a serving soldier in the 3rd Battalion of the Grenadier Guards. He was given the recruit number of 21499 and was now known as Private J.W.Hague. He took the King's shilling and in return, the recruiting officer was paid the King's Sixpence.

One amusing incident while Iron was there was that in the Short Service queue for Pontefract residents were two fifteen year olds. They were keen to sign up and join the army. The recruiting sergeant asked them there ages and they said nineteen. He then asked them where they worked and when did they start there. They had rehearsed their dates of birth but weren't ready for those questions. The sergeant leaned over and said "Listen sonny, I am not here tomorrow. Come back then but get your answers right" and so off they went, perhaps they did come back the next day. It was not necessary to produce evidence of age or even of one's name in order to enlist at the time.

Iron was given his travel documents to take the train to London reporting to the Guards training camp at Caterham situated, South of London,

Caterham is located in the Tandridge District of Surrey. It lies on the A22 Eastbourne road south of Croydon set in a valley cut into the side of the North Downs. The town had a railway station which was heavily used by the military for troop and supplies transportation.

The Barracks was the main depot for foot guards regiments and was created "on the hill" in 1877. It was the largest army depot of the Victorian age, home to the unique "Her Majesty's Foot Guards", the elite personal bodyguard of the monarch.

Once there, Iron was greeted by 2nd Lieutenant Pennington who explained the new

Grenadier Guard's third battalion – vest badge

regime they would now live and breathe by. He went on to explain that although hard, the training was also to assist them in their own safety. They would learn to work as a dedicated team and obey orders without question. He also explained the consequences of not doing so. The Regimental Sergeant Major then strutted up and down and explained how he would not accept any slovenliness. Beware any man who had to encounter his wrath. He would be watching them closer than a mother looks at her new born child, they had been warned.

He was issued with a uniform of standard battle dress with a web belt. There was no luxury of a Dress Uniform. What he got was what he had. If he ever left the barracks, he was expected to where his Battle Dress outfit.

Iron was to be subjected to some five months tough training in what was classed as a training battalion. He would learn drill, weapon training, minor tactics and field craft. Afterwards, he would join the battalion proper.

Despite joining up with the previous occupation listing as "miner", the word of Iron's former sporting prowess spread round the barracks. Within a week of being there, he was summoned before the officers. They confirmed with him his past history of boxing. They then stated they wanted Iron to take up fitness training once more and represent the regiment in a tournament or two. Iron was very receptive to this. His boxing career was a couple of years behind him now but he decided he would have a go. Tom Stokes was also in the Guards and was also earmarked for fighting duties in the ring.

The first fight that was arranged for Iron was a six rounder against Frank Wright. The contest took place on the 13th February 1915 to a full audience of Squaddies at the Guard's Tourney. Iron had weighed in at 13 stone four pounds. He carried his weight well with not a lot of the old fat that plagued him showing through.

Iron mastered the fight from end to end. He skipped around the ring like a lightweight. He used his left punch skilfully, catching the challenger out on many occasions. Whether by choice or mishap is not known but Iron could have gone in for the knockout on a couple of occasions quite easily but didn't. He won the fight on points very comfortably.

This victory gave Iron back some self esteem, the crowd and officers were firmly convinced that in the world of boxing "Iron was back".

He remained in training, being excused from some of the everyday duties his fellows had to endure. Part of that training saw him take part in a three round exhibition bout against Pat O'Keefe at Caterham on the 15th March 1915.

Such was the interest to see this new Guard fighter in action, it was decided the next fight would be at the West London Stadium at Edgeware. This was to be on the 27th March 1915. This time though it would be more of a professional contest. He was to be matched against Bandsman Rice.

Dick Rice hailed from Leeds from a family of boxers. His younger brother, Ernest, went on to become the British Lightweight Champion in the 1920's. Rice served in the Rifle Brigade and had his first professional fight back in 1909. His track record was very impressive. He had in the past defeated Lurie, Voyles and Rawles twice. He had fought Bombadier Billy Wells the previous April losing on points. On this occasion, the fight went the full twenty rounds. He was rematched against Wells on the 24th February 1915 where this time, he was knocked out in the sixth round. Although billed as "Bandsman" Rice, he was actually a sergeant.

Bandsman Rice in fighting pose.

It was set to be a challenging fight and Iron trained hard. For some unknown reason, further negotiation took place and the fight duration was reduced from twenty rounds down to fifteen. His followers were convinced that could now recover his lost laurels. The Fight Reporter printed that Iron was now back at the forefront after five years of obscurity. Further publicity was also put out that Rice demanded another re-match against Wells, with the English Title to be at stake.

The night of the contest saw a packed stadium. Iron entered the ring to great applause. The Guards were there in large number and were right behind him. He stood in his corner, waving back to his fans, with all the mannerisms of "the King is back again". The fight set off with Iron being quite guarded and managing to hold Rice off. This trend continued for the whole fight. Despite the fact that Iron prevented Rice from administrating any devastating blows he didn't do enough himself to score points. On a couple of occasions, he set Rice up to receive "Dirty Dick" treatment but failed to deliver.

The fight was given to Bandsman Dick Rice. The press reported that the fight was a little disappointing, the pro-Iron crowd were obviously there to see the Yorkshireman win in style.

Iron suffered from a lot of post fight regret. He felt he could have taken Rice and was angry with himself why he did not go that extra mile.

Nonetheless, he enjoyed the adulation and buzz of it all again. To that end, he sent word back to Mexborough that he wanted to talk to Frank Law. He wanted Frank to represent him once again.

Back at Mexborough, things were a little strained. The heart had been sucked out of the town with a large number of young men all being directed away into war efforts. Business was static, just ticking over. The bars of the town's public houses didn't have the same electric atmosphere feeling to them and the beer was much weaker

Tom Gunner.

Frank's reaction to Iron's request was a positive but with a difference. He saw it as helping out as opposed to a serious promoter opportunity. The war in any case, would ensure that the money was not around as in the past. Nonetheless he went about trying to arrange contests, so to establish a fight path forward. Iron was coming home soon for his final leave before he was sent overseas to France. Following instructions, Frank arranged a fight with up and coming youngster Tom Gummer. The fight was to be at Catchweight over ten rounds and would be at Carbrook, Sheffield on the 3rd July 1915.

Tom Gummer was also in the

Army and had the rank of Sergeant. He had been born at Kimberworth, Rotherham in 1894 and was barely 21 years old. Boxing skills ran in the family as his brother went onto be Welterweight Champion of the Mediterranean Fleet. He left school at 13 years of age and went to work in the local Pit at Droppingwell. He had a lot in common with Iron. He started boxing as an amateur with good success. In 1913 he entered the "White Hope" competition promoted by the Daily Sketch and Sporting Chronicle. He won the Yorkshire leg with a knockout. He turned professional in 1914 commencing with a fight against Willis Monks, the Lancashire White Hope winner, he won over six rounds. He had several more fights at the Carbrook Stadium notching up wins with them all. He had joined the 5th Battalion of the Yorks and Lancs Regiment and within a year, became Sergeant. He had watched Iron box two years earlier and he was very much one of Tom's heroes. He was in some awe to now be facing the man in the ring.

As often happens, even the best laid plans go wrong. Gummer had been given a weeks extra leave to go back to Rotherham and prepare for the forthcoming fight. Iron had no such luck.

A virus had gone round the Caterham camp, laying low many of the inhabitants. Iron was grounded so as not to spread the illness to others outside. He didn't leave camp until the day of the fight itself. The train service had become so irregular that time was against him so without further ado he took a taxi all the way home to Mexborough. Much to Lucy's great disappointment, Iron could only spend a short time at home before being whisked off again to Sheffield for the fight. Not a great start for the warrior.

The newspapers had certainly been bulling up the fight as a distraction to the daily war news, which slowly filtered through. With Iron's experience and his alleged pick up on form it, was predicted he would be the victor. The crowd attending Carbrook were some 5000 which was excellent considering the war situation.

The fight was one that didn't disappoint the spectators. It had all the qualities of a real grueller. Both boxers gave and received a lot of punishment. The first two rounds were Gummer's but by the third, Iron started to rally and then started to dish out the punishment. "Dirty Dick" hit home a few times followed by a hard left. By the last round, Gummer was badly battered and bruised. He launched himself at Iron in a feeble attempt to which Iron responded rushing in with a right. Unfortunately, the punch missed and the force of it launched Iron out through the ropes and down onto the floor. The impact bruised three of his ribs and pain soared through his body. Iron managed to climb back into the ring but dazed and breathless he paused a second and Gummer landed a right on the jaw and down he went. He was counted out with only three seconds remaining on the clock. The crowd were somewhat bewildered. Gummer was beaten to a frazzle yet he was the winner, spirits ran very high. This was one of Iron's worse experiences. As a true professional, he accepted the decision gracefully although inside he was very angry with himself. The newspapers headlined it next day "Certain winner comes a cropper".

After the fight, a damaged Iron returned home to Lucy but any reunion could only be brief. The next morning, Guardsman Hague had to catch a train to London, he was expected back in camp. He was sore and the jolting of the train made him squirm. A medical examination established that there were no broken bones and that time would be a good healer.

Despite the setback of the previous seventy two hours, another fight was announced on the 2nd August 1915. This time, it was to be in the open air at Stamford Bridge, Chelsea's Football Ground. It was to be a fifteen round "have a go "bout. The opponent this time was Sergeant Harry Curzon. He hailed from Bloomsbury, London. He was an occasional middleweight fighter, having had only seven fights in the previous twelve years, of which he had only won two. His last win was against Curly Watson back in 1909.

Iron had great advantage in both height and reach and was favoured to win the contest. Whilst in the dressing room, Iron was talking to several interested parties about his damaged ribs. One fellow was very interested indeed, asking Iron a lot of detailed questions about the injury. He stood there with his mouth open, listening intently. What Iron did not realise was that the man before him was non other than his opponent Harry Curzon.

This loose tongue was to prove very costly. From the off, Curzon concentrated on landing body slams. Not once did he try and land a punch to the head and face. He just carried on peppering away at the ribs. Iron appeared slow and heavy in the ring and his heart did not seem to be in the fight. The warrior of old was not there that day. He was forced onto the ropes on a number of occasions. In the third round, Iron was cautioned by the referee for holding. Curzon took advantage of the situation and landed a punch that put Iron's lights out. He was knocked out again.

It wasn't a great night for Mexborough as on the same bill was Tommy Stokes who fought Sapper Ashdown. He was stopped in the second round following injuries sustained, he was clearly out boxed.

Chapter 28
Off to France

The 8th August 1915 saw much activity at Caterham Barracks. The 3rd Grenadier Guards was at last considered fully trained and was now about to enter the theatre of war. The troops were driven to the railway station to make their way to the Channel ports for boarding a troop carrier for the short journey over the sea to France. There was a lot of excitement as, "this was it" this is what they had craved for, trained for, couldn't wait for – to get out there amongst it all. After arrival in France at the port of Le Havre, they were all transported to the Guards Division Base Depot near Harfleur. The No 10 camp in the Lezarde valley was newly established and Iron and his fellow troops were one of the first to use the base and its facilities.

By August 1915 there were four battalions of Grenadiers on the Western Front where they remained for the rest of the war. In camp, the boxing interest continued and an open air ring was set up. Iron acted as a trainer to some of the younger soldiers cutting their teeth in boxing. He had only been there three days when he was asked to take part in an exhibition match with Gunner Gray. He agreed and the regiment's top brass all watched it with great interest.

On the 23rd August, another exhibition was arranged and this time it was to be over six rounds. The other boxer was none other than Charlie Knock.

It was like an old friend's re-union. The bout was classed as a draw but it would be.

Grenadier Guards at Leisure awaiting deployment in France.

Both boxers were more interested in socialising after the event. Charlie was like family to Iron.

After pressure from the officers, a further bout was arranged between Iron and Gunner Joe Mills a Londoner (he was actually Cardiff born). Mills had previously fought the Bombardier in what was Wells' first fight after leaving the military service. Wells won on points of this six rounder. Wells, incidentally, had also rejoined the military and was in France acting as an advisor on physical training.

The fight took place on the 7th September 1915. The fight was quite mediocre until the third round when Iron stepped up the ante and got "Dirty Dick" in action again. Iron knocked his man clean out. Mills later developed an infection which led to pleurisy. He died on the 2nd November 1915. This early death did effect Iron in that he got to thinking that, had he not knocked him out, he may well have not contracted the virus. He firmly held himself responsible. It was absurd as there was illness going around the base and the reality was that Joe was just unlucky, it was nothing to do with Iron and the fight. One thing that this event did though was to make Iron decide to retire from boxing altogether. A long and illustrious boxing career folded. At least he went out on a win.

As September matured, the news was issued that the 3rd Battalion would be joining the 2nd Brigade and would be going into action at Loos. The 2nd Brigade was to be made up of the 1st Coldstream, 1st Scots and 2nd Irish Brigades. The fact that all Guards units made up the brigade was unusual but Lord Kitchener had encouraged it. He was hoping to form a unique unit that could act as a model army and be an example to the rest. The Commander was the Earl of Cavan. The Brigades emblem became the "Ever open Eye". At Loos they would be fighting alongside the 3rd Brigade as well as other non Guards outfits.

It was the first large scale use of "Kitcheners's New Army". On the 27th September,

The guard's medical tent set up with the ever watchful eye symbol shown on the right hand side.

Grenadier Guards cap badge

Iron, along with his battle kit, boarded a London bus, one of a large procession of buses specially commandeered for the war effort. They were all transported to the railway station at Harfleur accompanied by lorries carrying equipment and ammunition. From here, they all boarded the train for the ride. At the other end, they had more vehicles provided for the transportation part of the way but they had to march for the last five miles. The small town of Loos-en-Gohelle was to be found to the north of Lens.

It turned out to be a baptism of fire for Iron and his comrades as the preparations for the offensive were unfortunately poor. One of Iron's first jobs was to help extend the trench system, working at night.

Under the command of Lt Col Noel Corry with Major Montgomery as second in command, they hoped to advance over the third line German defences. One officer diarised how he found the 3rd battalion to be rather young soldiers somewhat struggling in the art of trench warfare. Their training had concentrated more on the

Earlier Guards recruits awaiting deployment.

open battlefield scenario.

The first assault failed miserably and heavy casualties were experienced. The next day they advanced again. To their great astonishment, they discovered that the Germans had dug in twenty to thirty feet down into the soft chalk strata creating an extensive trench system. Joined for the assault by the 1st Scots, they engaged in prior heavy fire and artillery shelling attacks but it was not effective.

The Germans, who were better organised, retaliated and almost surrounded them. They hung on for their lives for forty eight hours before being relieved. Losses were right across the board, officers and men. One of the fatalities on the second day was Watch Captain, Fergus Bowes-Lyon (The future Queen Mother's brother).

Action carried on over the summer months, the Germans employed smoke screens, gas attacks as well as concentrated artillery and machine gun fire.

The Germans had first used gas at Ypres on the 27th April 1915. In retaliation, the British decided to create their own gas attack capability. The inaugural use of this capability was on the 25th September 1915 at 5.20am at Loos. Unfortunately, the delivery system was crude. It consisted of fixed cylinders which released gas when manually opened instead of being projected into the area intended. The direction of the wind was obviously a key factor to deployment decisions. On that morning, unfortunately, after the valves were open, the wind and the gas released changed direction and blew it back over the British lines. This caused high casualties to the brigade and very little to the Germans.

Action at Loos finished on the 14th October 1915 by which time the combined British forces had suffered some 50,000 casualties. For three days, action was then heavy at Neuve Chapelle the eighteen pounders fired some 78,000 rounds in total. Like a Chinese water torture, the men could not escape the continuous bangs of the canon. Sleeping, eating, on duty or off duty the noise was always with them.

On the 28th October, Iron's battalion were to be reviewed by his Majesty King George 5th but he was laid low with an accident so it didn't happen.

On 8th November, Iron found himself deployed to the Neuve Chapelle sector. As spring then came to relieving a harsh winter, operations were moved to the northern part of the Ypres Salient. This was the quietest time of Iron's war service. His battalion were billeted in Laventie, only 1000 yards behind the front line.

A break in active service was enjoyed on the 5th March when the Guards were withdrawn for a temporary reprieve and training and transported to Calais. What a magnificent sight it was for Iron as he was able to look over the Channel to see England once more. The day after on the 6th March, they were inspected by Sir Douglas Haigh. Unfortunately, this short break was marred by late spring snow and shifting fog. On the 12th March, for light entertainment they organised a race day

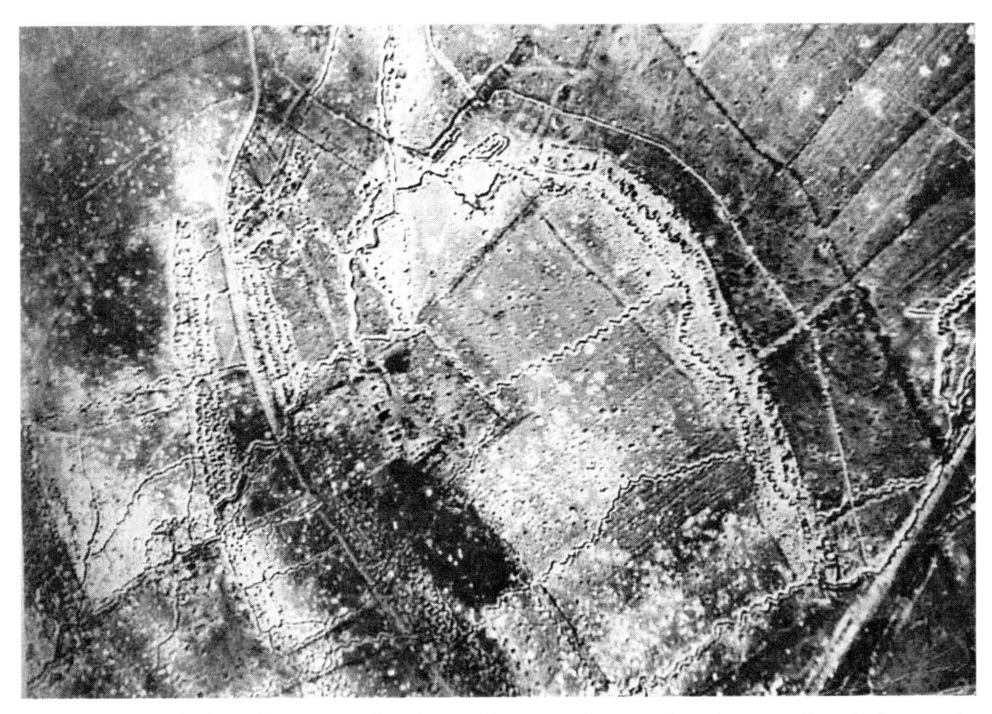

Arial picture of Chapelle Neuve the zigzag lines are the trenches dug out, the whole area is littered with craters from shell fire.

based on the wide beaches.

On the 20th March 1915, they were then sent back to Ypres. Holding this ground had cost thousands in casualties but a withdrawal would send out the wrong messages. The battalion were deployed into hundreds of cellars of the towns houses, which were mostly bomb damaged above ground.

The heavy bombardments that the troops had found themselves being subjected to meant a review of the uniforms. The new standard issue to the khaki battledress was a metal helmet. Although these were uncomfortable they were necessary to save lives. The area was well covered by German snipers and any careless exposure was swiftly met with gunfire. One difficult time manifested on the night of the 30/31st March when trying to relieve the Scots Guards. They were in a bad way after extensive shelling and the trenches were full of their dead. As most of the trenches were blown up positions were taken up in shell holes. The dead and wounded Scots were taken away during the few intermissions of shelling.

On the 12th April, several days of recoupment were enjoyed in Poperinghe which as a town was still standing. A return to Ypres was made on the evening of the 19th April, which was done under heavy bombardment. They remained on active duty until the 21st May. During this time, trenches were extended and bombardments carried out.

An Injured Grenadier guard is taken away.

Thereafter, the Guards returned for a month's rest at Volkeringhove. During this time, practices were held for a big offensive on the Pilkem Ridge. The trench system was recreated in miniature so everyone knew its layout. As it happened the assault was delayed.

Instead, they were deployed to assist a Canadian Division who had been subject to

Grenadier guards in their bombed out trenches with hospital units present.

continuous attack. After that it was a return to the front line at Zillebecke village.

In August of 1916, Iron learned that they were all to be deployed into the battle hell of the Somme. The opening day of the Somme battle had been on the 1st July 1916 and saw the British Army suffer the worst one-day combat losses in its history, with nearly 60,000 casualties. These losses back home had a profound social impact. With casualties from all over Great Britain there wasn't a town or village who had not lost a loved one. Many children were orphaned because of the Somme's attrition.

At the front, the conditions there were poor. Water was always knee deep in the trenches and the German's own trenches, in part, were only situated some twenty five yards away, meaning extra vigil. The incessant effect of water was impacted by corroding rifles, guns, ammunition and even rotted the uniforms on the Guards backs. Trench foot was quite common as was frost bite in the cold of winter, adding to the nightmare conditions. Commander Lt Col Bertram Segison-Brooke was in charge of operations for the Brigade.

Iron's outfit were encamped at Ginchy and at 6.20am on the 15th September, took part in a major "Over the top" offensive. The British Army were keen to try out their new invention "the Tank" in battlefield conditions. They joined in with the action. The Germans counter defended using smoke and the Allied lines became broken. Iron found himself as part of a smaller group under the command of a C.O from another unit, engaged in combat, grimly trying to advance the battle lines whilst hundred fell around them. German machinegun nests picked off the enemy as soon as they came into sight. Casualties were high, the fields of barbed wire made progress often very

Grenadier guards march behind the tanks which were then a new invention for war fare.

difficult. Lives proved to be worth little.

After forty eight hours of being "bang at it", the Brigade was rested for several days. It allowed the injured animal to lick its wounds. New drafts of Guards were fetched in to restore numbers. The attack on German lines was eventually successful with the village being taken but at what price? However, The Royal Munster Fusiliers suffered heavy losses in doing so.

On the 25th September 1916, Iron found himself back in action. This was at Lesboeufs. This village was situate some sixteen kilometres north-east of the town of Albert. It had first been attacked by the Guards Division on the 15th September 1916 and it was now hoped to finally capture the area.

Iron's Brigade were positioned at the extreme right of the advancing army. Advancing meant three lines of barbed wire had to be cut through, out in the open.

The plan was to pierce this, rush into the German trenches for hand to hand and bayonet fighting. Iron's battalion suffered greatly with about 45% casualties. The battle proved effective and the Germans did retreat back over open fields. On the 27th September, they were made up into burial teams. There were 3,136 casualties overall. Graves were dug and the decomposing bodies buried to stem the spread of disease and take away the smell. It was a hard task to undertake for any soldier.

Trench Duties. The conditions were often so bad that the wet induced a condition known as "Trench Foot".

The German army, after suffering ground losses, retreated several miles and re-established a front line along the Hindenburgh Line. Iron's unit were then moved to what would be known as 3rd Ypres or Passchendale after the town situated in the vicinity. Conditions were again appalling. The Guards fought in the north sector over a front of some 1500 yards. After a series of good victories saw them move forward some two and a half miles, the fight settled down. At the end of July 1917, the rain started falling. Once more, the trenches and the battlefield itself became a quagmire of mud. The trench system was continuously extended to create new dry ground but within forty eight hours of construction, the water had encroached there as well. The soldiers faced the same hell as at the Somme, incessant shelling, fields of barbed wire and water everywhere.

In October, the line tried to cross the Broembeek ridge, the front of which was marshy ground. The deep mud sucked in the boots and legs of the advancing troops, restricting further movements. Being laden with battle kit did not help the situation. Of the 4 Battalions, the 2nd suffered the worst casualties at around 30 per cent. The 3rd's losses, though great in number, percentage wise were much lower.

On the 20th November, Iron took part in a surprise attack on the Hindenburgh line at Cambrai. Tanks were used in large numbers with the troops walking behind them. Normally before an offensive 24 hours of incessant shelling took place to weaken the enemy both in numbers and spirit. On this occasion, it was decided to abandon this practice, so appearing out of the blue. Unbeknown to the Guards, the Germans were planning their own offensive and were stocking up on ammunitions, they had been preparing for weeks. The Germans launched their heavy offensive in response and gained three miles in no time. The Guards had to beat a fast retreat, the fully armed German war machine advanced at great speed.

The advance was finally checked at Gouzeaucourt. Counter attack plans were then put into operation. The action included hand to hand fighting both in the open and in woodlands accompanied by heavy shelling of the enemy.

The objectives were to retake the St Quentin ridge and Gauche Wood. Strangely, a unit of Bengal Lancers fought nearby and ended up being intermixed with the Guards.

As 1918 came, the Germans decided to have a final crack at breaking the British Army. The Guards manpower was severely depleted. Iron himself was not without injury. He had damage to the back of one his knees, caused by barbed wire catching on him and ripping open his flesh as he tried to weave his way through the sea of wires. He also had suffered lung damage through exposure to gas. The ending of hostilities on the eastern front, following the Russian revolution, released 1.5 million German troops to join their comrades on the western front.

In March of 1918, Iron found himself in Arras. His walking was painful but nonetheless, he was classed as being battle worthy. Here, the Guards were subjected to intense fire and attack. A tactical retreat had to be made. On the 19th June 1918, Iron's injuries were such that he was transferred to the rear echelon. Here, he undertook what was described as "some light work" the best he could, preparing supplies, etc, for the lads just down the road.

The Back battalion digging roads. Iron was sent here after his injuries became too bad for front line action..

In August, the 1st, 2nd and 3rd Battalions grouped together and proved effective in crossing the Canal du Nord on the Hindenburgh line . Iron rejoined his unit at the front on the 13th August 1918. The fighting conditions were, by then, more favourable to the Guards and they capitalised on it. As they advanced, they discovered that the Germans had been mining and had left quite sophisticated traps. The operation

The Middlewood Wharncliffe War Hospital, Sheffield.

SPECIAL VICTORY NUMBER. FINAL NIGHT EDITION.

ROYAL EXCHANGE ASSURANCE A.D. 1720 — FIRE AND ACCIDENT INSURANCES.

The Globe
AND TRAVELLER. Founded 1803.

ROYAL EXCHANGE ASSURANCE A.D. 1720 — LIFE AND MARINE INSURANCES.

No. 38,482. MONDAY EVENING, NOV. 11, 1918. ONE PENNY.

VICTORY!

GERMANY SURRENDERS.

OUR TERMS ACCEPTED TO-DAY.

LAST SHOTS FIRED AT 11 A.M.

Headline in the Globe newspaper.

finished with the capture of Maubeuge. The German dying efforts were overcome at great cost. The swelling of the Allied forces with US troops had helped tremendously. The German threat then disintegrated.

On the 3rd November 1918, Iron was sent back to England. His medical condition was such that he was transferred to the Wharncliffe War Hospital for medical attention. His papers show that his condition was described as being Aiii. This meant he would be ready to re-serve in the battalion excepting to his present physical condition, it was expected he would reach a sufficient fitness level in the near future. This was a very broad brush statement and not really representative of Iron's actual state of health.

Great celebrations were held all around the country following the announcement of the ending of the war. These Sheffielders were no exception.

Armistice Day – marking the ending of the First World War – was officially at 11am on the 11th November 1918. Peace reigned once again.

Great celebrations took place all over England as the news of the ending of the war became official.

Street parties, work's parties and official municipal parties were the order of the day. Although Iron was still detained at the hospital, he joined in with the merrymaking that took place all over the hospital complex.

By the end of the war, the Guards Regiments had suffered 11,915 casualties of which 203 officers and 4,508 other ranks were dead, seven VCs had been won and 34 battle honours awarded.

Chapter 29
Back To Blighty

The Wharncliffe Hospital was previously an asylum taken over for Military injury purposes. Some 35000 troops received treatment there up until 1920 when it was closed. It was situated in the Wadsley part of Sheffield. The atrocious nature of injuries sustained in the trenches caused severe mental problems and many patients went on to be treated in mental asylums. Post traumatic stress units did not exist. The hospital was staffed by the Royal Army Medical Corps, supplemented by voluntary workers, often organised by the local lady gentry.

Despite the categorising of his medical condition Iron's injuries were quite prolific. He would never return to the fit athlete he once was. He had damage to his knee joints which would never fully repair and they would act as a constant reminder of his time spent in the Great War.

Regular visitors were Lucy and daughter Jane who was now aged eight. The journey was irksome as they had to take a train to Sheffield and then take the Hillsborough Tram, then undertake a brisk walk.

Daughter Janie was clearly taking after her father in stature, now being quite tall for her age. To Iron, it was a great reunion as the last time he saw his daughter she was only four years old. Iron found out his young brother George, who he had sat on his knee in the victory parade of 1909, had actually in his absence, been married that

The Kings visit to the Middlewood Wharncliffe War Hospital shortly after Iron's arrival there..

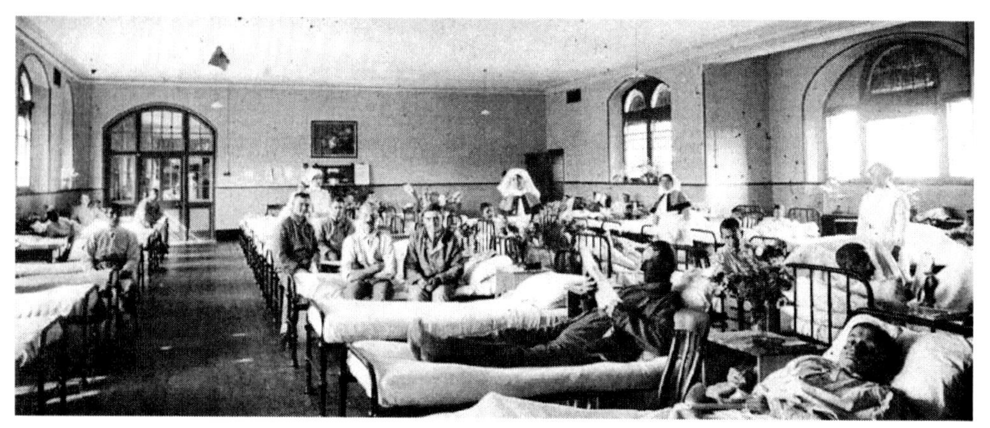

A ward of soldiers at Middlewood Wharncliffe War Hospital.

year to Emily Eliza Bisby.

Iron remained at the Hospital until the 9th January 1919 where after he was then able to return home to Mexborough. He now walked with a permanent limp and wore an elastic support on one knee.

This time, on arriving in town there was no hero's homecoming where the streets were packed with well wishers. Thousands of former soldiers from the area had made their own return and it was now a daily ritual. His family however, did organise a welcome home party which he attended. People could be forgiven for thinking that he had changed somewhat, that he appeared now to be quite reserved. Circulating through his head were the memories of the hundreds of lost fellow soldiers. His first hand witnessing of their demise impacted on him, strong comradeship had at the time, bonded them together. The horrific conditions of the battlefield had been part of his life for the past four years and it had destroyed good men, he was still traumatised. Over the years, he kept this part of his life private, he did not talk openly of his war experiences.

He found out he had lost many friends in the war who were in other regiments. He was unaware of many of their losses until his return home. They were unfortunately part of the total of 703,000 casualties that Great Britain had incurred, Iron was one of the 1,663,000 wounded.

Like most soldiers, Iron's all had been taken to the limits. Men he never knew before fighting at his side were badly wounded and many were shot dead, the stench of wholesale death frequently filled the air. Burying piles of rotting corpses who were once men like him was a frequent duty. His mind had been re-programmed into one of self survival and undying loyalty to the strangers fighting at your side. To just walk away from it and pick up the pieces was nigh on impossible. Many commented that their loved one's had not returned the same person.

Now back on civvy street, reality of his situation set in. Despite all the money that had passed through his hands in the past, there was nothing left. Like many, he now found himself out of work, less able and virtually penniless. He was grateful for initial family assistance but his deep pride would not accept it past his initial return. He had received news that he was to receive a war disablement pension of £2 a week, this would obviously help.

Needing employment and income, he scoured the locality trying to secure something. Luckily for him, he didn't have to wait long or travel far. His old manager Frank J Law was still at the Montagu Arms and came to his rescue again. He offered Iron a regular job behind the bar. Iron very gratefully accepted.

He soon got into the barman routine and was very popular with the locals and visitors who dropped into meet this former champion.

Iron was pleased that his old boxing gym, in the low drop at the Montagu was still being used by a group of new up and coming boxers. He often went down there watching them train, offering individual advice to them and discussing tactics. They were very receptive to this former boxing giant's suggestions and invariably asked him about certain memorable fights he had been in. He made the place buzz. Boxing was on a bit of a revival and Tommy Stokes was also training a couple of lads there. One young boxer on the scene was Herbert Crossley and Iron befriended him.

The next fight in town was to be at the Empire on the 1st February when Walter Stenton from Leeds faced Billy Hague of Oldham (no relation). They were fighting at bantamweight. Hague had billed himself as "Cast Iron Hague" much to the

The Montague Arms today.

The Castle Hills War Memorial erected at Mexborough – the building of the memorials was greatly supported . It was a cause Iron Hague and his brother Johnny felt was well deserved and they assisted in fund raising.

amusement of the crowd. Hague screwed up his timetable and travel arrangements and ended up stranded at Doncaster. Without further ado, he speed walked the eight miles so not to let any one down.

Iron was undoubtedly still a celebrity and pointed out everywhere he went. Being the former Heavyweight Champion was almost as popular as being the former Prime Minister. He still kept his interest in the boxing scene.

He really had a laugh though when the newspapers printed a headline that made everyone read it twice and think.

"Iron Hague to fight at Rotherham on the 15th February 1919."

There was a lot of activity about erecting war memorials so that the war dead who sacrificed their lives would never be forgotten. Iron was very keen to be supportive of the movement. He would never forget the past comrades and saw it as his duty to do anything to help immortalise their memory.

Sergeant Johnny Regan was trying to raise funds for a memorial at Rotherham and approached Iron to appear as a novelty attraction and he agreed. He did actually step in the ring that night and boxed a sort of three round exhibition against his brother, Johnnie Hague. Johnnie was well familiar with Iron's medical problems and worked round him with them. The crowd loved it and Iron received a standing ovation.

On the same show was Dick Lawton who was now billed as "The Ten Stone Pitman's

Champion". He fought Ben Evans from Pontypridd. Lawton got the decision as Evans had to retire, still suffering from gas injuries received serving in the War.

Bombardier Billy Wells had defended well and was still the English Heavyweight Champion. Unfortunately, he lost a fight on the 8th March 1919 to Beckett, the Southampton Gypsy fighting at the Holborn Stadium. Wells was then aged 32 and struggled against the youngster. The fight was recognised by the N.S.C so the title was actually lost by Wells. Reminiscing on his career in the National Reporter, Wells intimated that he was never confident of beating Iron Hague at the time, even right up to the start of the sixth round when he knocked Iron out. The Reporter speculated on that if Iron had managed just one of his pistol like punches on Wells, the fight would have been over. It likened Wells and Moir to being gymnasium men, scientific boxers and that they were not true prize fighters who entertained when they fought by giving the crowd a fight to talk about.

Following the publishing of the interview, a White City greyhound was named after the former champion. "Iron Hague" went on to win many races.

Iron next appeared in public on the 21st March 1919 when he refereed a bout at the Empire. It was a fifteen round contest between Bert Day of London and Arthur Tracey of Darwen. They were both rising welterweights who were progressing up the ladder towards appearing at the N.S.C. The pair had met a few weeks earlier when Tracey was beaten on points by Day. Tracey wanted to reverse this decision so clearing the way to fight Johnny Basham and win a Lonsdale Belt. The only time that Iron was called to duty was when he had to warn both men about excessive clinching. The fight went the full distance and he gave the verdict at the end to Day once more. The crowd whole heartedly backed his decision.

The following week, Iron was back at the Empire again, this time acting as timekeeper for the night on all bouts for a promotion being run by Tommy Stokes. Tommy was venturing into being a promoter and was hoping for great success. He came a little unstuck at the next show on the 5th April. This show coincided with the Lord Mayors Parade at Sheffield and a lot of the townsfolk had ventured to the city to witness that event.

That night, Iron refereed the top of the bill fight between Dick Lawton and Barney Tooley. Tooley

Bombardier Tommy Stokes who saw War service himself.

was, as it transpired, in poor physical condition and no match for Lawton on the night. It was a lacklustre fight. On the same bill previous had been a local fight between Thompson and Squires who were both from Mexborough. Iron stopped the fight in the second round awarding the contest to Thompson.

Being a barman has its downside as every job does. In July, Iron found himself involved in a fight in the Montagu Arms helping to protect company property. One of the drinkers, a stranger who had enjoyed one too many, objected to Iron calling time and not serving him so in protest, he threw an ashtray through the hotel window. Frank Law was there at the time and asked the man to leave and he would then deal with him when he was sober. The man refused to leave becoming abusive, swearing at the top of his voice at Frank in front of the regulars. Frank asked Iron to eject the man, which he subsequently did. Following his arrest after the police had been called, the man then later claimed he had been assaulted by Iron. Iron explained to the judge at Doncaster that he had not used any excessive force. The "brief" acting for the victim accused Iron of failing to identify that his client was incapable of defending himself, to which Iron replied "Well he was alright to throw ashtrays". The brief told the judge that Iron was a former English boxing champion but the judge would have none of it. He found that Iron had no case to answer for but the drunkard had. He fined him the huge sum of £70.

A family tragedy occurred on the 20th September 1919 when news drifted out that Iron's uncle, William "Mickey" Bennett had died. He was only 57 and it was unexpected. Mickey, like his brother had been a professional footballer playing for Sheffield Wednesday between 1888 and 1892. At the age of 53, he had volunteered for service in France in the Army Service Corps. The division was the largest unit in the British army. It provided logistic support for the army. With both his sons serving in France, he wanted to contribute with his own war effort. Unfortunately, he was invalided out after a 144 days service because of bad rheumatism. He continued his war efforts as a volunteer, manning the town's Fire Brigade. His coffin was born from the church to Mexborough Cemetery by uniformed fireman aboard one of the fire tenders. Mickey was described as being, fiery and quick of temper, quick to condemn but equally as quick to forgive.

After the war, the issuing of medals to service men and women took some time due to the sheer volumes. Iron received his 1914-15 Star medal on the 1st March 1920 and then received his Victory medal on the 25th July 1921. The issue of the 1914/15 Star was authorised back in 1918. It was awarded to those individuals who saw service in France and Flanders between the 23rd November 1914 and the 31st December 1915.

The Victory Medal was authorised in 1919 and was awarded to all eligible personnel who served on the establishment of a unit participating in an operational war theatre.

Campaign :— 1914 ,5.

(A) Where decoration was earned.

(B) Present situation.

Name	Corps	Rank	Reg. No.	Medal	Roll	Page
(A) HAGUE	1 Gds	Pte	21499	VICTORY	85/103	563
(B) Jack W.				BRITISH	Do	Do
				15 STAR	35/1A	18

Action taken

THEATRE OF WAR.

(1) France

11.8.15.

QUALIFYING DATE.

Correspondence.

Address.

Iron Hague's War Medal Card as issued by the Grenadier Guards.

Chapter 30
The Herbert Crossley Affair

Herbert was born in Queen Street, Swinton, in May 1901 and was the third of four brothers. His two elder brothers were the first to encourage his boxing talents and they worked tirelessly to further his career.

Herbert Crossly the boxer. Iron took a great interest in him.

From an early, age he used to hero worship Iron Hague. As a youngster, he used to listen in awe to his adventures and later on, came under Iron's eye. Iron took an instant liking to young Herbert and encouraged him in his boxing.

Herbert's first contest was in 1917 when he met a Rotherham youngster at Mexborough's Empire Theatre. His opponent, Quinn, was no match for him and was unable to continue on after just two rounds. He took on four more opponents over the year notching up victories on them all, Goldthorpe's Billy Crummack went down at Mexborough, Frank Rylands of Doncaster was beaten on points and Young Heyland of Wombwell retired after eight rounds and lastly, Billy Crummack was beaten from a second time on a rematch, on points.

Like many Mexborough area boxers, Herbert worked in the pits by day. He worked for the Manvers Main Colliery Company. Herbert was physically very able and his fitness enabling him to take part in contests in quick succession. He next fought and won, "Luggy" Rodgers, another Mexborough lad who retired after four rounds, Billy Crummack, who was seemingly a mug for punishment was beaten for a third time, Dick Hepworth of Goldthorpe, "Tosh" Price of Mexborough and Iron's brother, George, who were both beaten on points. Sam Hyde of South Elmsall held him to a draw. His only loss was to another Mexborough boxer, Jack Stanton, who became the first to beat him on a points decision. Stanton was older and was and much more experience than Herbert. Nonetheless, it was a hard fight and Herbert fared well.

Herbert used to train at the rear of the Plant Hotel on Wath Road, Mexborough. Iron was a regular visitor to watch the youngster train. He spread the word of this

Boxing Poster for Herbert's brother Harry Crossley for a contest at the Plant Hotel, Wath Road, Mexborough

up and coming boxer to all. The Plant Hotel, situated on Wath Road, had a bowling green attached to it which was utilised to stage boxing shows. In the absence of venues in town, it became in demand.

As the wins started to notch up, Herbert was approached by promoters from further afield who could arrange more lucrative fights. Herbert appeared on bills at, Sheffield, Doncaster and Manchester.

Iron sent a message down to Peggy Bettinson to invite this lad down to the National Sporting Club in London for the next Novice knockouts. Peggy sent word back that he needed more wins first to strengthen his past record.

During 1919, Herbert completed five successive points victories, his opponents were, Young Cliffe (Sheffield), Charlie Woodhall (York), George Twelvetrees (Worksop), Harold Male (South Elmsall) and Tommy Greaves (Rotherham). His next two matches were both draws. These were over fifteen rounds against Seaman Hudson (Worksop) and Rotherham's, Sunny Crofts.

Iron contacted Peggy once more. This time he agreed that Herbert would be invited to the National Sporting Club to take part in a Novice Heavyweight competition.

Iron went down to London with Herbert. It was the first time Iron had been back to the N.S.C since before the war. Peggy was delighted to see Iron again. Frustratingly, Peggy kept introducing Herbert to others there as "another Iron Hague" without saying his name.

The first two fights of the competition saw wins over Sergeant Hilton and Sergeant Thomas, both within the first two rounds. Herbert then qualified to meet Seaman Merrilees in the final. Fight fans had nicknamed the Portsmouth sailor "Man Eater" as earlier he had fatally injured Joe Beckett's sparring partner.

The "Man Eater" was not able to turn it on against Herbert and the sailor was beat with Herbert the winner. While all the razzmatazz was going on, Iron sat alone thinking back to 1909 when he was there as the winner. So much water had gone under the bridge since then. Life was like a fast flowing stream, it never stops for you, moments can only be looked back on as they are gone by before you realise it.

As boxers go Iron and Herbert had differing styles. Iron Hague was the strong man, the hard puncher who would use brute force, whilst Herbert used a more scientific approach. Herbert kept a fine physique and looked the part of an athlete but he lacked the killer punch. Iron didn't do science, he just had guts. He was very strong in his upper body and would wade in taking blows, so to be in position to throw the deadly punches.

What Herbert lacked in punching power though he more than made up for it with ring technique. Speed, stamina, endurance, pluck and ring cleverness were among his attributes, these were ways of winning without actually delivering a knockout punch. This told in that nearly all Herbert's wins were on points, there were very few men failing to go the distance with him.

Herbert's next ring appearance was at Doncaster against Tommy Stokes, now billed as "of Dover", not Mexborough. Stokes had by now took work at the Snowdown Colliery in Kent, although he did not remain very long. The fight was a bit of a farce lasting only three rounds ending in the Swinton lad being disqualified. It was Herbert's rash youth, enthusiasm and inexperience that caused the problem. Up to then, Stokes was well beaten.

Will Brooks from Aberavon, a well known heavyweight nationally, was the next fight. It was a fifteen three minute rounds contest at the Sheffield Drill Hall and Herbert took the verdict in what was perhaps, his hardest fight to date.

Although his two elder brothers had been looking after his affairs, they had limits as to their achievements so Billy Bridgewater of Doncaster took over as manager. There were no arguments about this. Bridgewater had the necessary contacts to further Herbert's career it was agreed that his brothers would still look after his ring business.

Herbert's next fight was against Windsor's Barney Tooley who was beaten on points as so too was Harry Curzon of Derby. Curzon had fought for the British Light Heavyweight against Dick Smith in July 1916, a few years previous losing to the holder.

Continuing his winning streak, Herbert returned to London for his next contest which was against Harry Drake of Windsor, another leading contender for the lightheavy title. Herbert showed great fitness, style and performance beating Drake on points.

Herbert's next opponent was the seasoned Tom Berry of Custom House, London, a cruiserweight well in his thirties at the time. The fight was on the same bill as Joe Beckett versus Bombardier Wells, British Heavyweight clash. The ageless Berry proved to be a difficult opponent, Herbert was beaten over ten rounds at the Holborn Stadium. Showing great longevity, Berry won the British Lightheavy title in 1925 when nearly forty years of age.

Bridgewater told Herbert they needed to wipe this loss out and a rematch was set against Berry at Manchester's Free Trade Hall. On the day, things went wrong. Iron told him to get a taxi after his train let him down. It was essential to travel as smooth as possible. This related to Iron's London taxi trip when in the Guards to effect a fight.

The pressure got to Herbert and he was in a tense condition, fearing he would miss the bout. Although the fight took place as planned, his below par performance only gave him a draw.

The next fight gave Iron some problems as he had a foot in both camps. He knew and respected both lads and would not take sides. He commented "they will have to sort it out in the ring between them, my congratulations are to the winner and my condolences are to the loser".

Tommy Gummer, the Rotherham favourite was up for this contest, right on his doorstep. It made great interest being a local clash between two respected fighters. Only a few months earlier, Gummer had won the British Middleweight title with a fourteenth round TKO over Jimmy Sullivan of Bermondsey, London. It was a great career fight for Herbert.

The fight was to take place at Carbrook, Sheffield and was for Herbert, the highest purse so far, namely £147. The resultant verdict was a draw. The crowd believed Herbert should have just "nicked it". Both men fought hard. For once, Iron sat quiet throughout, studying both men.

A further fight with Tom Berry was now arranged and they met for a third time at Doncaster. Iron told Herbert he needed to apply a bit more brute force if he was to beat this man. He was a bit of an old fashioned fighter and could shut down the action quite easily. With a good local crowd roaring him on, Herbert was able to beat Berry and thus square up the series. It was a convincing points win.

Gus Platts

Tommy Gummer's main rival for supremacy in the middleweight ranks was another South Yorkshireman, namely Sheffield's Gus Platts.

After the draw with Gummer, it was considered a good match, to put Platts in with Herbert. It was a well attended fight as there was always a keen rivalry between towns and districts in South Yorkshire and Sheffield. Iron, in the past, had won the crowds over and given them something to shout about. In front of heavily supportive Platts' fans, the Swinton teenager beat the

"Blade Hero" over twenty rounds. To finish the year off, Herbert, in December 1920 went to the north east, where he beat Harry Shoop of London in a fifteen rounds contest held at Sunderland.

For his first match of 1921, Herbert was paired with one of boxing's former heroes, Harry Reeve. In 1916, Reeve was a former light heavyweight champion who had returned from the war with a bad leg injury. He had no option but to relinquish the title.

After a while, he made some recovery and was to make a comeback as a heavyweight. Herbert fought hard against this old war horse and it was one of the rare occasions when Herbert actually damaged and stopped his opponent to achieve victory, the fight ending in the thirteenth round.

In March 1921, Herbert, back at St James's Hall, Newcastle fought Frank Ray. Ray's real name was Paul Murray. He was some 6ft 3in tall weighing in at fifteen stone, a real heavyweight. Ray had previously beat Tom Gummer. Crossley suffered a severe setback as it was the first time he had not gone the distance in a fight.

The referee stopped the fight in favour of Ray in the seventh round. One real hard right knocked Herbert down for the first time in his career and he was lucky to survive the knockout.

In Herbert's next trip out he fought a fifteen round draw against Gordon Simms of Portsmouth and then he lost on points to Arthur Townley of Birkenhead.

One thing that narked Iron over Herbert Crossley was that Peggy Bettinson and his men had never invited him back to fight again for something worthwhile at the N.S.C. "What's the point of it all?", Iron reasoned if there was nothing more at the end of it than a silver Rose Bowl. One problem was that Herbert had never been totally accepted by the old establishment. He was yet another Yorkshireman. Ideally, they wanted a handy Londoner to take the merit.

With the drying up of money in a stagnant economy spreading into sport, it was fashionable for top British fighters to cross the Atlantic and try their luck in America. Charlie Harvey, the American link man, had seen Herbert fight in London and wanted him to try his luck in the States. This was something that Herbert agonised over. He discussed it with Iron who had no hesitation in telling the young man "Go where the money is, you only have so many fights in you, why fight for a bob when you can fight for half a crown?"

Boxer Jimmy Wilde offered him the same advice and so he decided to make the trip. Sheffield fighter, Gus Platts, had already left the country for America and Herbert was to join him. Herbert sailed alone on 20 August 1921, joining up with the Platts' party shortly after embarkation.

On 26 September 1921, Herbert had his first fight in America against the legendary

Gene Tunney in fighting pose. He fought Herbert Crossley.

Gene Tunney. At this time, Tunney was the Light Heavyweight Champion of the Expeditionary Force. The fight was at the "Dykeman Oval", New York. The fight, scheduled for fifteen rounds, was cut during the evening by mutual consent to seven rounds because of previous bouts over running it. This meant their fight was delaying the principal event of the evening. Incidentally, Gus Platts was also on the same bill earlier in the evening, fighting Mike McTigue.

Gene Tunney was in a different class to most boxers and although Herbert gave a good account on his American debut, Tunney won the contest comfortably on points. (Only a matter of months later, Tunney won the American Light Heavyweight championship and then in 1926, he won the World Heavyweight championship from Jack Dempsey.)

Herbert wrote home regularly. In his letter of October, he mentioned that two American heavyweights, Jim Coffey and Frank Moran, wanted to hire him for sparring bouts. Coffey, who was living in New York, was from Roscommon, Ireland. He was 6ft feet 1 inch tall and known as "the Roscommon Giant". Coffey's only European bout was on the 1st May 1919 in Dublin when he won with a K.O against Cyclone Billy Warren.

Moran had already seen Herbert fight in England and had been impressed on that occasion. Moran had previously fought the legendary black boxer, Jack Johnson, for the heavyweight crown back in 1914 and gone twenty rounds. There was talk of a fight between Herbert and Coffey but the latter declined.

In Herbert's next contest, he fought Al Roberts and was unfortunately beaten on points over ten rounds. The press said "He lost the decision but won the honours", the referee's verdict being manifestly against the opinion of the press and spectators.

The same night, Herbert had a rocketing temperature and felt unwell. The next day, he was confined to bed with what was thought to be an attack of influenza. The illness was, in fact, pneumonia ending in septicaemia. This was a poisoning of the blood and believed to have been brought about because of internal injuries. His fights were too close together.

Herbert, still only twenty years of age, died in Roosevelt Hospital, New York, just a few days later.

Herbert Crossley's gravestone in Swinton St Margarets Churchyard.

The public back home in South Yorkshire were shocked that this immensely popular athlete had been so tragically taken when so young and still only in his primary period as a fighter. Just days before his illness, he had agreed a two year deal to stay in America which would have been very lucrative for him.

Iron was very bitter as to what happened and when asked by a journalist for his opinion he said " If that's how you come back from fighting in America then unpack your trunk." It was his belief that the Brits taken to fight in the U.S were being given hard fights. They became fashionable career notches, to assemble on the American's fight records.

Although Herbert never became a British champion, he had done enough in his short career to justify his ranking as one of the best heavyweights to come from the north.

The Herbert Crossley funeral about to set off from the funeral parlour.

THE TIMES, SAT

A BOXER'S BURIAL.

HERBERT CROSSLEY'S REQUIEM.

A Sad "Homecoming."

The body of Herbert Crossley, the ill-fated young heavy-weight boxer, brought from New York, where he died of a species of pneumonia, found a final resting place in the Swinton Churchyard on Saturday afternoon. The remains of the gallant young fellow were followed from his home in Highwoods Road by a great company of his relatives, friends and admirers, while the churchyard was thronged with crowds of curious sight-seers. Among the numerous mourners were many who had at one time or another been prominent in local sport, and particularly in boxing. The pall bearers were mostly men who had made a name in the prize ring. They included "Iron" Hague and his brother George Hague, Tommy Stokes, Percy Calladine, F. Calladine, Ben Stevenson, Jack Stanton, and Gus Richards. Gus Platts, the well known Sheffield middle-weight boxer, who was with Crossley in America, and was the last person over here to see him in life, came over to the funeral and followed with Mrs. Platts.

The personal mourners included Mrs. Ellor (mother) and Mr. Ellor (step father), Mr. and Mrs. F. Crossley (brother and sister-in-law), Mr. and Mrs. Ernest Crossley (brother and sister-in-law), Mr. and Mrs. E. Needham (sister and brother-in-law), Mr. H. Crossley (brother), Mr. J. Gilbert (brother-in-law), Miss M. Crossley (sister), Mr. J. Ellor (brother), Mrs. J. W. Booth, Mrs. W. Pilling, Mrs. R. Whitworth, Mrs. H. Law, Mr. Y. Greenwood, Mr. R. Greenwood, Mr. J. Crossley, Mr. W. Howarth, Mr. and Mrs. A. Hepton, Mr. and Mrs. W. Harrison, Mr. and Mrs. E. Thompson, Mr. and Mrs. W. Cramphorn, Mr. J. and Mrs. T. Cramphorn, Mr. J. Crookes, Mr. and Mrs. C. Cramphorn, Mr. and Mrs. F. Gratton, Mr. and Mrs. T. Stead, Mrs. J. Brown, Mrs. M. Lovatt, Mrs. A. Hollings, Mrs. M. Sindalls, Mr. and Mrs. J. Hiendley, Mrs. J. C. Shaw, Mr. and Mrs. M. Hall, Mr. J. Rawson, Mr. and Mrs. G. Eccles, Mr. J. Watson, Mr. and Mrs. J. Hague, Mr. W. Bennett, Mr. and Mrs. W. H. Wadsworth, Miss M. Wadsworth, Mr. and Mrs. Gus Platts, Mr. and Mrs. J. W. Crookes, Mr. J. Gratton, Mr. G. Eccles, Mr. W. Davis, Mrs. E. Arrowsmith, Mr. J. Cragg, Councillor J. Siddall, Councillor J. Rawson, Mr. A. Fearne, Mr. G. Fowler, Mr. T. Price, Mr. A. Houssian, Mr. E. Sully, Mr. F. Walker, Mr. J. Walker, Mr. W. Gibson, Mr. O. Senior, Mr. G. Lindley, Mr. G. Petty, Miss F. Dorrington, Mr. J. Chambers, Mr. C. Morriss, Mr. H. Calladine, Mr. F. Finnan, Mr. W. Lawley, Mr. R. C. Schofield, and many others.

Mr. J. H. White, Mexborough, was the undertaker.

The route, which was by Bowbroom and Queen Street, was densely thronged with spectators, and the funeral party quite filled the spacious Parish Church.

The service was conducted by Dr. F. Hutchinson, Vicar of Swinton, and he took the opportunity of delivering a solemn and earnest address. "This our dear brother," he said, "calls to you to prepare to meet your God," and he developed this theme with great sternness and emphasis. "This man," he concluded, "has been brought from the other side of the world that he may rest here among you, and you are here to witness to the noble and clean and upright life of a man who tried to lift sport to a higher level. You can only give perfect witness by copying that life. The death of this dear fellow, taken in the pride of his young manhood, is one more warning to us all. Many of you who are here would give much to hear his voice again. It is speaking louder than ever. See that you listen."

A great number of beautiful wreaths were sent, and among those who sent these tributes were his Mother and Step-father, Brothers and Sisters, Step-sisters, Mr. J. Gilbert, Mrs. Whitworth, Mrs. Law (Shawforth, near Rochdale), Mr. Y. Greenwood and Mr. R. Greenwood, Mr. and Mrs. Gus Platts, Joe Com, Charlie Harvey, and Al. Roberts (New York), Sid Turner, Holt, and Buckley (New York), Edlington Comrades, Hardy's Billiard Hall, Roman Terrace Working Men's Club, Roman Terrace F.M. Athletic Club, Friends at Bowbroom, Mr. and Mrs. Gratton, Mr. and Mrs. Hindley, Mr. J. Kitts, Jack Stanton, Mr. and Mrs. Eccles, Mexborough Comrades, Mr. and Mrs. Hollings, Mr. and Mrs. Walker, Miss Nellie Wileman.

The obituary from the newspaper for Herbery Crossley

As soon as Iron heard the news, he went round to the family home to see Herbert's mother and step-father at Queen Street, Swinton. What could he say? It was just very, very bad luck.

Herbert's body was shipped back and his funeral was held on the 10th December 1921. Iron organised for the boxers of the area to become pall bearers and give him a send off he justly deserved. The funeral procession set off from Herbert's Highwoods home, winding its way to St Margaret's Church, Swinton, where his body was to be laid. The large procession of family and friends followed the horse-drawn hearse as it wound its way to Swinton. It went via Bow Broom and Queen Street. It was a Saturday afternoon and the churchyard was swelled with more mourners. The pall bearers were Iron, his brother George, Tommy Stokes, Percy Calladine and F Calladine (these were relations), Ben Stevenson, Jack Stanton and Gus Richards. Immediately behind them was Gus Platts. He had been the last there to see Herbert alive.

The service was conducted by Dr F Hutchinson who was very solemn in his address to the assembled. "This man has been brought here from the other side of the world that he may rest here amongst you and you are here to witness to the noble and clean upright life of a man who tried to lift sport to a higher level. You can only give perfect witness by copying that life. The death of this dear fellow, taken in the pride of his young manhood is one more warning to us all. Many of you who are here would give much to hear his voice again. It is speaking louder than ever. See that you listen."

The wreaths included those sent by Joe Com, Charlie Harvey and Al Roberts of New York.

The Crossley Plaque erected by Swinton Heritage situate at the junction of Queen Street and Church Street, Swinton.

CHAPTER 31
EEKING OUT

Iron remained at the Montagu Arms for another 10 years. His involvement in the active boxing scene became a little less as the years drifted by. This did not however, stop the lads from far and wide nipping in to have a drink and a chat with "Iron Hague".

His popularity did not seem to wane over the years. One local journalist commented that up and down the country, as soon as people knew you were from Mexborough the first thing they would ask you was "Do you know Iron Hague?"

One highlight for Iron and Lucy was that on the 26th April 1922, a second child was born. This was another daughter whom they called Agnes. At the time, Iron was nearly 37 years old, Lucy was aged 36 and sister Jane was now aged 12. As the baby of the family, she was treated with great kindness, perhaps a little spoilt by them all. Daughter Jane was nicknamed "Big Un" and Agnes "Babs" by the Hague's.

What is very strange at this time is that Iron's brother Johnny disappears altogether from the scene. No more news reports, no death or marriage notices are picked up, he just disappears. Apparently, Iron never referred of him to his daughters as they grew up and his existence was unknown to them. Although he was on photographs, no one in the family knew who he was. They were so close why would this be? One can only speculate!

During 1926, the town of Mexborough was reeling was from the general economic

The Montague Square taken from the Bank roof. This area was certainly the hub of Boxing in the town..

downturn. The General Strike started nationally on the 3rd May 1926 and lasted for 10 days. The country, under the chancellorship of Winston Churchill, had reverted back to a gold backed currency system. This placed the pound at a high value and made exports very expensive and industry suffered. Locally, the mine owners were trying to lower the miners' wages and increase their hours in an economic retaliation. The Trade Union Congress instigated the strike in sympathy. There was a severe knock on effect locally to all this and trade was in the doldrums. John (Iron's Father) was 58 years of age and still working at Denaby Colliery. With no work and no savings, things soon started to prove very tight and John could not keep up the rent on his house. To assist the situation, John and Ann moved in with Iron's brother, William and his wife.

During 1929, Iron was interviewed for the Topical Times about the boxing scene. He gave the following advice:-

"To the young people who are contemplating taking up the noble art of boxing as a career, don't get it into your head that as soon as ever you put on a pair of gloves, you are a boxer. If you are successful in your first contest, which may be a six round affair, don't think you are a champion and capable of knocking Gene Tunney's head off. The road to a championship is very rough and long and the progress must be slow. If you make your early progress too quickly, you will want a bigger "game" before you really understand the business.

You may succeed in getting a match with an old experienced hand and more likely than not, he will give you a jolly good hiding. This may shatter your hopes for good. It will not be physically, where you have suffered but mentally.

I could give you the names of a dozen young boxers in my own district who had apparently a great future but they have bitten off more than they can chew, received a good thrashing, threw away the gloves and then returned to work.

If you do make headway and become one of the "shining lights" of the country, don't think because you are able to box that it necessarily means you understand every detail of the business side of the question. The financial side of boxing is a great business. A shrewd manager can put thousands of pounds into the pockets of a successful boxer. I learnt all this when it was too late.

And last but not least, keep off intoxicating liquor. A boxer's career, at the best of times is very short and by the time you have reached the age of thirty, you will possibly be "on the shelf". If you have been successful and are the proud possessor of a nice little banking account, then if you wish it, drink to your heart's content but leave it alone during the few vital years of your boxing career.

Having got that off my chest, the best thing I can do is to drink up and have another. So here is to good health boys and jolly good luck to those who contemplate taking up the noble art of self defence."

Iron was trying to be very genuine in his advice. He resented the situation that he had been abused by boxing managers over the years. The one man he had a great word for was Frank J Law. He had tried to organise the young wayward man into a financially gratifying future.

The year 1930 saw a family event in that Iron and Lucy's daughter Jane married Alf Winnard of Barnsley. The wedding was at Mexborough Parish Church and an expense he had to find. The couple went onto live at Kendray, Barnsley after they were married. They had three children, providing the first of Iron's grandchildren.

Despite his long term disablement as a result of his First World War injuries as a barman, he still had to rise to the rigours of the job when necessary. One such situation arose on the 28th February 1931, this time involving his cousin William Bennett of Charles Street. Bennett was charged with unlawful wounding but this was later reduced to assault. It was a Saturday afternoon and Iron was on duty in the Low Drop bar. A crowd of people, including his cousin, were becoming very boisterous. One man, a coloured gentleman, was present and started using bad language to emphasise his point.

Iron, wanting to avoid confrontation, went to fetch the landlord to let him decide what he wanted to do. On their return, the coloured man and Bennett were still there. Iron went round the bar to confront them again. As he got up to them, Bennett picked up a glass from the counter and smashed it over Iron's head. A large fragment hit a customer, Charlie Hodkin, causing him a wound just under his eye.

The case was heard at Doncaster Court. The barrister representing Bennett questioned Iron. He asked Iron to confirm that he was the former English Heavyweight champion. Iron did this, also confirming that he especially had no problem with coloured men. The barrister tried to infer that Iron held a deep grudge following his defeat by Sam Langford. Iron replied that this was ridiculous, he had met and fought coloured men and they remained his friends. Bennett claimed that Iron hit him on the nose first and that he was acting in self defence which Iron denied. The barrister then went on to say that Iron was a "chucker out" at the Montagu and his reputation was at stake. Iron denied this and said he was employed as a barman. There were further allegations that Iron had to be restrained by three of his relatives to prevent him from attacking Bennett further.

Charlie Hodkin, the customer, was called to the stand and he confirmed that it was Iron who was attacked and that Bennett and his crew should be ashamed of themselves.

Detective William Lee told the court that when he went to charge Bennett the next day. Bennett said he regretted using the glass. Bennett also said that he thought he had no chance against a man like Iron. Bennett told the court that he had only drunk three pints and was rational and sober the whole of the time.

Staff and Holiday makers at the Grangers Holiday Camp at Bridlington.

Inspector Redfern told the Magistrates that a lot has been said about Iron that day but from his experience, "He was not a callous brute." The bench decided that Iron was telling the truth and Bennett was duly fined forty shillings.

Shortly after this incident, Iron suffered a severe setback in that he developed double pneumonia. He was laid low for some time and lost his job as a barman.

Not to be outdone, Iron searched far and wide to get back into work. Surprisingly, he went to take up employment at a holiday camp at Bridlington. Owners, Ted and Margaret Granger, were quite revolutionary in the emerging holiday industry. Like their counterpart, Billy Butlin, they had opened a holiday camp where families could enjoy an inexpensive holiday by the sea. To the miners of the Dearne Valley, this

The Grangers Holiday camp abutted up to the sea south of Bridlington.

Holiday Makers and their children enjoy the sands near Grangers Holiday Camp. It was a great release from the mundane industrial strife of their hometown's.

gave a welcome break to the hours of underground toil they endured.

Lucy did all the cooking for the residents and Iron acted as "paraffin lad", filling all the chalet heaters up as well as carrying out general handyman duties. To take this position, they could not take their children so that twelve year old Agnes continued to live with her grandparents, John and Anne at Phoenix Street, Mexborough.

The camp was situated a few miles south of Bridlington. Access to the town from the camp was via a long walk along the cliff top and then catching a bus for a short ride. The accommodation generally consisted of small wooden chalets, which were described by visitors as being like dolls houses. Each chalet was individually named like "the Moorings". Some of the chalets were converted from railway carriages. There was also a wooden chapel on site where the local vicar took services in the summer for the visitors. As the work was seasonal, Iron and Lucy would return home in the autumn and winter.

After Agnes reached the age of thirteen, she left school and went to Bridlington to join her parents. She found employment in service to a Mrs Bainbridge who operated one of Scarborough's increasing number of hotels.

They all stayed at Bridlington for a few years before returning home to Phoenix Street, Mexborough. Once permanently home, Iron applied to Mexborough Urban District Council for a new property and took over a council house at 36 Washington Street. The deal was done and Iron, Lucy, Agnes, John and Anne all moved in. In the meantime, Jane's young husband had died and she decided to return to Mexborough to take on the tenancy of Phoenix Street.

Iron and his wife Lucy on duty at Grangers Holiday Camp

Daughter: Jane Hague

To sustain an income, daughter "Janie" secured employment at the Bull's Head on High Street, Mexborough. She had indeed taken on her father's stature of being well above any average size. She was tall and some twenty four stones in weight. She could carry fourteen pints of beer at a time, which was some feat. Her personality was lovely, a gentle giantess, she didn't drink alcohol or smoke and always had time for anyone who wanted to talk. On her other side, she would take no nonsense and got a reputation of being able to throw out a troublesome punter as easy as shelling peas. She was the "bouncer" there when things got rough. She could whip the troublemakers out like ninepins. Somebody would open her the pub door and out they would go.

The earnings of the last few years had only enabled Iron to eek out a living and on return, things were not good. Lucy and Iron were enduring great financial hardship as the late 1930's unfurled. This did not go unnoticed. Someone who knew Iron well contacted a reporter who penned an article for the press to highlight the severe plight Iron was in.

Someone then contacted Iron's old Regiment to see if anything could be done through them. The following letters were written;

AB.

GG/Docs/21499.
The Rev. E.B.A. Somerset, MA.,
I.S. & S.H. Society,
Mexborough Vicarage,
Rotherham,
Yorks.

22nd March, 1939.

Dear Sir,

The Lieutenant-Colonel Commanding the Regiment has heard that J.W. Hague, more commonly known as Iron Hague, an ex-member of this Regiment, is in distressed circumstances and in need of assistance.

He would be very grateful if you would endeavour to see the man and let him have details of his circumstances, and for this purpose I am enclosing one of our Regimental Forms of Investigation.

The man's address on enlistment was 22 Orchard Street, Mexborough, but he may have left this address, though it is known that he still resides in Mexborough. The attached newspaper cutting may possibly be of some assistance to you.

It is hoped that this request will not cause you any unnecessary trouble or inconvenience.

Yours faithfully,

Captain.
Regimental Adjutant Grenadier Guards.

AB. GG/Docs/21499

The Rev. E.H. Rawkins,

I.S. & S.H. Society,

Mexborough Vicarage,

Rotherham,

Yorks. 22nd March, 1939.

Dear Sir,

I have been informed by the Reverend E.B.A. Somerset that he has passed my letter to him dated 2nd March, to you, as you are his successor as the representative of the Incorporated Soldiers' and Sailors Help Society for Mexborough.

I should be very pleased if you will inform me whether you are able to accede to the request contained in the letter and let me have a report on the circumstances of J.W. Hague, an ex-member of this Regiment.

Should this be possible I should be grateful if you will report as soon as possible as the Lieutenant-Colonel Commanding the Regiment is anxious to deal with the matter without any undue delay.

Yours faithfully

Captain,

Regimental Adjutant Grenadier Guards.

Steel, Peach and Tozers works at Rotherham where Iron found employment.

Nothing apparently came from this as Iron was a very proud man and would not accept charity, despite all he had been through.

As the Second World War came in, Iron was determined to do his bit and volunteered as a fire watcher. He also obtained work as a gateman on the security staff at the Steel, Peach and Tozer works.

The company plant was at Templeborough. It was huge, being over a mile long and employing some 10,000 people. Iron and steel production had been on the site since the late 18th century. He stayed in this occupation for several years. One thing that interested him and that interested his employer was the Steel, Peach and Tozer Boxing Club. Iron used to wander over and watch the youngsters in training. One of the boxers there in 1946 was his great nephew, Richard James, who lived in Wharfe Road, Kilnhurst. He used to pass on tips to each fighter on a one to one basis and his visits were very welcomed.

He enjoyed a bit of a celebrity status with visitors to the works being introduced to the former English Heavyweight Champion.

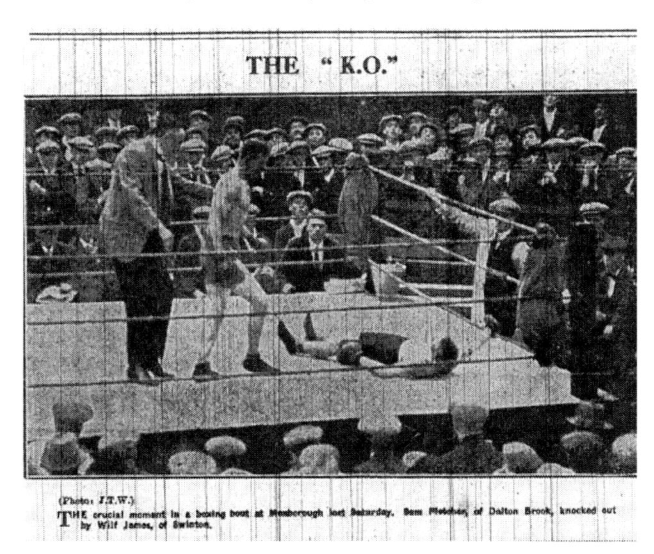

THE "K.O."

(Photo: J.T.W.)
THE crucial moment in a boxing bout at Mexborough last Saturday. Sam Fletcher, of Dalton Brook, knocked out by Wilf James, of Swinton.

Iron's relation ,the young Wilf James, knocking out his opponent.

One of his "party pieces" whilst there was still being able to pick up two 56lb weights, standing with one gripped in each hand with arms partly held out from his body. By this time he was aged in his 50's.

Family celebrations took place in April 1941 when youngest daughter Agnes married serving soldier Clarence Ruecroft. The wedding took place again at the local parish church.

John and Ann Hague (Iron's Parents) sat with their granddaughter Jane behind them holding their great grandchild.

After the wedding, they also moved into the Washington Street house.

A family bereavement took place on the 18th September 1942 when Iron's mother, Ann, died. Her funeral was on the 22nd September 1942. She and John were living with Iron and Lucy at their 36 Washington Street home at the time.

The ending of the war brought great celebrations but the following year, 1946, was a bad year for the Hague family.

It was in 1946, whilst at the Steel, Peach and Tozer works that Iron fell over and broke his hip. He was taken to Rotherham Hospital for treatment. This accident terminated his working career. The combination of this with his war injuries meant he had to heavily depend on a leg support.

After a bout of failing health, Iron's wife, Lucy, died on the 16th May 1946. She was 59 years of age. Her funeral was on the 19th May and it was well attended. Iron took her death very badly. He missed her so and his own health started to notably deteriorate.

One uplift for them all during this year was the birth of twins to Aggie and Clarence. Reggie and Jeanette were two more grandchildren.

Further tragedy occurred in 1946 when Iron's father, John Hague, aged 78, died on the following 11th December. His funeral was on the 15th December. His funeral eulogy remarked how he had been quite a sportsman himself in his

Iron's house situated on Washington Street, Mexborough.

early days. It also said how he had worked forty eight years underground at Denaby Main Colliery. Iron was unfortunately struck down with a virus and was unable to attend his father's funeral. This was very upsetting for him and demonstrates the seriousness of his illness.

The smaller house at Byron Road, Mexborough that Iron moved to from Washington Strreet.

Such was Iron's popularity at his former employer Steel, Peech and Tozer that he was regularly invited back by his old mates, particularly for matters to do with the boxing club.

One boxer Iron took a keen interest in and to whom he offered coaching tips was as mentioned previous, his great nephew, Richard James. Richard lived in Wharfe Road, Kilnhurst. He was related to Iron through his wife's sister. She was Richard's grandmother.

Richard trained at the Commercial Public House, Victoria Street, Kilnhurst. He started boxing training whilst in his early teens enjoying good success. He entered the Amateur Boxing Association's National Competition in 1947 and succeeding in becoming a junior champion.

Bruce Woodcock stands aside his "Winners Trophy"

Following the losses over recent years, Iron became very unsettled with the Washington Street house, probably too many sad memories for him. After some persuasion, daughter "Aggie" applied to move and they were re-housed to 13 Byron Road, Mexborough.

Aggie was very concerned about her father's faltering health and wanted what was best for him. Another grandchild, Ann, was born shortly after.

One visitor to Iron, whilst he was at Byron Road in 1950, was none other than boxing champion, Bruce Woodcock.

Back in July 1945, at the White Hart Lane football stadium of Tottenham Hotspurs, Woodcock had defeated Jack London to take the British and Empire heavyweight titles. Woodcock won by a knockout in round six. London had struggled and was down on the canvas three times previously in the final round. This win also secured the Empire title which, along with the British title, was held by Jack London. On the 29th July 1946 Woodcock won the vacant European title by a sixth round K.O over Frenchman Albert Rene.

Then in 1947 at Harringay, London, Woodcock showed gutsy determination when he fought Joe Baksi. Although floored three times in the first round and twice in the second, he kept coming back. The referee finally stopped the fight in the seventh.

On 2nd June 1949, Woodcock beat Freddie Mills in defence of the British and European and Empire heavyweight titles by a KO in 14/15.

As Iron had been a former holder of the title, he said it was an honour to visit and meet the former champion. The visit was spurred on by the media who had flagged up on Iron's failing health and yet another bout in hospital.

Iron appeared with him a couple of times at boxing shows when they were both introduced to the adoring fans. A film about boxing called "Champion" starring Kirk Douglas was shown at the Gaumont at Doncaster and Iron, accompanied by daughters Jane and Aggie and his grandchildren Reg and Jeanette, went on the bus to see it. He was specially invited as a guest of honour. Before the show, Woodcock and Iron had their picture taken together, standing on the steps of the Gaumont cinema. Also on the picture is Iron's great nephew, Richard James.

Iron is seen here at the Gaumont cinema in Doncaster with Bruce Woodcock to his left and Richard James to the right.

The rugged looking Bruce Woodcock.

An Elderly Iron shows Bruce Woodcock he is still able to punch the bag.

At the Gaumont Cinema Doncaster watching the new film

Iron was still held in high esteem by the town's folks and many children were taken to Byron Road to see this fine old gentleman – the former English Heavyweight Champion. Dave Caress remembers such a visit well. He resided nearby and all his brothers and himself were all treated to this. He remembers Iron sat in a large leather chair in the corner and how he always talked to the kids.

By 1951, Iron's health continued to deteriorate. He could only walk ten yards or so before having to sit down. He was down to just eight stones in weight.

He caught a chill that progressed into pneumonia and he became confined to bed. He then drifted into a coma. Aggie called the doctors out five times and each time they told her to expect the worst. In true "Iron" style, he took no notice of them and rallied each time.

The former and current Heavyweight champions meet.

Elderly Iron Hague in fighting pose.

On the 18th August 1951, Iron was laid down on the settee .The fire burned fiercely in the hearth to bring warmth to Iron's aching bones. Aggie sat in the chair overlooking her dad. He then suddenly called out " Babs, come and hold my hand", which she did. He then died.

Iron's funeral was no spectacular affair. The Daily Mail commented upon there only being a handful at his funeral. The only representatives from the world of boxing were Matt Wadsworth, a contemporary of Iron's and local boxing promoter, Sid Breeze. (Sid had boxed 1925 to 1927.)

Following Iron's death, the press started digging into their archives for past pieces on Iron's boxing career. One of the top boxing writers of the day commented, saying:-

"One factor that generally counts for more than any other in boxing morale is whatever other assets and deficiencies a fighter carries to the fray, it is the truism that he must carry optimism as well as a will to win. He must believe that he can do it, he must fancy the job!"

No one could ever criticise Iron for not believing in his own fighting ability. He would go wading in regardless of the size, colour, age or past performance of any opponent. He would without any fear, take on all comers.

Once when speaking regards himself and the past, he commented to a Mexborough audience how "he had always tried to not only put up a good performance but also to stand out, by making that extra effort." He told how it didn't always work out, but nonetheless, he had always tried and that was a lot to do with his success "

James William Hague

THE CHAMPION NOW RESTS.

Oil Painting of Iron Hague painted by Lancaster. It is believed it was painted in 1911 just before Iron's title defence.

Iron Hague – A Financial Evaluation.

Statuettes of Roman Boxers recovered from an archaeological dig in England.

Boxing had been carried out in contest form for centuries. The ancient Greeks held regular fight competitions, as did the Romans. Whilst one could argue that the fighters may have been slaves, history tells us they were well looked after.

In England, for centuries, the earnings of top fighters were recorded as being very respectable. The likes of James Burke, Thomas Sayers, The Tipton Slasher and Jem Mace, for example, all enjoyed financial success from the large amounts of prize money made available.

The trend for high purses continued even after the introduction of gloves. The public would always hand good money over to see a contested fight, particularly from two heavyweights. The Americans enjoyed considerable wealth from their success in the ring.

This was emphasised in the famous Jack Sharkey quote:-

"Dempsey hit me hardest, 'cos Dempsey hit me two hundred eleven thousand dollars' worth, while Louis only hit me thirty-six thousand dollars' worth."

Although not at the size of the American purses, the successful British boxers of Edwardian times did enjoy a substantial wealth.

The difference today is the additional sponsorship of media and television, which greatly enhances the pay days with the extra payments made for worldwide broadcast and TV rights .

Jack Dempsey famously said "When you are fighting, you're fighting for one thing......money."

However, just being a boxer was no guarantee of income. It depended on results.

Gem Mace

In Iron's case, I don't think this applied. I believe that taking part in the fight was his prime motivator, cash earnings came secondary .

He just loved being in the ring. Like a gladiator, he would face all comers regardless. He rose to the occasion. He would stare intently at his opponent, looking to strike up fear and then justify this in the fight with a series of hard smashing right punches.

Importantly, he had belief in his own abilities, he knew he was special, a force to be reckoned with.

The cash was very useful but he treated it as a by-product of the ring.

Below is listed the actual career earnings of Iron. Most are from official records but when absent, an average has been used. The figures take into account normal deductions made for trainer/managers and includes the customary donation also made to the boxer from the successful backer out of his bet winnings.

Often additional money would be earned by the fighter from placing bets through others on the outcome. This is not taken into consideration below.

Iron Hague Earnings summary

Date	***Opponent***	***£***
04.08.1904	A White	25
02.01.1905	Dan Lewis	25
c15.02.1905	Tommy Stokes	25
08.04.1905	Dick Parkes	65
04.08.1905	Albert Rodgers	50
00.09.1906	Tommy Stokes	25
08.12.1906	Charlie Knock	25
	Tommy Stokes	Lost (KO.3)
09.01.1907	Shoeing Smith Randall	50
16.01.1907	Trooper Gibson	50
30.01.1907	Tom Horridge	75
28.10.1907	Jack Scales	50
26.12.1907	Fred Drummond	25
15.01.1908	Seaman Frank "spoff" Drummond	0
16.01.1908	Tom King	0

20.01.1908	George Turner	0
20.01.1908	Jack Gibson	0
20.01.1908	Harry Croxley	0
20.01.1908	Alf Pearson	25
16.03.1908	Frank Craig	50
11.05.1908	Jack Scales	150
01.06.1908	Corporal Sunshine	75
19.10.1908	Charlie Wilson	75
14.12.1908	Ben Taylor	150
11.02.1909	Bob Fitzsimmons	200
06.03.1909	Canon , Walker and Hague	150
	Bob Fitzsimmons	Exhibition
19.04.1909	Gunner Moir	600
25.05.1909	Sam Langford	450
11.02.1910	Petty Officer Curran	150
21.02.1910	Jewey Smith	150
26.05.1910	Corporal Sunshine	150
15.08.1910	Private William (Brickie) Smith	250
07.11.1910	Corporal Brown	250
05.12.1910	Jewey Smith	250
02.01.1911	Corporal Sunshine	250
30.01.1911	Bill Chase	300
24.04.1911	Bombardier Bill Wells	350 (Weight Title)
08.07.1912	Jimm Robb	100
05.08.1912	Tom Cowler	also promoter

Career Earnings circa £4465

From this figure, one should deduct 10% to cover other costs, personal costs and regular sparring partners. This still leaves £4019 available funds over the seven year period.

Iron lived in low cost rented property and did not exhibit any personal extravagances. If one considers that his annual home expenditure probably ran to around £130 a year, this would account for some £910 over this period. This leaves an amount of money that Iron spent over this period of £3109. When you consider a man's annual wage was around £150 a year, it was a huge sum. It was equivalent to over 20 years' earnings for most of his fellow townsfolk.

This would amount to some £1,258,000.00 in today's prices; a large amount of surplus cash.

Iron's 'carry on' was like owning a special sports car. When the tank was full, he would drive as quick and fast as he possibly could. Anyone could ride in the car and many wanted to. As the fuel tank approached empty, the car was parked up and everyone disappeared. That is until money appeared once more to fill it back up, then off he would go again, that is until it emptied once more.

By the time he enrolled into the army, he was virtually fund less with no savings.

Iron had an enviable earnings record but possessed no financial skills, just like many of other fighters before him. He struggled to manage or hang onto his wealth. He was not versed in financial skills and had no-one to advise him, he struggled to even read and this made him easy pray for exploitation.

For investment, he could have, for example, quite easily have funded the building of several new houses. One house for him to live in rent free then drawing down regular rental incomes from the remainder. This would have given him a guaranteed income stream and something to pass on to his children. Back then, only 10 % of the population were homeowners. Iron well had the ability to have joined the property owner set.

In Mexborough in 1910, a building plot on Church Street, with permission to erect six cottages, was sold for £205 14shillings. The build cost of the cottages by G H Smith Building contractors was £675.

The trap he fell into was that befalling many a young fighter, the belief that he could go on for ever ..... it didn't matter spending your winnings as there would be plenty more to come.

Iron Hague Fight Record

Date	*Opponent*	*Location*	*Result*
1900	Tommy Stokes	Denaby	Won (KO – 4)
1902	Unknown	Mexborough	Won (KO – 2)
13.12.1903	William John Hewitson	Hooton Roberts	Won (Bare Knuckle)
04.08.1904	A White	Manchester	Won (Points)
22.11.1904	Jack Lamb	Warrington	Exhibition
02.01.1905	Dan Lewis	Doncaster Drill House	Won (KO – 3)
c15.02.1905	Tommy Stokes	Doncaster Drill House	Won (KO)
08.04.1905	Dick Parkes (Won Yorkshire Heavy Weight Title)	Doncaster Drill House	Won 5th Round
04.08.1905	Albert Rodgers (Defence of Yorkshire Heavy Weight Title)	Doncaster Drill House	Won 6th Round
00.09.1906	Tommy Stokes (Undertook to stop his man inside scheduled 8 minutes but failed and so lost on points)	Mexborough	Lost on Points – 8
08.12.1906	Charlie Knock	Victoria Drill Hall, Sheffield	Lost (KO – 3)
09.01.1907	Shoeing Smith Randall	Fulford Barracks	Won (KO – 4)

Date	Opponent	Venue	Result
16.01.1907	Trooper Fred Gibson	Fulford Barracks (York)	Won (KO – 1)
30.01.1907	Tom Horridge	Fulford Barracks (York)	Won (KO – 2)
28.10.1907	Jack Scales	Sheffield Carver St	Draw (6th Round)
26.12.1907	Fred Drummond	Sheffield Carver St	Won (KO – 2)
15.01.1908	Seaman Arthur “Spoff” Drummond	NSC London	No decision 4
16.01.1908	Tom King (1st series “Novices Heavyweight Competition”)	NSC London	Won (KO – 2)
20.01.1908	George Turner (2nd series “Novices Heavyweight Competition”)	NSC London	Won (KO – 1)
20.01.1908	Jack Gibson (3rd series “Novices Heavyweight Competition”)	NSC London	Won (KO – 2)
20.01.1908	Harry Croxon (Semi-final “Novices Heavyweight Competition”)	NSC London	Won (KO – 3)
20.01.1908	Alf Pearson (Won final “Novices Heavyweight Competition)	NSC London	Won (KO – 1)
16.03.1908	Frank Craig	Sheffield Carver Street	Won (KO – 4)
11.05.1908	Jack Scales	Sheffield Carver Street	Won (KO – 2)
01.06.1908	Corporal Sunshine	NSC London	Won (KO – 4)

19.10.1908	Charlie Wilson	NSC London	Won (KO – 5)
14.12.1908	Ben Taylor	NSC London	Won (KO – 1)
11.02.1909	Bob Fitzsimmons	Sheffield	Exhibition
06.03.1909	Canon, Walker and Johnny Hague	Hull Empire	Exhibition 3 Round with each
25.03.1909	Tom Stokes	Withernsea Assembly Rooms	Exhibition 3
16.04.1909	Dick Parks, Tom Stokes, Harry Fellowes	Mexborough	Exhibition 3
19.04.1909	Gunner Moir	NSC London	Won (KO – 1)
	(Won British Heavyweight Title – was formerly English Heavyweight Title)		
25.05.1909	Sam Langford	NSC	Lost (KO – 4)
03.05.1909	Charlie Knock	Hull	Exhibition 3 Night
??.12.1909	John WH Douglas	NSC London	Exhibition 3
11.02.1910	Petty Officer Matthew Curran	Plymouth	Lost (KO – 15)
	(Billed British Heavyweight Title – not recognised by NC as not held there)		
21.02.1910	"Jewey" Smith	Sheffield City Club	Lost (Points)
	(NB as for 11 February bout)		
17.03.1910	Jim Styles	Mexborough	Exhibition
26.05.1910	Corporal Sunshine	Liverpool (The Arena)	Lost (Points)
	(NB as for 11 February bout)		

Date	Opponent	Venue	Result
15.08.1910	Private William (Brickie) Smith (NB as for 11 February bout)	Attercliffe, Sheffield	Won
07.11.1910	Corporal Brown (NB as for 11 February bout)	Attercliffe, Sheffield	Won (KO – 18)
05.12.1910	Jewey Smith (NB as for 11 February bout)	Attercliffe, Sheffield	Won (Points)
02.01.1911	Corporal Sunshine (NB as for 11 February bout)	Mexborough Olympia	Won (KO - 9)
30.01.1911	Bill Chase (Official British Heavyweight Title)	NSC London	Won (KO – 6)
24.04.1911	Bombardier Bill Wells (Lost Official British Heavyweight Title)	NSC London	Lost (KO – 6)
08.07.1912	Jim Robb	Mexborough	Won (KO – 1)
05.08.1912	Tom Cowler	Mexborough	Lost (KO – 9)
1913	Inactive due to ill health		
1914	Inactive due to ill health		
04.08.1914	Outbreak of First World War		
21.12.1914	Joined Grenadier Guards as a Private, a rank at that time recognised in the Guards. It wasn't in favour of Guardsman until later.		

Whilst in Military Service

13.02.1915	Private Frank Wright	Caterham	Won (KO – 1)
15.03.1915	Sergeant Pat O'Keefe	Caterham	Exhibition 3
27.03.1915	Bandsman Dick Rice	Edgeware (West London Stadium)	Lost (Points – 15)
03.07.1915	Tom Gummer	Sheffield	Lost (KO – 10)
02.08.1915	Harry Curzon DCM (Derby)	Chelsea, Stamford Bridge	Lost (KO – 3)
11.08.1915	Gunner Gray	Harfleur (France)	Exhibition 3
23.08.1915	Charlie Knock	Harfleur (France)	Draw 6
07.09.1915	Gunner Joe Mills (better known as Bombardier Tamlyn)	Harfleur (France)	Won (KO)
15.02.1919	Johnny Hague	Rotherham	Exhibition 3
NB	Untraced but claimed – Bill Elliott	??	Won (KO – 3)

NB On 22 January 1910 "Boxing" Tom Duckett (Goole) claimed he won a knockout in round 2 over Iron Hague in a booth somewhere in Yorkshire, in what would have been Hague's first ever loss – this was very early in Hague's career. If true it would contradict "Iron" Hague's own statement (made many times) that he never lost a booth fight. Also the statement on 3 May 1909 in Sporting Life that Charlie Knock was the only man to beat "Iron" Hague ,until then. Strangely enough, Duckett's claim was never denied by either "Iron" Hague or his backers but the truth of the statement will almost certainly never be known.

Background to the Town of Mexborough

Mexborough was a growing town situated in the heart of the South Yorkshire coalfield. Its origins were early, prior to the Doomsday Book. A public park, Castle Hills, contains early earthworks, remaining from a motte and bailey castle.

The town had its own fifteen strong town council and offered electricity and gas to its residents. The town had several elementary schools and later a Grammar and a Secondary School. The Montagu Hospital opened in 1905. The Church of St John's had origins from the 12th century. The town had two Church of England Churches and several other places of worship.

The whole town was a hive of industry. The coalmines were undoubtedly the largest employer and their expansion saw many families migrate from all over Britain. The other chief industries were the Phoenix Glass works of Thomas Barron's, the New Don Glass Works of Peter Waddington, Cottam and Co's Spring works, Verity's Railway Wheel and Wagon works, Grocock and Sons Wagon works, Brickworks at Doncaster Road and Lower Dolcliffe Road, the Don Corn Mill, Guest's Boat Yard, The Times Electric Printing works and nearby were the South Yorkshire Glass Bottle works, Ellison and Mitchell Chemical works and the Hattersley' Brothers Iron Foundry.

The population in 1909 was 13261 with some 3000 houses. The town was serviced by the Great Central Railway and had a tram system linking it into Rotherham, Sheffield and other outlying areas. The town featured many pubs and Working Men's Clubs as well as a brewery.

It was very sports orientated with football, cricket and hockey teams competing in various leagues. Hampden Road made an attractive sporting ground.

Addendum-So what happened To ...?

1) Iron Hague's Managers/ Trainers/Backers
Francis J Law – Manager

After his final bust up with Iron Hague, he continued on his interest in local sports. He operated training facilities in boxing as well as promoting football and cricket for the town.

After 20 years of running the Montagu Arms, his health deteriorated and so he sold up and retired. His wife, Jane, with whom he had six children, (five daughters and a son) died, leaving him a widower. He remarried to Mrs Newbert, the widow of Mr T W Newbert, the former licencee of the Terrace Inn at Kilnhurst.

His retirement did not last long as after four months of boredom, he came out of retirement and took over the less demanding tenancy of the Woodman Inn at Swinton. He died in March 1928 aged 69. His funeral was held at Brampton Bierlow church. Iron Hague was present along with his wife Lucy as mourners at the funeral ceremony.

F J Laws gravestone sits in Brampton Churchyard.

Thomas Weston – Financial backer

Mr & Mrs Tommy Weston's Gravestone is the largest in Mexborough cemetery.

He remained as the landlord of the Reresby Arms (the Pig) Denaby until 1915 when he then retired. He then returned back to the Birmingham area from where he originally hailed. He rejoined the community he left and became embroiled in local sporting interests. He retained his interest in boxing throughout. His retirement was long standing and he lived in some style.

He died in the 27th November 1932 at the ripe old age of 85. His wife Elizabeth had died in 1927.

As per his wishes, his body was brought back to Mexborough to be interred in the cemetery alongside his son. Such was his standing amongst the local community that his funeral was a very large affair.

The Reresby Arms public house is also sadly no more. It was demolished in 2008. Its nickname of "the Pig" originated from the inclusion of pigs in the family crest of the Reresby family after whom the pub was named. The Reresby Estate, which owned the property, was based at Thryburgh. It was the major landowner around Denaby.

William Biggs Junior – Trainer and Manager's Assistant

After his Father had died, his business association with Iron Hague ceased. He had worked at the Bull's Head alongside his father and assisted in the boxing training and management in the past.

He continued at the Bull's Head, taking over the licence from his father but he did not have his same integrity. He ran an illegal bookmaking operation from the premises. After discovery, he was duly convicted by the police and lost his licence so vacating the premises. This offence was seriously frowned upon by the authorities at the time.

He did not learn the ill of his ways and was convicted again on the 16th October 1915 for the offence of street betting. To make matters worse, he had resisted arrest at the time, lashing out and attempting to escape. He was pursued and formerly arrested. He was charged both with illegal bookmaking and with assaulting a police officer. He received a month's prison sentence.

Upon release, he continued to live in Mexborough.

2) Iron Hague's Boxing Opponents

Frank Craig – The Coffee Cooler (fought 16th march 1908)

After he fought Hague on the 16th March 1908, US born Frank remained in England. He was treated as an equal in sport and continued boxing on a regular basis, right through the years until 1912. Thereafter, his long career of around 150 fights tapered off. In 1910, he became embroiled in a police case in London where a woman was killed. He had supplied a gun to a coloured woman who then shot another woman dead. The police considered him an accessory. He stated he had got her the gun as she was the only coloured woman in a tenement block and it was for her protection. As the police could not prove any other, he was later released without charge.

He remarkably reappeared in the ring in 1922, boxing against Jim Rideout of London. At the time, he was some 54 years old. He died in January 1943 aged 75 at Chelsea, London and is buried in Finchley Cemetery.

Samuel Langford – the Boston Tar Baby (fought 25th May 1909)

Jack Johnson in fighting pose.

Sam Langford was a boxer who fought greats from lightweights right up to heavyweights. He fought and beat many champions in the process. Surprisingly, he was never able to secure a world title for himself.

The main reason for this was that heavyweight champion, Jack Johnson, after winning their first match, refused any rematches back against Langford. Langford was considered by many to be the most dangerous challenger for the taking of Johnson's Heavyweight crown. Johnson always denied this and cited Langford's inability to meet his $30,000 appearance fee as being the reason.

Langford's most memorable fights were his numerous encounters against fellow black boxers, Sam Mcvey, Jim Johnson and Joe Janette. They were all great fighters who all experienced racial prejudice barriers during their long fighting careers.

Langford, over a long career, had many fights. For example, he fought Harry Wills on seventeen separate occasions. In 1923, Langford fought and won boxing's last "fight to the finish", gaining himself the Mexican Heavyweight title.

Legendary Heavyweight Champion Jack Dempsey said of him "The hell, I feared no man. There was one man I wouldn't fight though because I knew he would beat me. I was very afraid of Sam Langford."

Langford's last fight was in 1926, when his failing eyesight finally forced him to retire.

Sadly, Langford eventually went completely blind and was unable to fend for himself. He ended up penniless and destitute, living in Harlem, New York. He had to resort to begging on the streets. In 1944, a national article was published in the press highlighting his story and plight. As a result, money was donated by fans to help him. Eventually, funding was obtained to pay for successful eye surgery. He moved into a private nursing home where he stayed until his death in 1956. He was entered into the Boxing Hall of Fame.

Bombardier Billy Wells (fought 24th April 1911)

Wells was matched to fight the then current world heavyweight champion Jack Johnson in London in October 1911. Various organisations protested at the mixed race contest. The Church became embroiled, opposing the excessive prize money as immoral. There was a nationwide call for a ban on contests between mixed races. Responding to this public opinion, the fight was cancelled by the Home Secretary, Winston Churchill.

After this, a 'colour bar' was introduced and remained in British boxing until 1947. In December 1911, Wells fought Fred Storbeck at Covent Garden for the British Empire Heavyweight Title, winning with a knockout in the eleventh round so gaining his second title in one year. In 1911, he also published a book called "Modern Boxing" .

Billy Wells

Surprisingly, Wells fought Gunner Moir in a non title fight on the 11th January 1911, losing to him on a K.O in the third round.

Billy Wells with manager Jim Maloney

In June 1913, Wells fought the extremely talented Frenchman Georges Carpientier for the European Heavyweight Title. The bout was held in Belgium and Wells lost by a knockout in the fourth round.

Wells successfully defended his British Heavyweight title three times in 1913. In the December of the same year, he had a rematch with Carpentier for his European title. The bout was held at Covent Garden, but once more, Carpentier won, this time by a knockout in the first round.

Wells continued to box successfully defending his British Heavyweight title but was interrupted by the start of the First World War. In May 1915, Wells joined up for military service and was immediately made a sergeant. He continued to box in the army until 1917. He was sent to France to organise physical training amongst the troops.

After the end of the war, Wells resumed his boxing career. His fourteenth defence of his British Heavyweight title and of his British Empire title was against Joe Beckett, a boxer whom he had beaten on points two months previously. The bout was held in February 1919, in Holborn, London, Beckett won by a knockout in the fifth round.

Bombardier Billy Wells

Wells then had five more bouts, winning them all, before having a rematch against Beckett in May 1920.Once again, Wells was knocked out, this time in the third round.

Wells continued to fight, having eight more bouts, winning five of them and losing three. His last fight was on the 30th April 1925.

On 7 September 1912, Wells had married Ellen Kilroy, the daughter of a publican. They had five children before eventually separating and getting divorced.

In 1923, he published the book,

"Physical Energy".

Wells was also famous throughout the world for being the first person to fill the role of the "gongman" - the figure seen striking the gong in the introduction to J Arthur Rank films. In the 1950's, he kept the Fountain in Sandgate, Kent, situate between Hythe and Folkestone. His daughter at this time was a talented piano player.

He lived in Ealing, London and died there on 11 June 1967, aged 77. The Lonsdale Belt that Wells won was the original heavyweight belt and was crafted from 22 carat gold unlike later belts. The belt was kept at the Royal Artillery Barracks inWoolwich, South East London, but is now kept at Larkhill, Salisbury being the new home of the R.A. Unfortunately, it is still not on display to the general public at this time.

Gunner James Moir (fought 19th April 1909)

Gunner James Moir in a fighting pose.

He had joined the Royal Artillery at a young age. He took up boxing in the services, winning a middleweight competition in Cape Town, South Africa circa 1898 whilst undertaking Boar War service. Following his defeat at the hands of Iron Hague Moir, continued his boxing career but with mixed results. He astounded the boxing world when against all odds, he knocked out in the third round the undefeated Bombardier Billy Wells. This was on the 1st November 1911. This was apparently not a first as he was credited with a K.O over Wells in a gym spar session.

Over the next year though, he went on to lose his next three bouts. These were against Porky Dan Flynn, Petty Officer Matthew Curran and Hawker Wilson. His last fight was on the 18th November 1912 when he lost a rematch with Billy Wells. He then retired from boxing altogether.

He briefly went on into wrestling appearing on the professional circuit. He went into acting in the 1930's and appeared in Third Time Lucky (1931), Side Streets (1933), The Mystery of the Marie Celeste (1935), Mr What's His Name (1935) and King of the Damned (1935). Sadly, health started to deteriorate and he had to retire from films.

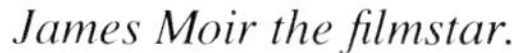

James Moir the filmstar.

James Moir with two fellow actresses

Moir in costume for a film.

He died on the 12th June 1939 at the relatively young age of 60. He was residing near Sutton in Surrey at the time. He left a widow and six children. He was buried in Tooting cemetery, Magdelen road, Wandsworth, London in a family tomb.

Tom Crowler – The Cumberland Giant (fought 5th August 1912)

After beating Iron Hague, Tom went onto wins against Bill Chase, Kid Jackson, Jack Daniels and Ben Taylor. With no opportunity for the English Heavyweight title materialising, he travelled to U.S.A and Canada. Here he fought Ed Martin and then William Casey Jones. This bout was promoted as being for the heavyweight crown of Canada. He won with a knockout.

On the 28th March 1914, Cowler was sentenced to a year in New Westminster Prison, U.S.A for participating in a strike riot and charged with assaulting a police officer. He had thought that by pleading guilty he would get a suspended sentence, not actual prison time. He thought wrong.

With the advent of the First World War, he found difficulty getting home. He had one more fight then travelled on to Australia. In 1915, he fought and won O'Donnell in Sydney, going on to engage in two further contests, both with knock out victories.

He returned to the U.S.A in July 1915, fighting Ed "Gunboat" Smith at New York. He had a further four fights in New York latterly with Dan Porky Flynn. In 1916, he went to Boston to fight Battling Levinskey where he lost.

He returned to New York and up to 1917, had a further seventeen fights with mixed results. He then boxed all over the U.S.A and even in Mexico, not returning to the U.K. until March 1920. He had a further eleven fights before fighting in Italy and returning back to the U.S.A in 1923. He then had eight more fights in New York and Philadelphia, finally retiring from the ring in 1924, aged 32. Of his 82 fights, he won

55 (46 by K.O), lost 24 and drew 3 .

He returned back to the U.K. He died in 1951 after ill health aged 58 at Broadmoor.

He did receive some criticism as to why he did not return to the U.K during the First World War.

(JOSEPH) JEWEY SMITH (FOUGHT 21ST FEBRUARY 1910 AND 5TH DECEMBER 1912)

Jewey's last fight against Iron Hague was on the 21st February 1910. He continued boxing in the UK until 1913 whereafter, he went to the U.S.A, settling in New York. With the outbreak of the war, he stayed in the U.S. He continued his boxing, going on right on into his 40's. His American manager, Harry Simmons, arranged him many fights. At the age of 41, he won three fights in succession, achieving praise from the national press. He is believed to have died in the U.S.

Jewey Smith aged 41 with his manager

Big Ben Taylor (fought 14th December 1908)

Big Ben was found dead on the 27th December 1916, the victim of a brutal murder. The day previous, Boxing Day, he had apparently been out drinking with his friends and no-one noticed anything untowards. He had been struck on the head by an unknown blunt instrument! It was believed the police of the day did not put themselves out greatly to apprehend his murderer as to them "Big Ben" was a problem removed. It does lend the question as to why he wasn't serving in the First World War.

John William Henry Tyler Douglas (fought December 1909)

He was a good all-round sportsman. After retiring from boxing, he continued with his cricketing career, captaining Essex until 1928. He played for England before and after the First World War, being named as Wisden Cricketer of the Year in 1915. He was the 'England captain' no fewer than 18 times.

He married in 1916, his best friend's widow.

He first visited Australia in 1911-12 and was captain of the M.C.C. team that went to South Africa in 1913-14. He next visited Australia in 1920-21, captaining the team and in the following season, led the English team at home in the first three Test matches against the Australians. His third visit to Australia was in 1924-25. He scored over 1000 runs and took over 100 wickets in the seasons 1914, 1919, 1920 and 1921. His highest score was 210 not out for Essex against Derbyshire.

He died aged 48 on the 19th December 1930 when, along with his father, he was one of the twenty two passengers drowned on the sinking of the S.S. Oberon. The ship was involved in an 'at sea' collision. It was seven miles south of the Laeso Trindel Lightship, off the coast of Denmark at the time. They were returning from a business trip to Finland where they had been on a timber buying trip. The collision was with a sister ship in fog.

The two captains were brothers and were apparently trying to exchange Christmas greetings with each other. Captain Eric Hjelt of the Oberon not only lost his ship but also his wife and their four-year-old daughter, the latter being frozen to death in his arms as he was swimming with her in the icy waters.

Both vessels belonged to the same line and ran a weekly service between Hull and Finland.

Petty Officer Matthew Curran (fought 11th February 1910)

He continued his boxing career until the outbreak of the war where he served in the Navy as a Gun Layer. He used to man the guns, aiming them at the targets be they on land or at sea. Each gun's projectile range was different and accuracy was quite an art. He remained on active service until the end of the war in 1918.

He then emigrated to Australia where he remained until his death in 1938. Many believe that the pre-1913 Curran was arguably one of the best white Heavyweights around in the world, that is,when he was in the mood. He was much maligned throughout his career.

Other Boxers

Richard James (Relative)

Richard James,who was Iron's great nephew, was born in 1929. As a youngster, he was overawed with the stories of his great uncle's success. He took up boxing himself in his early teens.

He received selective advice from Iron to help advance his ring career over the years, which he turned to good advantage.

On leaving school, Richard initially worked for Ralph Clayton's family butchers in Swinton. He took part in the Amateur Boxing Association's National competition in 1947 and succeeded in becoming a junior champion.

Joining the Cadets, he became the Army Cadet champion, going on to take the northern Counties A.B.A championship. In 1950, he reached the finals of the A.B.A's.

His National Service saw him joining the RAF where he continued to compete. He was assigned to the Military Police, seeing service in Malaysia and representing them in boxing tournaments.

After being demobbed in 1951, he eventually took up work at the Steel, Peach and Tozer Iron works at Rotherham. Whilst there, he continued his boxing training using the company gymnasium.

He was turned down by South Yorkshire Police recruitment for being 0.5 inch below height requirements so he joined the London Metropolitan Police instead. He became European Police champion, winning the title in a grand final at the Royal Albert Hall.

Richard died on the 4th February 1976 aged 46.

3) Other Boxing Sundry:-

Mr A F "Peggy" Bettinson
Manager of the National Sporting Club

Arthur Frederick Bettinson was dubbed "Peggy" by his brothers from when he was a boy. He was a very capable sportsman in a variety of competing activities.

Appropriately enough, he was born within a stones throw of Lords Cricket Ground and although he never became a first class cricketer, he did play a few games there.

He started his athletic career at a young age, becoming a swimming champion at 13 in races up to five miles. Later, he only just failed to win the British Amateur Championships over 100 yards distance with himself and the winner both beating the record standing at the time.

Aged 15, he joined the German Gymnastic Society. At the age of 19 years, he took up boxing seriously. He won the Amateur Light-Weight Championship of England in 1882, later on winning the Middleweight title.

His greatest achievement was the founding of the National Sporting Club in conjunction with another famous sportsman, the late John Flemming.

He was only 28 at the time and the year was 1891. The Club became a national institution. Its members included most of the greatest personalities in sport.

Peggy Bettinson

The Club operated trouble free apart from the police taking action against it once, on a charge of manslaughter following the death of an American boxer called Bill Smith (real name Murray Livingstone).

The Club was honourably acquitted and gained in reputation after being praised for its organisation of safety for fighters.

In addition to his association with the N.S.C, he became a manger of the leading amateur boxing club, the Belsize and vice president of the Amateur Boxing Association. He was also a level headed referee of both boxing and wrestling.

The era of big purses affected the ability of the club to compete with the outside promoters but the standards of the club remained unique.

In 1922, he published a book jointly with his son called "The Home of Boxing".

He had previously written "The National Sporting Club Past and Present" back in 1901.

Bettinson had been in failing health for several years and returned from Italy feeling unwell just before Christmas 1928.

He died at his residence in Fairfax Road, Hampstead, London on Christmas Eve, Friday 24th December 1928 only days later.

He was 65 years of age.

The National Sporting Club, Covent Garden, London

After Iron Hague's time there, business carried on as normal through the First World War and into the 1920's. During the Roaring Twenties, boxing became more popular and new venues with bigger crowds opened up all over the U.K. This exacerbated the old problem for the N.S.C. that professional boxers could appear at the larger venues and earn a lot more money.

Responding to the challenge in October 1928, the club reluctantly opened its doors to the public so to hopefully increase crowd numbers and ticket sales. The level of business obtained from this was insufficient and in 1929, the club was forced to close its premises in Covent Garden and move temporarily to the Stadium Club, at Holborn before finally moving to 21 Soho Square in the January of 1930.

In 1929, a new organisation, "the British Boxing Board of Control" had been formed to control the sport as a whole. Not unsurprisingly, most of the board of the new organisation were senior members of the N.S.C. The N.S.C. was given a permanent seat on the new Board of Control .

A new limited company was formed in 1930 to take over the N.S.C and try and revive the club's ailing fortunes. There were, at the outset, very ambitious plans to build a new headquarters and venue but these floundered. In 1936, boxing enthusiast, John Harding, set up a new committee, which took over the Empress Hall and put on boxing shows there in the name of the N.S.C. but it was not a commercial success.

Site of the former National Sporting Club today.

In 1938, the club moved again this time to the Hotel Splendide, Piccadilly. With 1939 came the onset of the Second World War. Adverse conditions followed thereafter. The country in crisis made it very difficult for all sports to thrive. As a result, the club struggled and went into voluntary liquidation.

A new N.S.C started up in 1947. It then took over the Empress Club in Berkeley Street in 1951 from where boxing shows were staged. In September 1955 it moved again this time to the Café Royal in Regent Street. It had no connection with the old club apart from the name.

Andertons Hotel

Andertons Hotel was built on the site of the "Horn in the Hoop" tavern which dated back to circa 1405. The hotel itself was founded around 1800.

In 1820, the hotel's front was described as having a central double door entrance with a wine merchants called Davis and Cooper occupying the front window spaces, the guest rooms being above and behind into the courtyard.

Being centrally located in Victorian London, it was a popular place. The Hotel was situated at 162-164 Fleet Street, occupying a very prominent position.

An advert of 1880 proclaimed "Anderton's is still in Fleet Street, beloved of Freemasons and literary men".

It was recorded that in 1882, the Press Club was founded there.

In 1888, the Football League was founded in its meeting room and in 1892, it was the venue for a meeting of a potential breakaway "Southern Football League".

In 1918, the Magic Circle made the Hotel their HQ with all meetings based there.

The National Sporting Club used to arrange rooms there for all their visiting fighters. It was not far from the club and was very convenient.

Its use as a hotel was unfortunately brought to a premature end courtesy of the Luftwaffe. The site is today occupied by banks.

The site of Anderton's Hotel is today occupied by banks.

4) FAMILY

Daughter Jane Winnard (nee Hague)

Jane died on 3rd July 1970 aged 59.

Daughter Agnes Bradley (nee Hague)

Aggie died 27th February 2004 aged 81

Iron Hague's daughter Aggie poses with Brian Anderson and Herrol Bomber Graham. Brian was British Middleweight Champion until he lost the title to Tony Sibson. He went on to join the prison service becoming a Governor , he is today still a senior administrator within the service.
Bomber Graham went 38 fights undefeated, winning the British, Commonwealth and European Light-Middleweight titles and the British and European Middlewight titles. He lost his unbeaten record in a European Middleweight Title defence against future world champion Sumbu Kalambay in 1987. Herol fought for world titles three times at Middleweight and Super-Middleweight only missing the title by the narrowest of margins. Today he is a fitness coach.

Post Death Honours to Iron Hague

Iron Hague was appreciated and his success admired, tributes and memorials in his honour were created over the years.

Iron Hague Fights on Radio Again - October 1969

BBC Programme Producer, Geoff Sargieson, combed the files of the South Yorkshire Times to piece together a story line of Hague's life. The fight narration for Iron's title win was done by Harry Carpenter as if he had been there at the time. It was a masterpiece containing story lines and sound effects of scenes. It contained interviews with Iron's brother, George, daughter Aggie and his childhood friend. The whole was retransmitted in 2009 by Rony Robinson as part of his BBC Radio Sheffield daily show. It can be heard by accessing the BBC website - highly recommended.

IRON HAGUE FIGHTS AGAIN – ON RADIO

MEXBOROUGH'S legendary British Heavyweight Champion, Iron Hague, fights again next Tuesday. Although he died 18 years ago, Hague will tread the canvas once more . . . . in the commentary of world famous sports broadcaster Harry Carpenter.

The night Iron Hague won his title will be re-created by Carpenter over the air as part of a special radio profile of the man who is still a household name in the Mexborough area.

Programme producer and researcher Geoff Sargieson combed the files of the "South Yorkshire Times" to piece together the life and times of Hague, who held the English championship from 1909 to 1911.

From canal bank

"Iron Hague began his boxing career on a canal bank at Mexborough," says Mr. Sargieson. "He fought his way into the boxing booths, where he took on up to 10 men in a single afternoon.

"While still in his 'teens he fought and beat some of the best boxers in South Yorkshire. At 23 he became the heavyweight champion of Britain. He held the title for two years, and then slipped quickly into obscurity."

The story tells how, for the next 40 years, Iron worked mainly as a barman in local public houses, and died in 1951.

The tale is told with the help of friends and relatives contributing to the programme—including Hague's younger brother, George, his youngest sister, Agnes, and his daughters, Janie and Aggie.

Mexborough-born folk singer Tony Capstick will sing "The Ballad of Iron Hague". The programme will be repeated next Saturday, October 18th.

219 BIRTHS IN NINE MONTHS

A TOTAL of 17 live births, eight males and nine females, were registered in the Mexborough urban district during September.

South Yorkshire Times article

A Play – "Scraps of Iron"

Conisborough poet, Benny Wilkinson, penned a play about Iron Hague's career. The storyline covers the time from childhood through to boxing success. The play was originally instigated at the behest of former professional boxer and local hero, Mr Tommy Joyce. The play is set in a boxing ring and is narrated in a South Yorkshire dialect.

Plaque Erected on the Montagu Arms, Mexborough

Councillor Ken Wyatt and myself operate Swinton Heritage. We felt that a plaque to Iron Hague in Mexborough to recognise his achievements was long overdue. It was our view that had Iron originated from the South of England, a plaque would have been erected years ago. To this end, we organised a fund raising dinner at the Swinton Civic Hall. The objective was to raise enough funds to also secure a plaque for Herbert and Harry Crossley. The night was a great success, it was a sell out. It was attended by Aggie as our guest of honour. Mike Lee of Constant Security Services also organised for a few past titleholders to also be there.

BRITISH BOXING GREATS

TRIBUTE TO MEXBOROUGH AND SWINTON BOXING GREATS

(TO EFFECT A MEMORIAL FUND)

IRON HAGUE	British Heavyweight Champion
HARRY CROSSLEY	British Cruiserweight Champion
HERBERT CROSSLEY	British Heavyweight Novices Champion Died in the USA after fight

DINNER DANCE
SWINTON CIVIC HALL
29th SEPTEMBER 1995

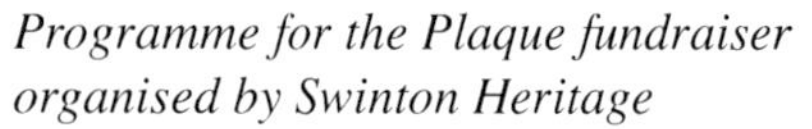

Programme for the Plaque fundraiser organised by Swinton Heritage

TOWN PAYS TRIBUTE TO IRON HAGUE

Plaque to honour former champion

By MARTIN FISHER

FORMER British Heavyweight Champion Iron Hague is to be honoured by the unveiling of a heritage plaque in his former headquarters.

Hague, from Mexborough, took the British Heavyweight title in 1909 at Covent Garden when he beat James Moir.

South Yorkshire Times Article

The Plaques were successfully purchased. Iron Hague's plaque was duly erected on the Montagu Arms. It was considered the best location, considering his long association with the building.

For the ceremonious unveiling on the 27th April 1996 at 1pm, local professional boxing referee Roy Snipe of Swinton, organised the then current British Heavyweight champion, Scott Welch, to travel up to Mexborough from Brighton to do the honours of unveiling the plaque to the former title holder. Unlike others over the years who asked for outrageous fees to do unveilings and the likes, he did this task for us entirely voluntarily which gave a measure of the man. He was very popular with the crowd that turned up to witness the event. He was a proper gentleman, just like a pugilist of the old school. The unveiling was also supported by former boxing and athletic greats.

Pictured outside the Montagu Arms are: to the far left Ken Wyatt Senior (former heavyweight boxer), Mark Epton (former Olympic boxer), Peter Elliott (Olympic runner), Scott Welsh (the then current Heavyweight British Champion), Graham Oliver (Saxon lead guitarist), Tommy Joyce (former commonwealth games boxer). Welsh carried out the unveiling ceremony.

Scott Welsh with the Heavyweight's Lonsdale Belt that Iron Hague fought for in 1911.

The plaque now mounted on the Montague Arms.

Race Horse Naming

An Irish racehorse born on the 25th April 2001 was named "Iron Hague". It was awarded the Jim Seely challenge cup for being the first South Notts qualified horse past the post.

New Headstone for Iron Hague's Grave

Councillor Ken J Wyatt, Mexborough businessman, Graham Schofield, Mexborough and District Heritage Society and myself got together and raised funds for a more fitting headstone to mark the grave of Iron Hague, which was in the Mexborough Cemetery. The existing stone only acknowledged the inclusion in the grave of daughter Jane, although it was the last resting place of father and daughter.

Dearne Valley Weekender, Friday, July 25, 2003

Headstone tribute to a boxing hero

ONE OF the area's most famous sporting sons is to have a new memorial—after lying in an unmarked grave for more than half a century.

South Yorkshire Times

The new headstone was to include a picture of Iron in fighting pose. The picture was made in Italy being placed into Italian ceramic. After consultation with the family, it was agreed to include the words "The Champion Rests" as well as having details of his birth, sporting achievements and ultimate death.

The gravestone was unveiled on Monday, 28th July 2003 in front of a large crowd. The unveiling ceremony was watched by Aggie (Iron's daughter), grandchildren, great grandchildren, other relatives, many local boxers past and present, members of Mexborough Heritage, Civic guests and other interested parties.

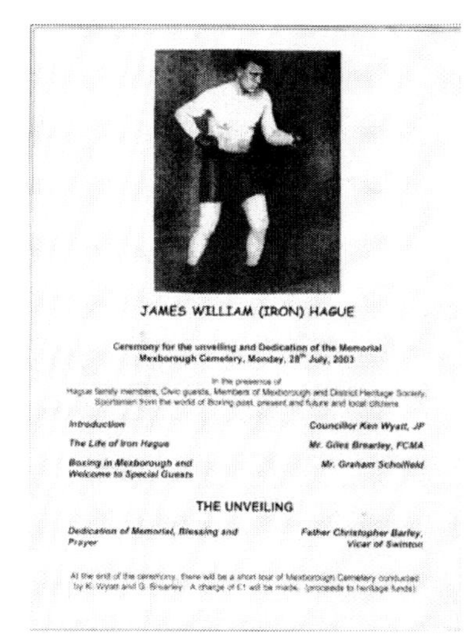

JAMES WILLIAM (IRON) HAGUE

Ceremony for the unveiling and Dedication of the Memorial
Mexborough Cemetery, Monday, 28th July, 2003

Introduction	*Councillor Ken Wyatt, JP*
The Life of Iron Hague	*Mr. Giles Brearley, FCMA*
Boxing in Mexborough and Welcome to Special Guests	*Mr. Graham Scholfield*

THE UNVEILING

Dedication of Memorial, Blessing and Prayer	*Father Christopher Barley, Vicar of Swinton*

The new headstone unveiling programme

A introduction was done by Ken Wyatt followed by a quick history of Iron Hague and his boxing achievements. Graham Schofield then gave a run down of boxing in the town and welcomed the special guests amongst us.

The actual unveiling was done jointly by the fund raisers.

Father Chris Barley, the Vicar of Swinton, then performed a dedication and blessing followed by prayers.

The new headstone in Mexborough cemetery.

Iron Hague's daughter Aggie proudly stands at the side of the new stone.

Boxing Board of Honour - Mexborough

Mr Graham Schofield, the operator and sponsor of the Mexborough Boxing Club, decided in 2008 to erect a board in honour of the many successful boxers the town had produced over the years. Iron Hague is included on the board.

Graham Schofield (centre of the picture) organised this gathering of former boxers, local historians and boxing supporters and backers, the author is stood to the left of the sign.

APPENDIX 1

The rules of boxing that Iron Hague fought under for his professional career.

Marquis of Queensberry Rules

Governing Contests for Endurance (1865)

1. To be a fair stand-up boxing match, staged in a twenty-four foot ring, or as near that size as is practicable.
2. No wrestling or hugging allowed during the bout.
3. The rounds are to be of three minutes' duration, and one minute's time between rounds.
4. If either man falls down through weakness or otherwise, he must get up unassisted, ten seconds are to be allowed for him to do so, the other man meanwhile to return to his corner, and when the fallen man is on his legs the round is to be resumed, and is continued until the three minutes have expired. If one man fails to come to scratch in the ten seconds allowed, it shall be in the power of the referee to give his award in the favour of the other man.
5. Any fighter hanging on the ropes in a helpless state, with his toes off the ground, shall be considered to be down.
6. No seconds or any other person are to be allowed in the ring during the rounds.
7. Should the contest be stopped by any unavoidable interference, the referee to name the time and place as soon as possible for finishing the contest; so that the match must be won and lost, unless the backers of both men agree to draw the stakes.
8. The gloves worn are to be fair-sized boxing gloves of the best quality, and new.
9. Should a glove burst, or come off, it must be replaced to the referee's satisfaction.
10. A man on one knee is considered down, and if struck whilst down is entitled to the stakes.
11. No shoes or boots with springs allowed.
12. The contest in all other respects to be governed by the revised rules of the London Prize Ring.

London Prize Ring Rules of 1838

(which succeeded and built upon the Broughton Rules of 1743)

1) That the ring shall be made on turf, and shall be four-and-twenty feet square, formed of eight stakes and ropes, the latter extending in double lines, the uppermost line being four feet from the ground, the lower two feet from the ground. That in the centre of the ring a mark be formed, to be termed a scratch; and that at two opposite corners, as may be selected, spaces be enclosed by other marks sufficiently large for the reception of the seconds and bottle holders, to be entitled "the corners."

2) That each man shall be attended to the ring by a second and a bottle-holder, the former provided with a sponge, and the latter with a bottle of water. That the combatants, on shaking hands, shall retire until the seconds of each have tossed for choice of position; which adjusted, the winner shall choose his corner according to the state of the wind or sun, and conduct his man thereto, the loser taking the opposite corner.

3) That each man shall be provided with a handkerchief of a colour suitable to his own fancy, and that the seconds proceed to entwine these handkerchiefs at the upper end of one of the centre stakes. That these handkerchiefs shall be called "the colours;" and that the winner of the battle at its conclusion shall be entitled to their possession, as the trophy of victory.

4) That two umpires shall then be chosen by the seconds to watch the progress of the battle, and take exception to any breach of the rules hereafter stated. That a referee shall be chosen by the umpires, to whom all disputes shall be referred; and that the decision of this referee, whatever it may be, shall be final and strictly binding on all parties, whether as to the matter in dispute or the issue of the battle. That the umpires shall be provided with a watch, for the purpose of calling time; and that they mutually agree upon which this duty shall devolve, the call of that umpire only to be attended to, and no other person whatever to interfere in calling time. That the referee shall withhold all opinion till appealed to by the umpires, and that the umpires strictly abide by his decision without dispute.

5) That on the men being stripped, it shall be the duty of the seconds to examine their shoes and drawers, and if any objection arises either as to insertion of improper spikes in the former, or substances in the latter, they shall appeal to their umpires, who, with the concurrence of the referee, shall direct if any and what alteration shall be made.

6) That both men being ready, each man shall be conducted to that side of the scratch next his corner previously chosen; and the seconds on the one side, and the men on the other, having shaken hands, the former shall immediately return to their corners, and there remain within the prescribed marks till the round be finished, on no pretence whatever approaching their principals during the round, on penalty of losing the battle.

7) That at the conclusion of the round, when one or both of the men are down, the seconds and bottle-holders shall step forward and carry or conduct their principal to his corner, there affording him the necessary assistance, and that no person whatever be permitted to interfere in this duty.

8) That at the expiration of thirty seconds (unless otherwise agreed upon) the umpire appointed shall cry "time," upon which each man shall rise from the knee of his bottle-holder and walk to his own side of the scratch unaided, the seconds and bottle-holders remaining at their corners; and that either man failing so to be at the scratch within eight seconds, shall be deemed to have lost the battle.

9) That on no consideration whatever shall any person be permitted to enter the ring during the battle, or till it shall have been concluded; and that in the event of such unfair practice, or the ropes and stakes being disturbed or removed, it shall be in the power of the umpires and referee to award the victory to that man who in their honest opinion shall have the best of the contest.

10) That the seconds and bottle-holders shall not interfere, advise, or direct the adversary of their principal, and shall refrain from all offensive or irritating expressions, in all respects conducting themselves with order and decorum, and confine themselves to the diligent and careful discharge of their duties to their principals.

11) That in picking up their men, should the seconds or bottle-holders wilfully injure the antagonist of their principals, he shall be deemed to have forfeited the battle, on the decision of the umpires or referee.

12) That it shall be "a fair stand-up fight," and if either man shall wilfully throw himself down without receiving a blow, he shall be deemed to have lost the battle; but that this rule shall not apply to a man who in a close slips down from the grasp of his opponent to avoid punishment.

13) That butting with the head shall be deemed foul, and the party resorting to this practice shall be deemed to have lost the battle.

14) That a blow struck when a man is thrown or down, shall be deemed foul. That a man with one knee and one hand on the ground, or with both knees on the ground, shall be deemed down; and a blow given in either of those positions shall be considered foul, providing always, that when in such position, the man so down shall not himself strike or attempt to strike.

15) That a blow struck below the waistband shall be deemed foul, and that, in a close, seizing an antagonist below the waist, by the thigh or otherwise, shall be deemed foul.

16) That all attempts to inflict injury by gouging, or tearing the flesh with the fingers or nails, and biting shall be deemed foul.

17) That kicking, or deliberately falling on an antagonist with the knees or otherwise when down, shall be deemed foul.

18) That all bets shall be paid as the battle-money after a fight is awarded.

19) That no person on any pretence whatever shall be permitted to approach nearer the ring than ten feet, with the exception of the umpires and referee, and the persons appointed to take charge of the water or other refreshment for the combatants, who shall take their seats close to the corners selected by the seconds.

20) That due notice shall be given by the stake-holder of the day and place where the battle-money is to be given up, and that he be exonerated from all responsibility upon obeying the direction of the umpires and referee; and that all parties be strictly bound by these rules; and that in future all articles of agreement for a contest be entered into with a strict and willing adherence to the letter and spirit of these rules, and without reserve or equivocation.

21) That in the event of magisterial interference, it shall be the duty of the umpires and referee to name the time and place for the next meeting, if possible on the same day.

22) That should the event not be decided on the day named, all bets shall be deemed void, unless again declared on by mutual agreement: but that the battle-money shall remain in the hands of the stake-holder till fairly won or lost by a fight, unless each party shall agree to withdraw his stake.

23) That all stage fights be as nearly as possible in conformity with the foregoing rules.

National Sporting Club Boxing Rules

Contests

1. All contests to be decided in a roped ring not less than 14 feet or more than 20 feet square.

2. Contestants to box in light boots or shoes (without spikes) or in socks. The gloves to be of a minimum weight of 6 ounces each. Contestants to be medically examined before entering the ring, and to weigh on the day of the contest

   Should Bandages be agreed to, the length and material of same to be approved and deposited with the Management of the Club at the time of signing Articles. The length of Bandage for each or either hand not to exceed six feet, and width not to exceed one inch.

3. In all contests the number of rounds shall be specified. No contest shall exceed 15 rounds, except Championships, which shall be limited to 20 rounds. No round shall exceed three minutes in duration. The interval between the rounds shall be one minute.

4. A contestant shall be entitled to the assistance of two seconds, whose names shall be submitted to the Committee for approval. The seconds shall leave the ring when time is called, and shall give no advice or assistance to the contestants during the progress of any round.

5. In all contests a referee and a timekeeper shall be appointed by the Committee. The referee shall award a maximum number of five marks at the end of each round to the better man, and a proportionate number to the other contestant, or, when equal, the maximum number to each.

   If a contestant is down, he must get up unassisted within ten seconds, his opponent meanwhile shall retire out of striking distance, and shall not resume boxing until ordered to do so by the referee. A man is to be considered down even when he is on one or both feet, if at the same time any other part of his body is touching the ground, or when in the act of rising. A contestant failing to continue the contest at the expiration of ten seconds shall not be awarded any marks for that round, and the contest shall then terminate.

The referee shall decide all contests in favour of the contestant who obtains the greatest number of marks

If at the conclusion of any round during the contest one of the contestants should attain such a lead on points as to render it an impossibility for his opponent to win or tie, he must then be declared the winner.

Marks shall be awarded for, attack direct, clean hits with the knuckle part of the glove of either band on any part of the front or sides of the head, or body above the belt; "defence"guarding, slipping, ducking, or getting away. Where contestants are otherwise equal, the majority of marks shall be given to the one who does most of the leading off or who displays the better style.

6. The referee shall have power to disqualify a contestant for any of the following acts. For hitting below the belt, for using the pivot blow, for using the kidney punch, for hitting with the open glove, the inside or butt of the hand, or with the wrist or elbow. For holding, butting, shouldering, intentionally falling without receiving a blow, wrestling or roughing, or for any other act which he may deem foul. The referee shall also have power to stop the contest if in his opinion a contestant is outclassed or accidentally disabled.

7. If in the opinion of the referee a deliberate foul is committed by a contestant, such contestant shall not be entitled to any prize.

8. The breaking of any of these rules by a contestant or his seconds shall render such contestant liable to disqualification.

9. The referee shall decide (i) any question not provided for in these rules ; (3) the interpretation of any of these rules.

CHAMPIONSHIPS.

Standard Weights.

Fly Weight.................. 8 stone and under.

Bantam Weight .... 8 stone 6 pounds and under.

Feather Weight .... 9 stone and under.

Light Weight .... 9 stone 9 pounds and under.

Welter Weight .... 10 stone 7 pounds and under.

Middle Weight............ 11 stone 6 pounds and under.

Light-Heavy Weight .. 12 stone 7 pounds and under.

Heavy Weight .... Any weight.

Acknowledgements

I would like to thank the following for their encouragement and assistance in the research and production of this book:-

A special thanks to Ron James, the Swinton Heritage archivist, who has spent hours trawling the various archives and was a big contributor to information and data.

Julia Ashby

Mexborough Heritage Society

Graham Oliver

Boxing Historian, David Bennett

Harold Alderman, MBE, who excelled with his great boxing history knowledge

Alan Downing

Lieutenant Colonel Conway Seymour (Archivist Grenadier Guards)

The National Archives, Kew

The British Library, London

The London Newspaper Archive

Joanne Rayner-Johnson and Cathryn Cartwright

Dorothy James

Jeanette Bradley (Iron Hague's granddaughter) and husband, Albert

Barry Crabtree

Ken Wyatt

And the late Ken Wyatt senior.

Bibliography

The Diary of a Champion, Barry Chambers

The South Yorkshire Times

The Mexborough and Swinton Times

The Doncaster News

Doncaster Free Press

Bombardier Billy Wells, The life and times of a Boxing Hero - Stan Shipley

The Times

Boxing News

Sporting Life

The Mirror of Life

Manchester Sporting Chronicle

London News

London Illustrated News

The Complete Boxer, J G Bohun Lynch

The British Grenadiers, Henry Hanning.

Refereeing 1000 fights- reminisces of Boxing, Eugene Corri

Thirty Years a Referee, Eugene Corri

Gunner Moir (Heavyweight champion of the British army) - The complete Boxer.

Alfred Liversidge- England's Fastest Man, G H Brearley

Boxing in South Yorkshire, Ronnie Wharton.

A century of Boxing Greats, Patrick Myler

Various works by Geoff Sargieson

Reminiscences of a Grenadier, ERM Fryer